Shadows of Scartongarth

Acknowledgements

Thanks to Members of Caithness Writers for help, encouragement and beta reading. My series would never have been written without them.

And many thanks to Sheona Campbel for the final proofreading,

By the same author

Raumsey Series

(books are mainly stand-alone)

Follow the Dove

The Broken Horizon

The Road to Nowhere

Isa's Daughter

Mary Rosie's War

Novella

Song for an Eagle

Anthology

Gone With the Tide

Author's note.

This book is the culmination of months of dedicated research. I delved into several memoirs written by survivors of Japanese POW camps and watched numerous YouTube documentaries on the subject. While I've only lightly touched on the full extent of the horrors experienced in these camps—this book isn't intended to explore them in any detail—the insights gained have influenced the narrative.

The fictional Island of Raumsey, located just across the water from Scapa Flow, draws from the memories my parents and grandparents shared of their lives on a similar island.

Any mistakes I have made regarding the legal process in Scotland at that time are on me. (but then it is fiction.)

Email Catherinbyrne@aol.com

Published by
Overtheord Publishing

Chapter 1

Annie: Raumsey July 1939

Annie Reid set aside the letter she had received from her friend, Tess.

'How's she doing?' Annie's mother slipped another bannock onto the iron griddle.

'She's gone back to the nursing. They need nurses more than ever since it seems war's inevitable.'

Isa paused and turned to look at her daughter. 'You wish you were there, too, don't you?'

'I'll admit I miss the city, but the islanders are in sore need of a district nurse and,' she looked down at her sleeping baby, 'DeeDee needs to be here, where it's safe.'

'I'm glad you're being sensible,' said Isa. 'What else has Tess got to say?'

'The British Union of Fascists are holding regular meetings at the entrance to Queen's Park. They're spreading nationalistic and racist views. It's awful.'

'Is Tess still involved with all that?'

'She's not giving too much away, but there seems to be a genuine fear that things will get bad. Glasgow is preparing for war, she says.'

Annie knew it wasn't just in the cities. All across Britain, preparations were being made. Around nearby coastlines, lookout towers were being erected and, across the water,

Scapa Flow had been of immense importance during the Great War and would be again. Daily, large warships sailed through the channel.

'You don't mind me staying here, do you, Mam, when I now have a nice little nurse's cottage?' As the first state-paid district nurse on the island of Raumsey, she had been afforded accommodation and a bicycle to get around. Since her experience and skill were welcome, the islanders forgave her for the sin of returning home with a child and no husband.

'How could you even ask? Donald and I love having you here. It's a big manse, plenty of room. Furthermore, you do need us to watch Dee. It's far more convenient.' She lifted the bannock with a spatula and set it on a plate. 'Butter a couple of slices, while I get the tea.'

Annie lifted a knob of butter and spread it over the bannock where it melted and glistened.

She had no sooner drunk her tea and eaten her bannock than David Donald, affectionately known as DeeDee or just Dee, woke, demanding attention. After feeding and changing him, she placed him back in the cot and lifted her jacket from the back of the chair.

'I've a couple of calls to make,' she said, 'but I shouldn't be long.'

'Take as long as you want, love. The wee man is no problem.'

Magnus Munro, Tess's brother, caught up with her as she wheeled her bike along the road. His unruly hair, the colour of wet straw, fell over his deep blue eyes, fringed with the longest lashes she'd ever seen. He pushed his hair back with the heel of his hand, his smile as wide as the sea as he looked at her. Since he'd returned from the Great War, injured and broken, he'd gradually gained the strength and confidence to become the attractive man he once was. Despite having a limp and a twisted arm, he continued to work effectively as both a farmer and a fisherman.

‘I was hoping to catch ye,’ he said. ‘Have ye thought any more about my proposal?’

‘I can’t answer right now,’ she said, uncomfortable. He had asked her to be his wife and saying yes or no involved making a final decision. How could she explain that she cared for him, valued his friendship, would miss him if he left, that he would make a great husband and father, but she craved more? After experiencing a deep, heart-stopping love once, she didn’t know if she could ever settle for less.

‘Ach, come on, if it’s a definite no I won’t mention it again, but ye’ve kept me waiting around for far too long.’

Annie didn’t want to lose him, but at the same time, she could not commit.

‘I’m sorry I can’t give you an answer. I do care about you but I don’t think I’ll ever marry.’

‘If you change your mind…’ He gave her a longing look. ‘But don’t leave it too long.’ He turned away. Annie watched him walk along the road with his shoulders hunched and felt a moment of regret. If she accepted him, they would live amicably she was sure, but would that ever be enough for her?

She answered her own question. Her eyes turned to the far distance, to the road where the ghost of Alexander Garcia still lingered, and she knew Magnus would never be enough.

Chapter 2

Alexander: Aberdeen July 1939

At that exact moment, Alexander Garcia drifted down the rain-filled street in Aberdeen as if in a trance. The war in Spain had changed him and what had it all been for? He had damaged the sight in one eye and had watched his cousin die all for a cause they both believed in. He had come home, leaving his heartbroken aunt and uncle back in Spain, suffering more than they had before. And nothing had changed. His parents wanted him to return to teaching, but he knew that was no longer for him.

When he reached the offices of the *Aberdeen and World News*, he stopped and caught sight of himself reflected in the window. He had lost a lot of weight, his face was drawn and his eyes held the devastation of things better left unseen.

Looking away, he took a determined step towards the door. By writing, he could spread his message to the world. If he were lucky, he would get a column of his own.

A young woman, looking fresh out of school, sat at the desk in the foyer. Her hair was short and curled, and her smile friendly.

I've come to apply for the Reporter's job advertised on Friday,' he said.

'One minute, sir.' She lifted the telephone and spoke into it.

A tall man in his fifties entered through a back door and walked towards him. Alexander grasped the man's outstretched hand.

'I'm John Fitzgerald, managing editor of the *Aberdeen and World News*. And you are?'

Alexander introduced himself.

'And you want a reporting job? What experience have you got?'

'I was a schoolteacher, but have done some freelance work. I've just returned from Spain and I've written several pieces about my experiences there if you'd like to see them.' He didn't feel the need to explain that he'd been fighting; he was one of many young men eager to stop the fascists and he guessed his appearance said it all.

'Come into the office.' Fitzgerald led him through a narrow corridor.

As Alexander followed him, Fitzgerald looked over his shoulder. 'You may be in luck. We did advertise for a reporter, but we've had few applicants. Undoubtedly, more of our staff will be called up now that war with Germany seems a certainty. Have you brought your work with you?'

Alexander removed the folder from under his arm and handed it over.

'Sit down, sit down,' Fitzgerald took a seat behind a heavy desk and indicated the chair on the other side. He flicked through Alexander's folder, pausing now and then to read a passage. 'Could you leave these with me? If we like them, you can start as soon as possible. Your reports on the Spanish war might make a good weekly column, but we will need someone to report local news as well. Are you up to it?' He peered over his glasses as if in doubt.

'I absolutely am, sir,' Alexander could hardly contain his delight. He hadn't expected this to go so well.

'Then go home and have a good meal and a rest, you look as though you need it. Come back tomorrow.'

'I will, sir. I'm sick of resting up.'

Not wanting yet another lecture on his wasted education, he didn't tell his parents what he intended to do. Not yet.

'Report to personnel,' the receptionist said the next day when he returned. 'I'll phone ahead to tell them you're here. Ask for Callum.' She pointed to a door. 'End of that corridor, on the right.'

Callum, a tall, spare man with thinning sandy-coloured hair and a rather prominent nose, greeted him with the briefest hello. He pointed towards a desk with a typewriter and a stack of paper. 'I've read your reports on the Spanish War, and we are impressed with your style of writing. What have you been doing in the last few months?'

'I was injured. I was recuperating and trying to decide what to do next.'

'And you decided to work here?'

'I've always been interested in writing.'

Callum nodded. 'Now's your chance. There's been a report of a disturbance outside the town hall. Oswald Mosley's Black Shirt Fascists are in town. Go and see what's going on.'

Alexander left the building with his notebook in his pocket. He just realised he had not asked about wages.

Once the bus stopped on Broad Street, he jumped off and limped to where the rumpus was taking place. Anti-fascist groups had built roadblocks which had led to a clash. Sir Oswald Mosley's Blackshirts, part of the British Union of Fascists were as active in Aberdeen as in other parts of the United Kingdom. Alexander stopped and took a few deep breaths. While he understood Mosley's disillusionment with mainstream politics, he could not agree with his support of fascism.

'You are here to do a job,' he told himself through gritted teeth. 'You are no longer at war.'

A small boy around nine or ten years old stood pressed against the wall. His face was dirty and his clothes were a size too small. Alexander looked around for an adult, but the child seemed to be alone. This was no place for one so young.

Before him, the mood was growing increasingly ugly as the Blackshirts marched down the street. A well-dressed man before him shouted obscenities in support of the fascists, his aggressive fist punching the air, the upward motion of his arm lifting the tails of his jacket to reveal a bulging wallet in his trouser pocket.

The small boy darted towards him, snatched the wallet and turned to run. Alexander stepped forward and grabbed his arm. The boy yelped, eyes bright with fear. The child was thin and no doubt hungry. With a quick glance at the obnoxious man before him, Alexander released his grip. 'Get home,' he said, his teacher's voice loud above the din. The lad needed no second telling. Clutching the wallet and dodging among the rioters, he disappeared. Alexander gave a wry grin, imagining the fury of the man on finding his wallet gone, but without any regret for his actions.

Back in the office, Alexander wrote up an article on the notes he had taken, trying hard to stick to the facts and remain impartial even as the revulsion coursed through his veins.

Sitting at his desk in his bedroom that night, thoughts of Annie Reid distracted him from the words he meant to write. She had never been gone from his mind, but these memories had grown more intense since he'd returned from Spain. The desire to see her again, to tell her he had survived and to find out about her current life was strong. Yet, he still hesitated. There was every chance she was married and he had no desire to disrupt her life. She had a child by another man so she'd already loved again. No, he realised bitterly, a woman like Annie Reid would never wait for a man like him, someone so steeped in his own beliefs, that he had been totally unbending, while she, with her free spirit had been eager for change.

The last time he saw her, he had meant to ask her to wait for him but he'd swallowed the words, knowing that he did not have that right. Yet, he had regretted walking away, so much so, that he had penned a letter before he left the country, asking her to keep in touch and, if she wanted to reply, she could reach him via his parents' address. He clung to the hope that upon his return, a letter would be there to greet him. But there had been nothing. The silence told him all he needed to know. Then why did he still have this sense of something unfinished?

Chapter 3

Annie: Raumsey August 1941

By August 1941 the war had been raging for two years. Tess's letters still came regularly telling dreadful stories of returning servicemen, many without limbs, sight, or even their sanity. The latest catastrophe was the Clydebank Blitz in March of that year. Tess was in the middle of it all. Annie's young cousin, Mary, had joined the WAAF, and their adventures filled Annie with vague discontent. She could have been so useful as a nurse, yet becoming a mother had changed her. Keeping her child safe was her key priority. But something else weighed on her mind that sunny July day.

As she entered the manse kitchen, she set her bag in the corner. 'Where's Dee?' she asked her mother. Her four-year-old son usually ran to greet her.

Isa sat by the black-leaded range in the over-warm kitchen, listening to her Glenn Miller record of *In the Mood.* The kettle murmured in its ever-ready state and, in the corner, the grandfather clock clicked away the minutes.

'He's away with Grandpa Donald to do a bit of visiting. A favourite with all the old biddies, that lad is. A real wee charmer.' Isa pushed herself to her feet more slowly than Annie remembered and for the first time, she noticed how heavily her mother's age was settling on her. 'Is your back still bothering you?' asked Annie. 'I hope Dee isn't too much.'

Isa set down her knitting and moved the kettle to the

hottest part of the range. 'Heavens no, I'm just a bit stiff, that's all,' she said, glancing at her daughter's troubled face as she did so. 'What's wrong, pet?' Her brow crinkled with worry.

At first, Annie wanted to lie, to say nothing was wrong, but what was the use? Gossip is whispered and spread on the wind and would be all around the island soon enough. She shrugged. 'Nothing, it's just...well...' She stopped and sighed. 'Jeannie Sinclair's expecting. It looks like Nick will have another child.' The words soured her mouth.

With her hand suspended over the tea caddy, Isa paused. 'Wait — expecting? My goodness. Mind you, I'm surprised it hasn't happened before now.' She reached over and turned the gramophone off. 'But you'll no have to tend to her, surely?'

'Me?' Annie's eyes grew round. 'Nick's saying there's no way I'll get anywhere near his wife and that suits me just fine. He'll be taking Jeannie to the mainland. He's already booked her into the nursing home for the delivery. After what happened to Bel it's the best thing, anyway.'

'You'll be relieved.' Isa patted the cushion on the fireside chair. 'Come and sit down and I'll get you a cup of tea.'

'You know what this means,' said Annie, taking a seat and wishing her mother had offered to pour her a wee tot of whisky instead. The news had jolted her.

'That there'll be an heir to Scartongarth?' Isa's slim figure bent forward, carefully measuring how much tea to put into the pot.

'Not a legal heir. He cheated us out of our inheritance.'

'Don't dwell on it, lass. I know it'll bring back memories, but there's not much we can do about it.'

'I suppose as a minister's wife, you'll forgive and turn the other cheek. But I don't believe you've forgotten.'

'I've not forgotten any of it. But with the war and all we've got more to worry us,' said Isa.

The war worried Annie, too. After two years there seemed

to be no end to it and Scapa Flow to the north was constantly under attack, as was the garrison town of Wick on the mainland. So far the enemy had been held off, but they might still invade from Norway.

There were food shortages all over Britain but especially the islands. The floating shops did not risk sailing from Kirkwall in case of torpedoes and the only shop on the island was very low on supplies. Faced with that, the fact that Nick Sinclair's wife was having a bairn paled into insignificance.

'Aye.' Annie shrugged. 'I suppose you're right. I still miss Bel though.' Bel was Annie's cousin and Nick Sinclair's first wife, who had died in childbirth. 'We took her baby in good faith. Nick could have never cared for her.' Annie experienced that hitch in her heart whenever she thought of the child she had loved as her own, the little girl she had been willing to bring up, but who had been too good for this world.

'Don't blame Jeannie, it's not her fault. She no doubt married him in good faith and believes the lies he tells her. She had a hard time as a lassie herself, so we mustn't judge her too harshly.' Isa opened the oven, pulled out a tray of scones and served them with the tea. 'I was lucky to get enough flour for these the day.'

'It just threw me a bit, you know?' Annie grasped her cup and stared at the pale brown liquid. 'It was always Dad's dream, to come home to Scartongarth.'

'It's true your dad wouldn't be happy nor any of the Reid boys for that matter, but what's done is done.'

'Since Bel's child isn't here to inherit Scartongarth, it should have been Dee's.' Annie turned her gaze to the window and into the soft light of a late summer afternoon. A few feathery clouds reached across the sky. Beyond the undulating countryside dotted with cottages, outhouses, sheep and cattle, the firth lay blue and still like pearly glass.

When she saw her son running up the path, her heart swelled. Dee was the anchor that bound her to this land. Her stepfather, the Reverend Donald Charleston, came behind him, wearing the indulgent smile that appeared whenever he looked at the lad.

Annie opened the door, swept Dee into her arms and nuzzled his soft cheek.

'I took a cow to the bull,' he told her excitedly.

Annie looked at her stepfather in horror. The farming children learned early about the circle of life, but not at four years old.

Donald laughed, a deep baritone laugh. 'Honestly, Annie, you should see your face.'

'Well…,' she said hesitantly.

'Don't worry, Freddy was joking, the cow won't be introduced to the love of her life till much later in the year. He was just changing fields so that she was nearer the house.' His eyes crinkled, mischievous eyes, the eyes that had won her mother's heart despite their religious differences. He was still tall and spare although slightly stooped, and had managed to keep most of his hair. With his amiable smile and forward-thinking, the islanders had taken him to their hearts.

'I'll have to have words with Freddy, saying things like that to a bairn,' said Annie, then laughed. 'It's just that he's so young.'

'Annie, my dear, we live on an island with farmland. It won't be long before he starts to ask questions about all sorts of things. But that's your domain and I wouldn't tread on it, would I? And I'm sure Freddy won't either.' He lifted an eyebrow.

'I know.' She turned to lead the way into the kitchen. The question she dreaded when it came, the one from her son she least wanted to answer, was why he did not have a dad.

Reverend Donald Charleston bent to kiss his wife's cheek before sitting at the table. Isa's eyes grew soft and her face relaxed as she gazed at him. The warmth between them was not lost on Annie.

Although she'd had reservations about her mother marrying again so soon after her father's death, Donald had been good for the family, and Dee could have no better male role model. Better than the man who had fathered him, that was a certainty.

As they ate their meal, Annie updated her stepfather with the latest news.

'I know I shouldn't let it get to me,' she said. 'But it still rankles the way that man cheated us.'

Donald was quiet for a long moment while he chewed his food. 'You know, pet, I had a lot of contact with Jeannie's family when I first came here. Her father was a staunch churchgoer but a very hard man nonetheless. Jeannie's not had an easy life. I always felt sorry for her.'

'I feel sorry for her being married to Nick Sinclair,' said Annie. 'And at her age, a first pregnancy might be risky.'

'Aye,' said Isa, 'An old cow doesn't produce a strong calf.'

Annie couldn't help but laugh at that. 'It's nothing to do with me and I'm glad of it.' She stood up. 'Once I've put Dee to bed, I've to organise the ladies for the knitting circle, if you don't mind. We're collecting odd wool to knit socks for the troops.' The impending birth of another bairn in Scartongarth was best put out of her mind. Her mother was right. Whatever the future held, there was nothing they could do about it.

'You're a Godsend for the island,' said Donald. 'Not just a nurse, but the organiser of get-togethers, concerts and group meetings. You're a grand girl.'

'I need to boost sagging morale. Too many telegrams with bad news have already arrived. All this worry is driving the women into a new low, and that doesn't help their physical well-being either.'

'You'll cheer them on right enough. I'll be here to watch the bairn,' said Donald, looking over the top of his glasses at his wife. 'No doubt you'll want to go with her.'

'Thanks, dear,' said Isa, with a fond smile. 'I do want to help Annie. I'm good at the tea making, if nothing else.'

Later, as she lay in bed searching for sleep, Annie considered Jeannie and chastised herself for her uncharitable thoughts.

She had hardly noticed Jeannie before Nick Sinclair married her and knew very little of the life the girl had suffered.

As she drifted between waking and sleeping, her mind was pulled back to the past, when she first arrived at Scartongarth. Along with her mother, she had returned to Raumsey after the Great War had claimed her father and the drought had devastated their land in Alberta. The island, too, was struggling for survival, but Scartongarth was a farm of their own with rich, green pastures and only her cousin, Bel, left to run it.

Her father had spoken about the place so often she felt she was already connected to every stone and every blade of grass.

With all the selfishness of youth, the excitement of her new home and a budding relationship with the dashing young schoolteacher with the Spanish name, why would she notice the pale, shy girl who seldom left the house?

In reality, she did not know Jeannie at all.

For the first time, she wondered what kind of life the girl had endured to turn her into the sad recluse she had become.

Chapter 4

Jeannie: Raumsey

Jeannie Sinclair lay in bed in the kitchen of Scartongarth searching for sleep, moon rays pushing through a space between the curtains. Since the first day she had told Nick about the pregnancy, he had not graced her bed, but slept in the best room, or the parlour, as he called it. 'Bad for the bairn,' he said, while looking at her with uncaring eyes.

The sickness was long behind her, but her back ached and she was tired, so tired. If only her memories would stop dragging her into the past, she might find peace. Yet try as she would, they plagued her both night and day as if revisiting that time might somehow change the outcome. As she fought to find a comfortable position, she was back there, spiralling downwards through time.

The year was 1926. She saw herself as she was that day. Sixteen-year-old and heaving the pail of frothy milk onto the tabletop, fighting the urge to throw it over the old man in the bed. 'Any better the day, Paw?' she said.

Gus MacKay raised his head, his scrawny neck straining at the effort and said, 'What's going to become of ye once I'm gone?'

Jeannie always gave him the same answer.

'I'll be fine, Paw.' She longed to add, I'll be better off not having to look after ye.'

His eyes appeared more hollow that day, his skin more yellow and more tightly stretched over his cheekbones.

'I have to see ye all right. Ye know I'm dying.'

She turned to stoke the fire. 'Aye,' she said aloud.

'How will ye manage?'

'I'll manage fine.'

'Ye'll no be able to stay on in Stonehill.'

The shock of that statement halted her. She froze momentarily, then spun around. 'What? Why?'

Sucking in a breath, he shook his head. 'I've been meaning to tell ye, I've no intention of leaving it to ye. What could ye do? A woman alone? Run a croft? Hah.'

'But this is my home. My inheritance. Ye always said.' She turned cold, the strength went from her legs. 'Ye've no one else to leave it to.' She doubted he had any love for her; he had never held women in high esteem, but she had always assumed the croft would be hers one day. Dreams of that day lulled her to sleep each night, even when the pain of the welts left by his leather belt rendered her incapable of lying on her back. Most of the time she did not know why she'd been punished, perhaps she'd looked at him the wrong way, or he'd had a poor day's fishing. It could never be anything she said, as she'd learned to remain quiet in his presence, but sometimes, even that silence was perceived as insolence.

'Ye'd need to get wed and I doubt if any man would look at ye twice.'

The words stung as they always did. 'I've never had the chance, have I? Ye never let me out except to get tobacco for ye.'

'I've been taking care of ye. What man would want ye for anything other than a good time behind the haystacks and only then in the dark?'

Her lip trembled, but she would not give him the satisfaction of seeing her cry. If she did, his words would become even more bitter. 'So ye'll see me out in the cold?' The heat of anger rose. 'I've looked after ye since Maw died and never a kind word and is this the thanks I get? Why did ye lead me to believe that all this would be mine one day? Do ye hate me that much?' Tears filled her eyes and panic filled her breast. She had always seen herself here, in this house, even planned the changes she would make once the choice was hers. There was so much that needed doing. The thatch on the roof leaked and green mould streaked the walls. Her plan was to rent out some of the lands thus cutting down on the work and still making enough to live on. Sometimes she even dared to dream that, after all, a man would come along who could love her, unlikely though that seemed.

'No, no, I don't hate ye. I wish I could have been different, but I've never been a man of words. After yer mother did what she did, the light went out of me. But she would want me to see ye right.'

Ye mean after ye drove her to take her own life. The words remained trapped behind Jeannie's teeth. Instead, she said, 'And how are ye going to see me right if ye're leaving the farm to someone else? And who is that someone else, I'd like to know?'

Her eyes strayed to the poker by the fireplace and, for a minute, she wished she had the courage to lift it and bash his head in. Just as quickly the flash of rebellion died and left her with a deep disillusionment and a vision of the inevitability of having to leave the island to live in a public assistance institution. She thought of her mother, wading so slowly into the sea that it finally rose above her head with hardly a ripple. Why had that been her only option? No longer able to control herself, Jeannie began to weep, covering her face with her apron, something she hadn't done since that terrible night.

'I'll sort it for ye, I owe yer mother that,' came the rasping voice from the bed. 'It would help if ye had the looks to attract a man, no a face like a cow and the body of a pig.'

Sticks and stones will break my bones but words will never hurt me, beneath her breath she recited the words her mother had taught her. But her mother had been wrong. Words did hurt. They cut like knives and damaged the soul.

My mother's looks didn't help her in the end, did they? Again, the reply formed in her head but a lifetime of subservience stilled her tongue. Her mother had been beautiful. Jeannie took after her father, big-boned and heavy-hipped with a square face and lumpy body and she'd always been tongue-tied and awkward with people she didn't know, especially men. With the onset of Paw's illness, it seemed she would, at last, be free, and this had brought a guilt-ridden sense of relief.

'I've been running the croft single-handed since ye've been laid up and I managed that fine.'

'No, no. Running a croft is no job for a woman. Ye'll be all right. Don't worry.'

She didn't speak but glowered at him and dropped into the armchair, her father's chair, the only one in the house that provided any degree of comfort. The quiet tick from the clock on the mantel gave the only welcome heartbeat. The sun slanted through the window and danced on the reflection of the clock's glass face and the photo frame to the side of it.

What had happened to the family in that portrait? They sat so stiff and still, almost as if they were not real people at all. She could hardly bear to look at her mother, face pinched, sitting upright, hands clasped on her knee. Her father, large and healthy then, his square jaw and bristly hair so like her own, looked good on a man. She hardly recognised the child between them as herself. Hair in ringlets over her shoulders and tied up in a large ribbon, a smock dress that had been handed down from a distant cousin, looking almost sweet.

She remembered how she had to sit so still for that photograph, how her leg had itched in the rough-wool stockings, how she didn't scratch for fear of a slap. That was the only time she was taken to town. Her father had had a good season, he said, and he had treated them to tea and sandwiches in a restaurant by the seafront where they sat at the window and watched the mighty herring boats fill the harbour. That had been a good day.

She cried so rarely back then and when she did, her mother would hug her as long as her father wasn't there. If he was, he would reprimand her for *spoiling the bairn.*

She rose, walked to the window and clutched the ledge until her knuckles glowed white. Staring down the slope at the small houses, at washing fluttering on lines, at sheep and cattle grazing as they always did, at all that lay between her and the grey, gurly ocean beneath an endless sky, she considered her life, all she'd ever known. She couldn't leave this house, this island. She just couldn't.

Her head hurt and the suffocating odour of the sick room almost choked her. Desperate for fresh air, she pulled on her jacket and ventured outside.

After an unseasonable spell of fine, dry weather, winter had come with sudden, unrelenting winds that swept from northern shores. Lifting her face to the chill she closed her eyes as her hair whipped around her face. The fresh, salt-tinged air cleared away her father's odours that seemed to cling forever in her nostrils.

Chapter 5

Annie: Raumsey 1941

The news of Jeannie Sinclair's pregnancy was on everyone's lips, as they speculated and gossiped and cast Annie sly looks. With only the dismal prospect of an escalating war, Jeannie's imminent birth and how that would affect Annie's claim to Scartongarth provided a diversion for them to chew on.

Annie pushed the shop door open, the bell tinkled above her head and the familiar smells of earthy potatoes, paraffin and dried fish assailed her. Her friend, Ada, greeted her with a wide smile as she retrieved her change from Connie.

Nelly More, a woman who seemed to be a permanent fixture in the shop, leaned forward so that her heavy breasts rested on the counter, and said, 'I'm that glad for them. I know Sinclair's no an easy man, but losing his first wife and bairn like that...he's had a hard life. And that Jeannie, she's a strange one and no mistake. This may be the making of her.' Her voice faded as Annie walked to the counter.

Nelly's voice had been loud, deliberately Annie thought, so that she heard every word. But she'd expected nothing less and laughed inwardly at their chatter. The majority of the islanders were not like Nelly and her friends.

'Ah, Annie, ye'll have heard the news?' said Nelly, a malicious glitter in her eye.

'If ye mean about Jeannie, it's all over the island, how

could I not?' Annie replied. 'Just a half loaf if you've got it, Connie.' She set the money and her ration book on the counter. Ada, who had been on the verge of leaving, gave her a sympathetic look.

'Ye're in luck,' Connie said. 'I've just the one left. I don't know what I'm going to sell my customers tomorrow.'

'We'd better take advantage of the supplies as long as we can,' said Annie.

'Ye're right there, lass. Last time, they couldn't even get flour to bake a loaf themselves,' said Connie.

'The islands fare better than the cities.' Helen. a woman who habitually came into the shop to simply pass the time of day, added her opinion. 'There'll always be fish and rabbits, eggs and hens.' She gave a snort. 'That's if the government don't take all the eggs for the troops.'

'At least on an island, we'll be well warned if any government official is on his way over,' said Connie.

'Aye, there is that,' replied Helen. 'We've got to look on the bright side as my Sidney always says.'

Annie thought Sidney was a sour old bugger who wouldn't look on the bright side if he found a pot full of gold.

'Aye, but other supplies, like the ingredients used in baking are no readily available. My wee shop is pretty short on provisions,' said Connie.

Harriet, another of Nelly's friends who already had her shopping in her basket, looked at Annie. 'There'll not be much chance of ye getting Scartongarth back for yer bairn now, Annie,' she said with a smirk.

Annie felt a frisson of irritation. 'I don't care. I'm well set up where I am.'

A look passed between the elderly women.

Nelly shook her head. 'That's as maybe, but Owld Dan Reid built that house with his own hands. Do ye mind, Connie? And a grand house it was, too. We all thought ye'd move back once Bel died.'

'How would I have time to run a croft and do the nursing?'

Annie wished they'd let the matter drop.

'Will ye be tending to Jeannie?' asked Helen.

'I believe they're going to the mainland and that's as it should be. A first bairn and her no that young.' Annie tried to keep her voice steady when what she wanted to say was, *I wish you'd all stop. I've had my fill of Jeannie Sinclair*. She picked up her loaf and change. Thankfully, one more patient to visit and then she could go home, bathe her son and play with him before bed.

Ada followed her out. 'I'll walk along the road with ye,' she said. Once beyond earshot, she turned to Annie. 'Look, pet, don't mind the gossips. They've nothing better to do than stick their noses into other people's business. With the men either away fighting, or working twice as hard to keep the land producing or catching fish, the women are all alone at home, and those three, well they're widows and all. What I'm saying is, they're sad souls, ye mustn't let them get to ye.'

'Thanks, Ada. It's fine, honestly. I expected it. It can sometimes get quite amusing, but I must admit it's getting a bit wearisome.' Annie forced a smile. 'The ladies of the knitting circle avoided mentioning it last night. They're not so direct.' The previous evening, a sudden silence had descended when she entered the hall and a few guilty looks passed between the younger women. 'Where were you last night, anyway, Ada? I needed moral support.'

'It's our Margaret. She got me all upset. The lads aren't nearly so much trouble.' Although Ada was the same age as Annie, she already had four bairns, Margaret being the oldest and the only girl. Annie was very fond of Ada's daughter and thought her friend rather strict.

'What's she done now?' asked Annie.

'She wants to get married and she's only sixteen.' She laid her hand on Annie's arm, 'Look, never ye mind about what folk are saying about Jeannie Sinclair. Bunch of old busybodies.'

'I don't,' Annie said. 'I'm sure they've said worse about

me when I came back with a bairn and no man.' She gave a short laugh. 'I'm away to see your mam now.'

'Our Margaret will be there. See if ye can talk some sense into her because I can't. Sixteen's far too young to get wed.'

'I'm the last one to talk sense into anybody,' said Annie. 'But I'll see what I can do.'

She bade her friend goodbye. She wondered what was so wrong with Margaret wanting to get married; Ada herself had married young.

Chapter 6

Alexander: Aberdeen 1941

Meanwhile, in the kitchen of his parents' home in Aberdeenshire, Alexander Garcia tried to placate the angry woman before him. 'I'm sorry, Mama,' he said, 'I can't settle here. At first, I was glad that I wouldn't be called up because of my injuries, but my job doesn't satisfy me anymore. Please understand.'

Sofia wrung her hands. 'Pah,' she exclaimed. 'Is it not bad enough that you have worried us all these years? You can get a teaching job as you promised. But no, you have to go to war again. Haven't you done enough fighting? '

'I thought you were happy in your job,' said his father, much more reasonably. 'Think things through.'

'Sorry, Dad. My editor obviously thinks I can do this and, to be honest, I want to. It's an offer I can't refuse.'

He didn't tell his parents that the previous war correspondent had been badly injured. It was enough for them to grasp the fact that he was going somewhere more dangerous than the British Isles.

'I wanted to see you settled down with a nice Catholic girl and giving me many grandchildren,' said Sofia. 'But, not you, off you go to war again. Was Spain not enough for you? Is dodging bombs in Scotland not enough for you?'

'It's not like Spain. I won't be fighting. I'll be writing reports that's all.'

He hated to see his mother so upset. 'I'm just not ready to settle yet, Mama. Let me go with your blessing.'

His father stepped forward and extended his hand. 'Good luck, son,' he said. 'I wish you weren't going, but I do understand and it seems there's nothing I can say to stop you.'

'I am sorry to worry you, but you brought me up to know my own mind. I love you both. I'll have to hurry or I'll miss my train.' He opened his briefcase and took out the letter he had hoped to post on the way to the station, but after all the time spent trying to explain to his parents, his time was precious. 'Will you do something for me, Dad?'

'Of course, son,'

'Post this letter.' He handed the envelope to his father.

Robert nodded. 'Good luck, son.'

Alexander turned and left quickly. He could see his parents were close to tears and felt a lump in his throat. He had asked them not to come and see him off and he was glad of that. One of his friends from the newspaper had offered to drive him to the station and sell his car for him after he had gone and he now sat waiting outside.

'You're cutting it fine, mate,' he said.

Alexander grimaced. 'My parents still treat me like a child.' He felt a guilt-ridden sense of relief at being free from parental shackles. They hadn't wanted him to go, but the restlessness in his soul refused to let him stay at home.

His father had survived the Great War and the great depression, working his hands into gnarled parodies of what they once were. Finally, forced to sell his farm, he had enough money to move to this cottage on the boundaries of Aberdeen where they both meant to live out their days.

Alexander understood how they felt, in part. He was their only child and he had suffered that weight of responsibility all his life. His mother's constant fussing, yet pride in his academic achievements, his father's disappointment that he had not been interested in taking over the farm. He knew they hoped he'd get married to a good, god-fearing girl, live nearby, and give them grandchildren. Nothing could be further from his mind. Brought up a strict Catholic, he had lost the only girl he had truly loved, partly because she did not share his faith or values and, yes, the fact that his parents would have never accepted her had somehow affected his choices. But things he had experienced in Spain, the death, the destruction, the hopelessness of the underdog, had seriously tested his faith. Would things have been different if he had been more open-minded back then?

After his time in Spain, he had to admit that he missed the terrible excitement of the moment, being part of a larger force, the rush of adrenaline. He guessed that was what fuelled his eagerness at this opportunity.

In Union Square, Aberdeen, he bade his friend goodbye, grabbed his case and sprinted towards the railway station.

Once Alexander had left, Sofia turned from the window and snatched the envelope out of Robert's hand.

'No, Sofia.' He tried to retrieve it, but she held it away from him.

'You see who this is addressed to?' she asked, her voice a shriek. 'Annie Reid. That woman!'

'He's a grown man, Sofia. We have to let him make his own decisions.'

'He has broken my heart and now he plans to do it again. Elisabeth was so right for him and he threw her away for what? A Protestant!' She spat out the word as if it were a bad taste in her mouth. 'And the Spanish girl, Maria, I did not like her forward ways, but at least she was one of us. No, you will not post this letter and bring that woman back into his life.'

'Sofia, give me the letter back,' demanded Robert with more determination than he had exhibited ever before when faced with his feisty wife. 'I agree with you but it's not up to us.'

'I cannot give it back. You don't understand.'

'What don't I understand? That you still want to run your son's life?'

'You can't post this letter — they will find out and he will hate me forever. I can't stand it.'

'What are you talking about?'

Sofia sniffed and stared at the envelope in her hands, clutching it so tightly that it crinkled beneath her fingers.

'Sofia, what have you done?'

She glared at him, as if surprised at his tone, ripped the letter in half, threw it onto the fire, then burst into tears. 'I did what I thought was for the best. She wrote to him when we were still on the farm. I replied that he was married to Maria and had gone to live in Spain.'

'What?' He glared at her. 'You did what?'

'Think of it,' she shouted, grabbing his arm as he made to dive past her to rescue the burning paper, 'not only a Protestant but one with loose morals. She has a child. A fatherless child and you would help our son fall back into her clutches? You have lived in Scotland too long. Your blood runs tepid. We who have brought him up to be a devout Catholic and obey all the rules of the good book! I thanked the good Lord the day he parted from that one.' And then she burst into a fresh bout of weeping. 'So you see, he can't write to her again. To expose my lies. I can't have him hate me.'

Robert put an arm around his wife. 'All right, Sofia, don't get in such a state. But you've got to realise he is a forty-five-year-old man. He'll never be your little boy again…' His voice trailed away. He would have posted the letter and was horrified at what his wife had done, but deep down he agreed that Annie was wrong for his son and experienced a fleeting relief that Sofia had taken the decision out of his hands. 'But what if he writes to her from wherever he is posted?' He had a feeling this was far from over.

As if this had never occurred to her until now, Sofia gasped, covered her face and began to sob in earnest.

Chapter 7

Annie: Raumsey 1941

Ada's mother, Eliza Moodie, lived by the roadside not too far away and she welcomed Annie with a broad smile on her soft, wrinkled face.

'How's the leg today?' Annie asked as she walked into a room that permanently smelled of barley broth and boiled tea, and closed the door behind her.

'It's paining me pretty bad.' She sat on a rocking chair with her foot on a stool.

'Come on then, we'll see what we can do.'

'Och, I've had my day. I'm no long for this world and I know it. It's Margaret I'm worried about. Ye'd think she'd be happy now that her mam and da have finally agreed to her marrying Freddy. But Ada's adamant that she should wait till she's at least seventeen. That's no too much to ask is it?'

At that moment Margaret came into the kitchen carrying a basket of eggs. 'No many the day, Granny. I'll swear all the explosions over Scapa are putting them off the lay.'

'Shove the kettle on love,' said Eliza. 'Annie'll be wanting a cup of tea.'

'I'd better make a fresh cup,' said Margaret. 'The teapot has been on the stove so long it'll walk out of the pot.'

'That would be grand.' Annie smiled as she set to dressing Eliza's varicose ulcer.

'You'll be more comfortable now.' Once she had finished, she eased the leg back onto the stool, then took a long look at Margaret. The girl's pretty, usually smiling face did have a despondent look. 'I hear the wedding's on the cards, then,' said Annie, lightly.

Margaret's face almost lit up. 'Aye. Mam and Da's agreed. But they want us to wait.' Her sand-coloured hair curled around a heart-shaped face speckled with pale freckles, what Eliza called, 'fair and tickled.'

'It'll soon go in,' said Annie. 'Taking your time might be best all round.'

'But what if Freddy gets called up? He's eighteen in a month and he's no the oldest son so it's no like he's needed on the land.'

'I believe there's a six-week training period and then they get leave before they're posted. Maybe your mam will relent by then if she sees you're determined. There'll be plenty of time to fit a wedding in surely,' Annie said.

Margaret shrugged. 'I suppose so. I just wish it could be sooner, you know? Mam wanted to give me a big wedding one day. She's had her heart set on it. Honestly, ye'd think it was her who was getting married the way she goes on. But I suppose waiting till after his initial training is the least I can do.' She swilled the teapot out with fresh water before adding tea leaves. 'Hey, what do ye make of Jeannie Sinclair then? Maybe this will put a smile on her face. Honestly, she goes around as if someone slapped her with a wet kipper!'

Annie couldn't stop a smile at this. 'They don't speak to me, so I'll have little to do with it.' She accepted her tea and then changed the subject. 'Tell me more about the wedding. Who's your bridesmaid?'

'Actually, Annie, I was going to ask ye.'

'I'd be delighted, but what about your own friends, Nancy and Dolly?'

'Nancy's going to join the WRENs, so she'll no be here, and Dolly, well, she's as lazy as they come, she wouldn't be any help. I doubt if she wants to anyway. She's been spiteful, telling me I'm a fool to tie myself down. Planning to be a land girl on the mainland, so she is. Having a good time with all the service men more like. I think she's just jealous.' She tossed her head. 'Ye've been that good to my granny and me, too, Annie, that time I had my appendix out. Please say ye will.'

'I'd be honoured.' But not wanting to upset anyone, Annie worried about Dolly. She wasn't that bad; funny, bubbly and flirtatious and had been good friends with Margaret before the engagement. 'Mind, you can have more than one bridesmaid if you make up with Dolly.'

Margaret smiled thinly. 'I know,' she said. 'I want to make up with her, but ye know… she flirts with Freddy like ye wouldn't believe.'

'That's just her way. She doesn't mean anything by it. You've been friends since school. Maybe she's offended ye haven't asked her. Think about it.'

'Do ye no mind the way she is with Magnus?'

'Magnus and I are just good friends. And no, I wouldn't care even if we were closer. He sees her as a silly wee lassie.'

'Are ye no finished yer tea yet? Ye'll no doubt be wanting your tea leaves read.' Eliza claimed to have the second sight and she liked nothing better than reading tea leaves.

'I do have a wee bit of time,' said Annie. It cost nothing to humour the old lady — she did like a bit of company.

'I suppose you've seen a wedding in Margaret's cup, then?' Annie finished her drink and turned the cup upside down on the saucer.

'She'll no let me, the besom,' said Eliza. 'Says it's bad luck.' She shot an accusatory look at her granddaughter. 'Now, Annie, turn the cup round three times, then hand it to me.'

Annie complied. Eliza pulled her brows together. 'I see a gathering of some sort and ye'll be very involved in it.'

Annie nodded at Margaret. 'Your wedding,' she said.

'Na, this is sooner than we planned, very soon actually.' She continued to study the cup. Then her face tensed and she handed the cup to Margaret. 'Nothing more in there, I must be tired.'

'Eliza, what is it? Don't say you saw something bad.' Annie didn't believe in the second sight but something that felt like a cold spider running down her spine made her shudder. Eliza's expression concerned her.

'No, no.' Eliza shook her head, but she looked disturbed and Annie wished she'd never allowed the reading.

Margaret studied the cup for a second, then looked at Annie. 'Now ye know why I never let her read my tea leaves. She's aye doing this kind of thing. Granny, ye've worried Annie now.'

'No not at all,' said Annie, although she did feel unnerved. 'Are you all right?' she asked Eliza who had gone very pale.

'I saw danger, Annie. Caw canny. Be careful, will ye?'

'Of course I will.' Not wanting to hear any more, Annie stood up. 'I'll need to get on. Margaret, remember what I said about Dolly.'

Margaret smiled thinly and nodded. 'Maybe ye're right. Who are ye going to see next?'

'You know I can't talk about my patients.' Annie threw her a smile.

'I bet it's Denis. I just love that lad,' said Margaret. 'Tell him I'm asking for him.' She walked Annie to the door. Denis was thirteen years old and, despite the doctors' valiant attempts to save it, they removed his leg because of tuberculosis. It was healing well and Annie was pleased with that, but it was the lad's mood she was worried about now. 'Not today,' she said. As she mounted her bicycle, she looked over the rigs towards Scartongarth and wondered if Nick treated his new wife any better than he had Bel.

Above her, the gulls cried with the familiar keow-keow, and from the beach, the high-pitched peep-peep of the oystercatcher. Sheep and cattle grazed in the fields, a dog barked, a milk pail clattered, and a female voice, not too far away, sang a haunting melody. She turned her face away from Scartongarth, memories of what should have been and the pain of what had happened all those years ago still tugged at her heart. And now there would be another baby.

Suddenly, the high-pitched wail of a siren from the shores of Scapa Flow reverberated over the water, pulling her into the present. Soon the sound of gunfire and exploding bombs would shatter the peace.

Chapter 8

Nick: Raumsey 1926

Thirteen years earlier, in Scartongarth, the farm he had acquired after his first wife, Bel, died in childbirth, Nick Sinclair dipped his hand in the basin and shuddered as he splashed cold water on his face. Bel always had warm water and a flannel ready, followed by a hot plate of porridge topped with fresh milk. The fire would have been burning, the kitchen already cosy.

He ate a crust of dry bread, washed it down with weak tea, then walked out into the chill of the early day.

Looking across the fertile fields of Scartongarth, he considered how much work it would take to get the ploughing and seeding done, as well as going to sea for lobsters and fish.

Again, a stab of bitterness twisted in his heart when he thought of his brother Dougal's good fortune in having a stout woman, two sons and a well-run croft when all he had was an ailing daughter whose birth had killed his wife. Bel's cousin, Annie Reid, had offered to bring up the child and that suited him. He couldn't even look after himself, especially with everything else he had to do and it was no job for a man – bringing up a bairn. Furthermore, he had no desire to even look at the scrawny creature who had caused Bel's death.

The cow, her udder full and heavy, moaned and the hens ran around his feet. They needed feeding, jobs Bel would have done. Damn it all, he needed another wife.

He had already considered the eligible girls on the island and even chatted to a couple a time or two, but most girls needed courting and he had little time for that. He was seriously contemplating advertising for a wife from the mainland. That was his next step.

A young lad who did deliveries for the shop ran up to him, his tow-coloured hair standing up in the wind. 'Mr. Sinclair,' he shouted, 'Gus MacKay sent me to ask ye to come and see him.'

'What does he want?' Nick had never been friendly with Gus MacKay. He found him a rude, cantankerous man. Gus's farm bordered Nick's father's property and there had been a constant feud over a strip of land over which each claimed rights. They had not spoken for years.

The boy shrugged. 'He said he'll give me a ha'penny if ye came.' He wiped his nose on his sleeve and looked at Nick hopefully.

'Well, ye're getting no ha'penny from me,' Nick replied.

The lad sniffed, waited a further minute, then, as if realising there would be no charity here, made to run away.

The cow bellowed again. Nick shouted to the boy. 'Hey, you, can you milk a cow?'

The lad stopped and turned to face him. 'Aye, I can that.'

'Then milk my cow and I'll give you a whole penny. The bucket's in the kitchen.'

The boy's face lit up and he nodded before scampering into the house.

That was one job taken care of. Nick's eyes turned towards Gus MacKay's cottage, perched as it was on the edge of the moor.

Who did the man think he was, demanding to see him? If it had anything to do with the bordering land, it was no longer his concern. When his father died, he had left everything to Dougal. The oldest son was always the heir but Nick had hoped for something, anything, to prove that the man had some love in his heart for his youngest child, something that had been sadly lacking in his childhood. But there had been nothing. He shouldn't have been surprised. The only attention he ever had from the man was at the buckle end of his belt. His mother was even worse. She stood there and let it happen, a strange smile on her face.

It was later in the day that a curious Nick made his way to Gus's croft.

Jeannie answered the door, her eyes widened and she took a small, quick step backwards.

'What does your father want with me?' he asked.

Her face reddened. Avoiding his eyes, she shrugged, her hands twisting together. 'I…I don't know…he doesn't tell me anything.'

He studied her shapeless body and it seemed she'd tidied herself up since the last time he'd seen her. She was wearing a pale blue cardigan over a white blouse and a navy skirt. Her hair shone where it caught the sun and she wore it loose, falling past her jawline, framing her pale, broad face.

'Ye'd best come in.'

The atmosphere in the room was thick with pain and disappointment. For an instant, he wanted to turn and run but curiosity held him fast. In the box bed, Gus was propped up against several pillows, his emaciated face as grey as mist, his sunken eyes shut.

'Paw,' said Jeannie and crossed to put a hand on his shoulder. 'Paw, it's Nick Sinclair. Ye wanted to see him.'

Gus started awake. He blinked and narrowed his eyes. 'Ah, aye, Nick Sinclair,' he said, his voice broken and crumpled.

'I heard you wanted me.' Nick did not go any closer. Although the room was clean, the smell drifting from the bed was of old man's sweat and piss.

'I'm dying,' Gus replied.

'And what's that got to do with me?'

'I've got a proposition for ye.'

‘Which is?’

‘I want ye to marry our Jeannie and look after her.’

The air audibly rushed from Jeannie’s lungs. Her cheeks became as red as a cooked lobster. ‘Paw!’ she exploded and turned to look at the bemused Nick. ‘I’ve no part in this.’ She spluttered as she spoke, hands flying to her face. Anger blazed in her eyes and she became more animated than Nick had ever seen her. She turned to the old man in the bed. ‘That’s why you wanted to speak to that wee boy. I’d have never brought him to ye had I known. I need no one to look after me.’

But Gus acted as if he hadn’t heard her. ‘Well?’ He looked at Nick who stood unable to speak. The proposal had taken the wind from him. This was the last thing he expected.

‘Maybe if you thought there’d be a fine acreage of land and a house in the deal.’ Gus struggled to sit up. ‘Marry her and the croft will be yours, the house and all.’

Jeannie gasped and raised a shaking voice. ‘Ye can’t do this, Paw. I can run it myself; other women do. Paw, please.’

‘A woman can’t run a croft, now haud your wheesht. Be quiet.’

‘No, Paw, no. It should be mine. I can do the work of a man, I really can. Paw, please.’ Her growing distress caused her lip to shake and her eyes to become wet. She blinked and dashed her fingers across her cheeks and her furious eyes turned to Nick in a soundless plea.

Nick held up his hand to silence her. ‘And what else has she got to offer?’ Although she was homely, the deal sounded good, but he could not appear too keen.

‘She’s a damn good worker. A good cook, too. She may look shapeless, but she’s all muscle. Ye’re a man alone with a motherless child to raise and ye could do a lot worse.’

Nick turned to look at Jeannie who pulled her shoulders back and took a deep breath. ‘I. Do. Not. Need. A. Man.’ Her voice rose. ‘I swear, I knew nothing of this, Nick. Pay no attention to him. He’s nothing but an old fool. I’m capable of running this place by myself and it will be mine.'

'I'll not dismiss the idea lightly.' Nick turned his attention to the man on the bed as if he hadn't heard her. 'But I'll no take a woman who doesn't want me.' He looked at Jeannie, his eyebrows raised in question.

'I know ye wouldn't look at me twice.' Jeannie sniffed and chewed her bottom lip before she spoke. 'And don't go studying me as if you were considering a cow at the sales and finding it wanting. I'm no piece of meat to be bought and sold.'

He was taken aback at the venom in her voice. This mouse had a bit of fire in her and that at least gave her a modicum of interest.

'Well, Nick, what's it to be?' Gus totally ignored his daughter. 'I'm sure there are other young men who would jump at the chance of owning my croft.'

'I'll need to think on it,' Nick said. 'Ye took me completely by surprise.'

Glancing once more at Jeannie, he noticed her eyes glistening, her angry breathing fast and audible, her nostrils quivering, her lips pressed firmly together. He winked at her and said, 'We'll talk later,' and, with a nod to the old man on the bed, he left the croft house.

Marry Jeannie, eh? Nick's step speeded up. 'And why should I do that?' he asked himself. He had never considered Jeannie as a prospect, had forgotten her existence until now. She didn't have the looks to attract a man and hardly a word of conversation. Shaking his head, he smiled. To be honest, she hadn't looked that bad today and she seemed strong and healthy; no doubt she'd be able to bear children, children who would do much better than Dougal's brood. He doubted she'd ever had a lad interested in her, so she should be grateful to have a fine specimen such as himself. It was highly possible that she wouldn't even complain if he strayed now and then, should the opportunity arise.

Thoughts tumbled through his mind. If he owned Gus's

land, he would be right next door to Dougal and with Scartongarth as well, he would be bigger and better, almost as big as the Mains. The more he thought about it the more the seed of possibility grew.

He laughed out loud. ‘It’s a fair proposition,’ he said to no one. ‘I’ll go back and take the man up on it, but I’ll let him stew on it for a while.’

Chapter 9

Annie: Raumsey 1941

When Annie returned home, she found her son playing with a collie pup and Magnus Munro on his knees beside him.

'Look, look, Mammy,' Dee shouted. 'Him called Rags.'

'A doggie,' she said and turned to the young man sitting by the fireside.

Magnus looked up at her and pushed the swathe of hair aside with rough, calloused fingers.

'I came to ask ye if it was all right, Annie, but ye weren't here.' His head was angled giving her a soft look. 'It's the last of Bess's litter. They're good dogs. Well-bred.'

She bent down and fondled the dog's ears. The puppy jumped at her, pink tongue lolling and small tail whirling enough to take off. 'He's lovely, but you should have asked first. Maybe my mam and Donald don't want a dog in the house.'

He had the good grace to look embarrassed. 'He can stay in the shed if not. I thought it would be good for Dee to have a dog of his own.'

'It's good of you, Magnus, but you spoil my son. You can't keep giving him things. You've already given him a pet lamb. What next — a cow? That's definitely not coming in the house.' She gave a short laugh without humour.

'I didn't think.' He stood up. 'Do you want me to take him

back?' He made to pick up the pup and Dee began to cry.

'No, want the puppy.'

Annie relented; she could deny her son nothing. 'We'll see what we can do,' she said. 'But I'm still not pleased. Where are my parents?'

'Parish business. I offered to watch Dee. Look, I'm sorry if I overstepped the mark. I really didn't think you'd mind a dog. Ye seem to like them.'

'I do like dogs, but I'm out a lot and it's not my house. I know you mean well, it's just ….' She shrugged. 'It's been that sort of day.'

'Ye know I'd never do anything to upset ye. I just didn't think about the pup. That's me, just a big gormless brute, stumbling in where I'm no wanted.'

The sudden look of a little boy lost got to her and she softened.

'Ye just sit there and I'll make ye a cup of tea. I live alone, mind, I've learned to make a grand brew,' he said.

'Ach, Magnus, sorry I snapped. You're that good with Dee and a good friend to me.' He was her rock in many ways and she knew he was in love with her, but she also knew she could never fully return that love.

'Is there something else wrong? Ye're like a prickly wee hedgehog these days. Ye know I'm always here for ye, Annie.'

She took a deep sigh. 'You know about my cousin Bel, all that?'

'I know there was bad feeling between ye and Nick Sinclair when Bel died. And then losing Bel's baby too, it was a terrible time for ye and him. Is that it? Has Jeannie having a bairn brought it all back?'

Annie nodded. How could she explain the depths of despair that Nick Sinclair had plunged her into? When Bel had died in childbirth, the infant had been sickly and Nick rejected her. He said he could never love a child that had taken Bel's life. Although she'd been only seventeen, Annie had been willing to take the baby and bring her up as her own, but within a year, little Sina had joined her mother in the graveyard.

It was after that, that Annie and Isa found out Bel had signed Scartongarth over to Nick before her death, something she had no legal power to do. But Annie, devastated that she had been powerless to help either mother or baby, decided to pursue a career in nursing.

Three years later, with her nursing diploma intact, she'd returned to the island, pregnant and with no ring on her finger. She'd gone out of her way to avoid Nick Sinclair, not something easy to do in a community this size.

'I hate him,' she said, as if that was all the explanation needed.

'Ye're a lovely person, Annie. Ye're so good with the patients, everyone loves ye. I've never heard ye speak like that before.' He handed her the tea and poured one for himself.

Only because I've kept my feelings buried deep, she wanted to say, but didn't.

He pushed his hair out of his eyes. 'You've changed this last wee while,' he said, his voice low.

'No, no, I've not.' But it was true. With the news of Jeannie, all the past memories had flooded back to engulf her, forcing her into a low.

'Ye know I want to marry ye.'

When she opened her mouth to speak, he held up his hand.

'Listen to what I have to say. I've got a farm and a boat and I manage them both even with my gammy leg and bad arm. I love Dee like my own and, well, it would be good for him to have a brother or sister. Don't tell me you don't want more bairns. I know you don't feel the same way about me, but we get on so well. It makes sense. I've already held my tongue for years.'

It did make sense and she wasn't getting any younger. She would love more children and she wanted to give Dee a father who would be there for him through thick and thin, who would protect him from the wagging tongues and the name of a bastard. And being married to Magnus would protect her from the lecherous eyes and evil tongue of Nick Sinclair, the man who her made inside cringe whenever his eyes raked her body as if he could see right through her clothes.

But much as she cared for Magnus, she couldn't forget the rush of blood, the tingle of anticipation and the devastation of being separated, all feelings she had experienced with her first love. Was she daft to hope she could feel that way again?

'I've always thought I might go south again one day, maybe once the war is over and Dee is older. I do love Raumsey,' she said. 'But it's more of a place to come home to.'

'You can't leave.' His eyes rounded in horror.

'What future will Dee have here? He seems right clever. I hope he'll stick with his studies when he's older, go to university one day.'

'He'll do that right enough,' said Magnus. 'There are loads of young folk from the islands going to university now. It would make sense if we married.' There was a touch of desperation in his voice that unnerved her.

'I can't say yes right now. I have been honest with you.'

'Is it still Garcia?' he asked bitterly. 'Or Dee's father. Ye've never told me about him.'

A sharp intake of breath. 'I told you Dee's father was a moment of madness. Not worth speaking about.' Simon had been no more than a salve for her wounded pride. But she thought he loved her, and would have married him when she knew she was pregnant. The look of horror on his face when she told him, was hard to get over. The humiliation of that scene still brought a flush to her cheeks. She had never seen him again.

'And Garcia?' Magnus asked.

'For goodness sake, it's been years. He'd be a stranger to me now.' Clenching her fists, she wished he would shut up about the past. Her foolish younger life was not somewhere she wanted to revisit.

Magnus took a deep sigh. 'Did you ever hear from him again?'

'Enough about Garcia. His mother wrote to me. He's married.' And yet, something about that letter had not rung true. She would have liked to have heard it from his own mouth, or even written by his own hand. It wasn't like him to have her find out from someone else.

Here she was, she reprimanded herself, a fool for wasting the best years of her life carrying a torch for a man who had chosen to marry a Spanish girl. 'Can we speak about something else, please?' she said.

The happy laughter of Dee and the yapping of the puppy as they played together filled the room.

'Think about what I said.' Magnus stood up.

'Will there come a time when you have to go to war? I believe they are taking older men now.' She was determined to change the direction of the conversation.

'I'm a farmer, but I doubt if they'd have me anyway.' He patted his bad leg. 'And my arm has never been the same. That's how the last war left me. Yet I was one of the lucky ones.'

'At least there's that. Have you heard from your sister?' Tess had always been Annie's best friend, but her letters had become less regular.

'Aye, Tess is as happy as a pig in the proverbial that ye and I are getting close. She'd be over the moon if we got wed. I'm going now, Annie, but think on my proposal. We're neither of us getting any younger.'

With mixed emotions, she watched him walk along the road and over the hill, his familiar limping gait seemed more obvious today. She did find an attraction in the warmth of his eyes, his ready smile and the way his unruly hair flopped over his forehead. He was a good and kind man who would never let her down, and she enjoyed his company. Maybe it was time to accept that that was enough. Maybe that was all there would ever be for her now. Look how losing her head to a couple of men had turned out.

Chapter 10

Annie: Raumsey 1941

The lack of food had been an issue since the floating shops had stopped sailing and, with so many men away fighting, growing enough crops and catching fish was increasingly difficult. One of Annie's ventures was making sure that no one went hungry. The islanders were only too happy to contribute to the elderly with no family. Every Saturday she arranged a meeting in the hall so the islanders could discuss their ideas of how to make things easier for everyone. There were a few people who didn't take part, mostly the infirm, and others who kept themselves to themselves such as Nick and Jeannie Sinclair.

'Any spare fish, the day?' she asked old Hughie as he hoisted himself from the boat onto the quay.

'I can spare a couple of herring. These waters aren't the safest with German U-boats and all.'

'Are you up to giving us a tune on Friday night?' she asked.

'Another concert, is it?' Hughie was only too happy to show off his expertise on the accordion.

'The dance was good last month,' she said.

'Aye, but all these young lassies dancing with each other.' He shook his head. 'Not natural that.'

‘Not much else they can do when all the young men have gone. Anyway, dancing’s good for the soul,’ said Annie. ‘Is your Bessie coming to the sewing circle tonight?’

‘My Bessie can sew and knit in the house. Why should she come up to the hall in the dark?’ he grumbled.

‘Because when we get together we can have a gossip and a laugh. It’ll do her good to get away from the house.’

‘Aye and leave us men to fend for ourselves. And tear us apart with yer tongues, no doubt.’

‘You get together with your friends to build and sail your model yachts and you play dominoes up in the shop. Why is that different?’ Annie knew that the main reason only the younger women attended her clubs was that the older men left behind liked to be waited on hand and foot. ‘Apart from sewing, we women knit socks and roll bandages for the troops,’ said Annie. ‘And doing it together is more fun.’

Every get-together was a positive thing, especially when there was joking and laughter as the strength of the women shone through.

Tonight was the women’s sewing circle, where those good with the needle taught the young girls. Isa had loaned her a sewing machine for use in the hall. No spare bit of cloth was wasted, even if it was only fit for rag rugs or mismatched patchwork quilts.

Later that night when Annie and Ada were making tea and sandwiches to serve halfway through the meeting, Ada leaned towards her friend and confided, ‘Ye’ll never guess what that lass of mine wants to do now.’

‘What?’ asked Annie.

‘She wants to join the WVS.’

‘The Women’s Voluntary Service? She’ll need to go to the mainland.’

‘Aye. Says she’ll go wherever they need her.’

‘Does she still want to get married?’

‘Oh aye. Her idea is that since Freddy will have to go away

to do his bit, she should be doing something too. It would be different if she was married, according to her, though what difference that would make beats me.'

'I think it would do her good.' Annie remembered how much her time in Glasgow had opened her eyes to so many things.

Suddenly Ada leaned towards her and whispered. 'Did you notice Jeannie coming in?'

'Jeannie, no, where?' This was indeed unusual, as Jeannie had become even more of a recluse since she'd married Nick.

Annie lifted her head to see the pale, frightened face of Jeannie Sinclair peering around the door. 'You go and welcome her,' said Annie. 'She looks daggers at me. It's enough to strip the flesh off my bones.'

Ada left Annie's side and crossed the floor to where Jeannie stood in the doorway glancing from left to right as if she might bolt away at any minute.

'Come away in, Jeannie,' she said. 'We're about to have a break. Ye'll have a cup o' tea and a sandwich. We've got salmon paste the night.' She took the other woman's arm and led her to a spare seat. 'Are ye any good with a needle yerself, Jeannie?'

Jeannie nodded. 'Aye, I had to be, otherwise I'd not have had a stitch to put on when I was a bairn.'

Connie, who was next to her, shoved a bunch of rags towards her. 'We're sorting these out,' she said. 'Some are good enough to make a pair of knickers for a wee girl, others for a rug. Chinty there is awfully good at designing them. She does the drawing, see,' she pushed a sheet of paper in front of Jeannie, 'and we just follow the lines.'

Jeannie nodded. This was something she could do, she thought, suddenly interested. Trying to ignore the fact that Annie Reid was in the same room, she began to pick through the rags, finding as many of the same colours as possible. It was hard to stop her hand from shaking as Nick's cruel words when she told him she was going out still reverberated in her head.

'Ye'd go to something Annie Reid organised? Are ye a fool? These women are a bunch of interfering busybodies. They don't like ye, don't imagine they ever will. They laugh at ye behind yer back but ye're too stupid to realise it.'

She took a deep breath. 'I don't care. I've got to find something else to do. I feel like a prisoner here.'

He turned away with a sneer. 'Well don't blame me when ye come home humiliated.'

She hadn't wanted to go after that, but couldn't give him the satisfaction of staying at home. Sometimes she felt she was going mad.

As she walked home, she realised she'd enjoyed the evening despite all that Nick had said. However, she doubted she would go again; the atmosphere in the house as Nick sulked for the next few days would not be worth it. She thought of how her father and Nick Sinclair had bargained her life away. Why had she let it happen? Suddenly, the years fell away, and she was back in the past on that fateful day.

Chapter 11

Jeannie; Raumsey 1926

In the kitchen of her home in Stonehill, after Nick Sinclair had gone, a deeply humiliated Jeannie turned on her father, angrier than she had ever been. 'Ye had no right to offer me to Nick Sinclair. Why didn't ye tell me what ye meant to do? He won't want me, croft or no.' Dryness coated her mouth and a heat suffused her body. She should have questioned him when he offered that lad a ha'penny when he had never needed someone to do an errand before.

'I knew ye wouldn't go for it. But I've made the will, there'll be no changing it. Whoever marries ye will get the croft and if ye are unmarried at my death, ye'll have three months to find a man, otherwise, the farm goes to Tavish O'Malley.'

'Tavish O'Malley!' The name exploded from her. 'That wee weasel of a man. He only worked for ye for a year.' Her breath caught and she could say no more, such was the outrage and pain in her heart.

'He was a good worker,' said her father.

'He was a … a pig.' Jeannie thought of the skinny, muscly little man, half a head smaller than her but strong as an ox. He had tried to drag her down in the hayfield one day. The stink of stale sweat and tobacco clung to him. Visions of his open, toothless, drooling mouth coming towards her made her stomach heave anew. With a surge of energy, she had lifted her head with all the strength she could muster, hitting his mouth with her forehead and splitting his lip.

When he sprang up, coughing and spitting, and calling her a string of foul names, it gave her enough time to scramble to her feet and run away, shaking and crying and missing her mother more than ever. There was no point telling her father. He would have made some nasty remark about her looks and accuse her of lying.

'Why Tavish O'Malley?' she cried in dismay.

He looked at her, his eyes small and malevolent. Her father enjoyed tormenting her, but she never thought he'd do this. 'Ye could always marry him,' he said with a slight laugh.

'What have I done that ye hate me so much, Paw?' she asked, the rage within her causing her to tremble.

'Hate ye…hate ye? Why would I hate ye? There's no way ye could manage the farm on yer own, so it's marry Nick Sinclair or Tavish O'Malley, or go to the poor house for all I care.'

'Ye should have told me that was what ye were planning. I'm fair ashamed, so I am.'

'Nick'll come back and ye'll marry him. Ye're no likely to attract a man yerself, and a woman is little use alone. Now go and change into yer working clothes and get my tea on.'

For a moment she considered defying him. Leaving him to starve, but a lifetime of obeying her father's every command was deeply embedded in her psyche. She felt physically sick. 'He'll be laughing at me,' she said, cringing at visions of him telling the other fishermen and them all laughing uproariously. *Jeannie MacKay, the very thought.* Facing any of them again would be impossible.

'I know the man. He's greedy. He'll want the land, and marrying ye is the price he'll have to pay. Ye'll do it.'

Muttering under her breath she went into her room and stripped off her Sunday clothes, the clothes her father had ordered her to wear today, then returned to the kitchen.

Gus raised his rheumy eyes. A glob of phlegm caught in his throat and he hawked it, his hand waving frantically in the air, searching for his spittoon.

For one mad moment, Jeannie considered emptying the contents over his head, then walking away and leaving him to fend for himself. But he still had enough wits about him to leave her with no options at all. She ran outside and pressed her back against the stone wall, a wave of hopelessness washing over her. She could have gone into service but she had stayed, stayed because her father had held out the promise of the croft being hers one day.

Many a time her dreams had taken flight. There was no doubt her father had a tidy bit put by. Being as active in the whisky running as the rest and not being a drinker himself, he had to have stashed it somewhere. He wore the same boots until they were more mending than boot and neither she nor her mother had a stitch of new clothes except what mam had weaved and knitted from the sheep's fleece every year.

One year Maw had bought them each a new outfit from the floating shop after selling eggs and salt fish. She lied about how much money she had received and Paw had accused her of allowing the boatman to cheat her. Jeannie remembered that quarrel, remembered sticking her fingers in her ears and curling up beneath her blanket as her father stormed and raged while her mother sobbed and pleaded for mercy. Only Jeannie and her mother knew the outfits, a blouse and skirt for Maw and a dress for Jeannie was in the loft. It had taken many months before they dared to wear them and by then Paw had forgotten the argument and didn't even notice. Why would he, when he never really looked at them? Maybe that's why he didn't notice her once healthy maw getting paler, growing thinner, disappearing into her mind until she no longer had the strength to rise from the bed. But she had found the strength from somewhere that last night, hadn't she?

Jeannie returned indoors and stared at the emaciated

figure on the bed. He was asleep, his head back, his mouth open, his breath a deep rumble in his chest. 'Ye drove my maw to an early grave,' she said quietly. 'I'm not doing this anymore.' Her head spun and she felt she was floating above herself. She reached behind him and, removing the spare pillow, the pillow where her mother once laid her head, she covered his face, slowly, almost tenderly, and pressed it downward. 'Sleep tight, Daddy,' she said.

Chapter 12

Alexander: 1941

Alexander Garcia stood on the quayside in Greenock waiting to board the liner. The scent of saltwater and engine oil spread among the melee of sailors, soldiers, dock hands, and horses with carts bringing in goods to be loaded into the holds of the ships. The sounds of grinding gears and screaming machinery competed with shouted orders.

Already embarking further along the dock were, what appeared to him, hundreds of nurses. He watched them file aboard a large passenger steamer and suddenly started, his heart giving an unexpected jolt. He thought he recognised a nurse with black hair and a certain way of walking. 'Annie,' he shouted and, leaving the queue, he struggled through the lines of troops and dodged behind huge cranes as they swung their cargo above his head.

'Garcia,' came a shout from behind him. 'You need to get over here if you're coming with us.'

By now the nurses were mostly on board, and the nurse he had tried to reach turned her head, just long enough for him to realise that she was not Annie.

Fighting his way back to his ship, he reprimanded himself. He had to stop this act of self-torture, of imagining her at every turn. Anyway, if she were still interested, she would have replied to his letters. He had hoped to find at least one when he returned to Aberdeen. If she was still on Raumsey, she would have received the latest letter he had written by now and, as soon as he had another address, he would write to her again. If he received no reply this time, he would finally put the past behind him and move on.

Remembering her as having strong views about social injustices he wondered what she was doing now and whether she was using her nursing skills to volunteer in this war. Maybe not; she had a child, he remembered with the jolt of pain the thought of her loving another man always brought.

A burly sergeant stood at the top of the gangway, checking papers. Alexander handed over his documents. The sergeant scrutinised them, then looked up. 'Alexander Garcia? The war correspondent?'

'That's right.'

The sergeant nodded and handed the papers back. 'Welcome aboard, Mr. Garcia.' He checked his list. 'As a correspondent, you'll be pleased to know, you have been allowed officer status. You're assigned to cabin B-14. It's below deck, starboard side. Your cabin mate should already be there.'

Alexander stepped onto the ship. He made his way through a group of soldiers who were exchanging nervous glances and whispered words. Each face told a story. Fear, determination, hope. *It's my duty to capture them all, to bear witness to their trials and triumphs,* thought Alexander. He took a small notebook from his coat pocket and began to jot down his impressions. Beneath his feet, the ship creaked and groaned under the weight of cargo and passengers.

Below deck, dim lighting lit his way along narrow corridors lined with doors, each marked with a small brass plaque. He found B-14 and gave a brief knock before entering.

Inside, the cabin was cramped but orderly with bunk beds bolted to opposite walls. On one bunk, sat a man in uniform, scribbling notes in a ledger balanced on his knee. He looked up as Alexander entered.

'Ah, you must be Garcia.' The man rose to his feet. He was slightly taller than Alexander, broad-shouldered, with close-cut auburn hair and a square jaw. His eyes were a deep blue, sharp and assessing. 'Captain Edward MacLeod,' he said, extending a hand.

Alexander shook it firmly. 'Pleasure to meet you, Captain. Hope you don't mind sharing quarters with a civilian.'

MacLeod lifted his eyebrows. 'A fellow Scot, I wasn't sure what to expect with a name like Garcia. I don't mind at all. Have you been a correspondent for long?'

Alexander smiled and explained. 'I do have Spanish roots, hence the name. This is my first trip.'

'You'll find no shortage of material, I assure you.' MacLeod sat down again and began shuffling through the papers in his folder. 'Don't mind me,' he said, 'But I do have rather a lot to do before we set sail.'

'Do you know where we're going?' Alexander asked.

'Even I don't know that,' MacLeod said.

Alexander placed his kit bag on the opposite bunk and began unpacking. MacLeod had his head lowered over his paperwork and it seemed there would be no further conversation.

The ship's horn produced its resonant tone, powerful and commanding, deep enough to cut through all the other noises. The vibrations of the engines reverberated through the cabin, signalling imminent departure.

'I'm going up to the deck,' said Alexander.

Without looking up, MacLeod gave a brief nod. 'I'll probably join you in a bit.'

As the ship sliced through the water leaving the port behind, Alexander joined a group of young soldiers at the rail and watched Greenock fade into the mist, both smoke and fog shrouding the buildings. He experienced a mixture of fear and excitement; what stories was he yet to uncover? He spent the rest of the day on deck, talking to the recruits, taking notes and trying not to think of the threat of submarines.

He had hoped to make a friend of MacLeod but found the man pleasant but distant. Therefore, he only used the cabin to sleep. Alexander didn't want to bother his companion any more than he had to and, in the absence of a desk, the deck was as good a place to write as any.

Several weeks later, after many diversions to navigate the most dangerous waters, a call went out for all men to assemble on deck. A tall man in a captain's uniform stood before them, his expression grim. The murmur of the soldiers quieted as they turned to face him, forming a rough semicircle.

'I am Lieutenant General Harrington.' His voice, clear and commanding, carried over the sound of the waves and the engine. 'We are approaching our destination. Ahead lies the British stronghold of Singapore.'

A ripple of murmured conversation spread throughout the deck and excitement stirred in Alexander's veins. After such a long sail he had expected to land in Egypt or elsewhere in North Africa. Singapore had always been considered an impenetrable fortress, a symbol of British strength in the east.

Lieutenant Harrington continued, his tone serious. 'Our mission is to reinforce the garrison there and prepare for a possible attack. Intelligence reports indicate that Japanese forces are advancing rapidly through Malaya. I won't lie to you, lads, the situation is not good, but we have our orders, and we'll carry them out with the bravery and determination expected of us.'

Captain MacLeod appeared at Alexander's side. 'Now we know,' he said, then stepped forward, his boots clanging on the metal deck. 'Sir, do we know what we're looking at in terms of enemy numbers?'

Harrington sucked air through his teeth. 'We have no way of telling for certain how many there are.'

The men exchanged uneasy glances. A private, Bertie Campbell, a young Gordon Highlander Alexander had befriended, clenched his rifle tighter, his knuckles white. 'I hear it's a good place for the nightlife,' he said lightly, but an undercurrent of fear ran beneath his words.

'I believe so,' said Alexander, and continued sarcastically, 'I can hardly wait.'

A few days later, the crew and passengers stood on the deck as the large ship sliced through the dark, choppy waters, its engines a low, steady hum against the wind. The predawn sky was a mottled grey, with a hint of crimson peeking through, signalling the coming day. Alexander joined a group of Gordon Highlanders, clad in drab olive jackets and Gordon tartan kilts as, along with other regiments, they lined the rails on the deck, faces taut.

As the ship drew closer to the shore, the outline of Singapore became visible. The city's skyline, with its colonial buildings and modern structures, stood in stark contrast to the dense jungle surrounding it. The docks bustled with activity, ships loading and unloading supplies; troops moving with purpose.

Lieutenant Harrington's voice cut through the clamour. 'We disembark in one hour. Check your gear, stay with your units, and be ready for anything. Remember, we're not just fighting for a piece of land. We're fighting for the people of Singapore, for our comrades, and our country. Good luck, lads. Dismissed.'

The soldiers broke rank, moving with a renewed sense of urgency, now fully aware of their destination and the imminent danger. The fate of the city and perhaps the entire region hung in the balance.

'I guess this is goodbye for now,' said Captain MacLeod, extending his hand to Alexander. 'No doubt we will meet again as our destination is the same.'

Alexander shook the proffered hand. 'I hope we do,' he said, 'And hopefully in favourable circumstances.'

Chapter 13

Jeannie: Raumsey 1926

After her father lay still, his scathing voice finally silenced, Jeannie had no feeling left, nothing. Every movement was automatic. She rearranged the pillows beneath his head so that they looked as if they had never been disturbed, then trudged up the brae, dragging her feet through the damp grass, to where Willie Firth the undertaker lived, knocked on the door, three sharp raps, then stood back, waiting. A herring gull yelped, a ewe bleated, a curlew emitted a forlorn flute that echoed a hollow place in her heart.

Willie's wife, Olive, opened the door. 'Why, hen, what's up with ye? Ye're as white as paper so ye are.' She ushered Jeannie into her parlour. The room was warm. A fire burned in the grate and the chairs at either side had cushions. The oil lamp, already lit, emitted a soft glow through the early dusk. So different from the cold, damp cottage she had grown up in.

'I'll make us tea,' said Olive, and lifted a couple of china cups and saucers from the shelf of the dresser. The kindness from the woman loosened something in Jeannie and thawed enough of the ice inside her to make speech possible. 'My paw's gone,' she whispered.

Olive set the cups on the table. 'I thought as much, lass.

But he's in a better place. He suffered towards the end.'

Jeannie said no more.

'Ye drink yer tea and I'll away and check him over. Willie will be in in a wee while and he'll come and measure him for the coffin. Take yer time, and when ye're finished yer tea, go away down to the Post Office and get them to phone the doctor.' She glanced at the window. 'He'll no likely come right away. It's getting gie late and there's a swell in the firth.'

Jeannie was glad to let someone else take charge, to relax and let it happen.

Vera from the Post Office was equally kind. All this kindness, all these fussing women making tea and ushering her into warm rooms was something she had never experienced before, and she revelled in it.

'I'll tell Hughie to take the post boat and go for the doctor first thing in the morning. I'll phone and let him know what's what,' said Vera. 'And tonight, ye'll stay here. I'll guarantee ye'll still be in shock.'

Jeannie nodded, grateful. She had no wish to return to the scene of her crime while her accuser lay there. Rubbing her upper arms as if she were still cold, she forced a half-hearted smile.

Vera lit a fire in her spare room and put a heated stone bottle in the bed, brought in a towel, a jug of water, a basin and one of her own nightgowns. 'There ye go, lass,' she said. 'Ye make yerself comfortable, and if ye need anything give me a shout, I'm just in the next room.'

Next morning Vera bustled into the bedroom, carrying a cup of steaming tea and a treacle scone. 'How did ye sleep, lass?'

Jeannie hadn't slept well although the bed was the most comfortable she had ever known. 'Off and on,' she said. 'I couldn't settle, but yer bed is lovely.'

Vera looked at her with such concern that she wanted to

stay here forever.

'Ach, it's understandable. Ye take as long as ye like. That's Hughie away over for the doctor. I've some porridge on the stove when ye're ready.' With another kind smile, she left the room.

Jeannie sipped the tea and when she finished, she looked through the window, her stomach in a knot as the small boat ploughed over the firth. Her angst grew all the time. What if the doctor could tell what she had done? At his last visit, he said that her father still had roughly six months. What if there were marks on the body? There would be no need to worry about who would inherit the croft then; she would be thrown in jail, or worse still, hanged. Her stomach turned and twisted. The porridge smelt lovely, but she couldn't bring herself to eat a bite.

Two hours later, when Doctor Anderson arrived, he sat in front of Jeannie and leaned towards her, his voice soft, his eyes kind. 'Can you tell me what happened, my dear?' he asked.

Jeannie's throat and lips were dry but she managed a few panicky words. Why hadn't she rehearsed this? 'I…I…don't know. I found him like that. I was milking the cow.' It was the first thing that came to mind. She dry-swallowed, then took a sip of the now-cold tea that sat beside her.

'It's all right, Jean, take your time.'

'He wasn't breathing. I went for Willie Firth.'

'You did the right thing. We'll go up and see him now. Do you feel up to it?'

Jeannie nodded and rose to her feet. She couldn't stop whatever happened now. Outside, Hughie waited for them in his truck. When he saw them, he got out and cranked the engine up with the starting handle. 'Get in quick before it stalls,' he shouted.

In Stonehill, Doctor Anderson studied her father. He seemed

to be looking for signs of life, although it was obvious there were none. Jeannie rubbed her hands up and down her upper arms frantically as her anxiety rose — he seemed to be taking forever. She watched, her breath ragged, as he studied the face, then turned and stared straight at her. Her legs shook and threatened to fold. The breath stuck in her throat and she wanted to be sick.

'You found him dead?' he asked, his tone, she thought, almost accusatory.

Avoiding eye contact, Jeannie nodded, her head snapping up and down, her bottom lip trapped between her teeth. Her voice was too thick in her throat to get past it.

Doctor Anderson said nothing for a long moment but she could feel his eyes on her. 'He wasn't an easy man to live with. I always knew it. And it was hard on ye, that last while and it was hard on him, too. It's God's mercy that he's gone. He's at peace now.' He turned away, set his briefcase on the table and extracted a large pad on which he began to write. Eventually, he straightened himself, folded the pages and put them into his pocket. 'I'll see to the death certificate,' he said. 'And you'll get a copy in due course. Now I'd best get going before the tide turns.' He set a hand on her arm as he walked past. 'Take care of yourself, my dear.'

When the door closed behind him, Jeannie finally was able to breathe.

'Now off ye go, lass,' said Olive, 'I've to wash and dress the body. Have ye somewhere to stay the night?'

'Vera said I can stay as long as I want.'

'Ye'll be comfortable with Vera. She's a fine woman.' Olive patted Jeannie's arm.

The following morning dawned fresh and clear. 'Good morning, pet,' said Vera when Jeannie came into the kitchen after the best sleep she'd had in ages.

'I've made porridge and put fresh cream on it and all.'

'It's good of ye, I didn't eat a thing yesterday.' But even

now she wasn't hungry. She felt strange, detached from reality, yet inside something sang, *I'm free, I'm free.*

'Ye'll need to eat today. I'll leave it here and get the tea.' Vera bustled over to the stove and spooned the tea into the pot.

'I'll need to go home,' said Jeannie, wishing she didn't have to.

'Ye don't look very well,' said Vera, 'Mind, ye can stay here until the funeral if ye want.'

'Thanks, Vera, I ...I would love that.' She had no desire to share the house with a dead man. 'But I'll need to get my clothes and feed the hens and milk the cow.'

'I'll take ye in the jeep then.' Vera pulled her coat from a hook behind the door.

In Stonehill, Olive had done a good job. Gus was laid out in a plain wooden coffin, dressed in a white shroud. His face had been washed and his hair neatly combed.

Jeannie remembered something she had been told when her maw died. *Kiss her forehead. It stops the bad dreams from coming*. But bad dreams or no, Jeannie could not bring herself to even stand beside the coffin.

If Vera thought her behaviour was strange, she didn't remark on it.

Chapter 14

Jeannie: Raumsey 1926

On the day of her father's funeral, Jeannie wore a black cardigan that had been her mother's and fastened on a brooch handed down by her grandmother. She had washed her hair and tied it back in a knot, then applied a wee touch of rouge she had bought from Connie's shop. Her father's sneering voice still echoed in her ears. '*Ye'll never make a silk purse from a sow's ear*,' one of his favourite sayings whenever she tried to improve her looks. Feeling no sorrow at his passing, she worried that she couldn't pretend to.

She had baked pancakes and scones and made a pot of tea. The mourners came, not for the love of the man, but because it was tradition. Fishermen carried the coffin on crossed oars supported shoulder high, down to the graveyard where they buried him alongside her mother. Few women came to sit with her and those who had, extended their condolences and drank their tea quietly. Once the men had left with the coffin, Jeannie offered the women more tea. Only Olive and Vera accepted a second cup. The others smiled awkwardly, offered to help her in any way they could, 'Ye've only got to ask,' they said, and one by one, made excuses to leave.

Who gives a damn about them, any of them, thought Jeannie, relieved that this ordeal was nearly over. She was grateful for Olive and Vera's company, however, but knew the women were only staying out of the kindness of their hearts.

'Will ye be all right, dear?' Olive asked. 'Do you want a hand with the dishes?'

'I'll be fine,' she answered. *Yes, I'm perfectly fine*, she thought, by now wishing they would drink up and go. She had loved staying with Vera and wished the invitation had been extended, but she knew it couldn't go on forever. The sooner she got used to being on her own, the better it would be.

'I don't need a hand, thank you. It'll give me something to do.' Now that the coffin had gone, she had to start clearing out her father's things and burn them. There was nothing of him she wanted to keep.

'If you need anything, we are just over the hill. Anytime,' said Olive, setting down her cup and saucer.

'And I'm in the Post Office,' said Vera.

Jeannie offered a thin smile and a nod and saw them to the door.

When she was finally alone, she looked through the window at the sad state of the croft. How strong was she really to wield a scythe or manage a plough? Had her father been right all along?

Then she sat down and cried. The tears were not for her father, but for the knowledge that now she was totally alone. She had no one. Nothing. Not even a friend. The fact that within three months she also would lose the only home she'd ever known struck her anew. If she went to the mainland, she could gut herring for a living, she'd gutted enough fish in her lifetime to make her an expert.

She could have done better. Her mind took her back to the day when her father took her to one side. 'Ye're going to have to leave school,' he said. 'Yer mam's getting worse and she's no fit for the work anymore.'

Something caught painfully in her throat. She liked

school. She was good at her lessons and it was the one place where she felt she could escape from the drudgery of her life.

'I can do the work when I come home.' Desperation had crept into her voice.

Her father shook his head. 'Ye can read and write. That's all ye need to do. I've already spoken to the headmaster. Ye'll no be going back anymore.'

No, she wouldn't shed a tear for Gus. He had ruined her life.

But the truth was, she didn't want to leave the island. She didn't want to face the unknown. Why had fate been so unkind to her? But what was the use of wishing? Or tears.

She had three months to sell as much as she could in order to get enough money for lodgings until she got a job. The one thing she was an expert at was living frugally and that would stand her in good stead in the years to come.

But farming was all she knew, and the unknown terrified her. She couldn't be turned out, she just couldn't. She pulled the framed family portrait from the wall and worked the back from the frame, meaning to cut her father's image out, burn it and only keep that of herself and her mother to carry with her wherever she went.

As soon as she removed the backing, a large, thick envelope fell out. She picked it up and slipped open the seal, carried it over to the table and edged the flap open. Then gasped. There was a wad of £20 banknotes.

She sat down and counted them out. £400. A fortune. A laugh started in her throat, a laugh that rose and grew and became hysterical. Who cared if she had to leave Stonehill? She could buy another croft of her own. The money wouldn't last forever, and it wouldn't buy her the thing she most craved, love. But it did mean that she wouldn't starve.

'Oh, Daddy,' she said out loud, 'Did ye forget about that money or did ye just die before you could give it to Tavish O'Connor?

I don't need Nick Sinclair, she thought. *Or any man.*

Chapter 15

Alexander: Singapore 1941

The open truck jolted along a rutted road in Singapore. Alexander sat side by side with the young recruit, Bertie Campbell. His comrades had long since stopped talking to each other as the heat and exhaustion stilled their tongues. Having been awake since before dawn, most were dozing as much as they could, but Alexander's mind was too full. *What would his parents think if they could see him now?* He closed his eyes as the unforgiving sun strobed through the palm leaves on either side, the scorching air thickened with the scent of flowers and eucalyptus trees, and noises: the mutter of the motor, the whisper of the wheels as they threw up dust, the sound of twittering and hooting birds, the clicking of insects, all very different to the noises on the ship.

Bertie stirred, woke up and shifted his position. 'Can't wait to get a proper bed,' he murmured. 'Whatever the barracks are like they can't be worse than those damn cabins. Bloody hell, but we were overcrowded. They gave me a hammock. I hate the bloody sea, that's why I'm in the Army, not the Navy.'

Alexander looked at the young man, his fair complexion already turning red, the sweat beading his brow, and noted the worry lines belying his words.

'They seem to be doing all right out here,' he said as they passed posh bungalows with manicured lawns bordered by palm trees.

'Not much sign of war,' remarked Bertie, wiping his brow.

The heat was searing, worse than Spain in the height of summer, Alexander thought, although the dreich days back in Scotland may have influenced his outlook. He had already read about the rubber plantations, the way of life here and how fortunes were being made and was glad to finally see it for himself although maybe not in these circumstances.

'I hope we get some time off. This looks great.' said another recruit. By now they were travelling past exotic buildings, with every race of people filling the streets.

'We'll be lucky to get any time off,' said another.

A few miles further on, the driver looked over his shoulder. 'Don't let the vision of ex-pats living the good life fool you. There's a lot of unrest among the natives. I'm not too hopeful about the future of the Great British Empire. Now hang on to your seats. The road's going to get pretty bumpy from here on to your barracks.'

Once they were in the outskirts, jostled and jolted along the uneven roads, they saw a different side to this rich country. The poverty in many of the native villages, built of wood and bamboo, existed in stark contrast to the rich European lifestyle they had left behind in Singapore. Suddenly they were in the open country, with rice fields and banana plantations, and the searing sun beating on their heads.

Finally, when the men were drenched in sweat, and their tongues were stuck to the roofs of their mouths with thirst, they reached their barracks. Selerang, modern-looking blocks, seven of them, built around a square. One by one the men jumped from the truck, staggering, not yet fully confident on their land legs after being so long at sea.

'Looks fairly comfortable,' said Alexander as he gathered up his equipment. He meant to write a piece about the troops' living quarters before booking himself into a hotel in

Singapore. He had orders from his newspaper not to find anything too expensive, assuming that there were hotels in whichever region he was sent to. They were footing the bill. But for now, he was allowed to check out the soldiers' accommodation and share a meal.

'After a stint in the bases I've been in before and that bloody ship, this is like a holiday camp,' said Bertie.

The lads collected their kit and were directed to the dining room. Despite reservations when he saw the Chinese waiters, the meal consisted of very British fare, sausages, mashed potato and garden peas, followed by sponge pudding. After they had eaten and drunk weak tea, Alexander joined the troops to be welcomed to Singapore by the commanding officer, who, as well as reminding them of the important job they had been given, warned them of the dangers outwith these gates.

'Thanks for letting me look around the barracks,' Alexander said, impressed with what he had seen so far.

'Hope you give us a favourable write-up,' said Captain MacLeod who had been present at the talk.

'I certainly will,' said Alexander.

'I'll get my driver to take you to your hotel,' MacLeod said. 'I have been instructed to book you into Adelphi Hotel.' He gave a wry grin. 'I guess they were afraid you would choose Raffles if left on your own.'

That stung. Alexander felt aggrieved that he wasn't trusted to choose a reasonably priced accommodation on his own. He shrugged.

Expecting something basic, Alexander was completely taken by surprise at the classic, sophisticated design of the hotel, both outside and in.

'You mean Raffles is better than this?' he asked, amazed.

The driver shrugged. 'I'm surprised as well,' he said. 'I don't think you'll find anything to complain about. I'll leave you now to get settled.'

Alexander bade him goodbye and retrieved his key from

the desk, surprised when a porter picked up his case and carried it upstairs for him. 'I could get used to this,' he muttered to himself.

If the foyer had impressed him, he was awe-struck by the room, decorated in the colonial style, with deep greens and burgundies and floral wallpaper. A small wardrobe was provided with ample space for clothing, and a radio sat on a side table.

Oriental rugs covered the floor of polished wood, a plush armchair, upholstered in rich velvet sat near a small, writing desk complete with a typewriter and a lamp with a brass base. The bed was large and covered with a decorative bedspread, and matching wooden nightstands, each holding a lamp with a fabric shade, sat on either side. He felt the bed and fought the urge to lie down and sleep in the soft comfort.

The bathroom facilities were equally impressive. He filled the claw-foot tub, stripped off and sank into the warm luxury. After the cramped space in the cabin, he felt like a king, yet he was uncomfortably aware that at any time the situation could change.

Once he had bathed and unpacked, he went downstairs for something to wash away the lingering dryness of his throat.

The bar room featured warm, rich colours, deep mahogany and dark green, complemented by soft lighting. Elegant ceiling fixtures with brass accents cast a warm glow over the room.

British colonials dressed in semi-formal attire, well-dressed ladies, military officers, and personnel from various allied forces were either seated or standing, drinking and speaking in low voices,

Alexander ordered a beer, exchanged a few words with the barman, and looked around at the other occupants.

'A fellow Scot,' came a loud voice from behind him. He turned to see a large man with several chins and a bloated belly. 'Wilbur McCormac.' He held out a sweaty palm.

‘What are you doing over here, lad?’

‘Alexander Garcia, a correspondent for the *Aberdeen and World News*.’ He grasped the hand.

‘Let me pay for your drink.’ Wilbur clapped him on the shoulder. ‘I was born here, but my father came from Edinburgh. You must come and have dinner with my family. I own a rubber plantation on the outskirts.’

Alexander tried to refuse. He had already eaten and was eager to get his first article typed up and back to the newspaper, but Wilbur would have none of it. Finally, he agreed to go the following evening.

‘Good, good,’ said Wilbur. ‘I’ll send my driver, Zi Han, for you at seven.’

Chapter 16

Jeannie: Raumsey 1926

Jeannie clutched the £400 to her chest, enjoying the feel of the crisp notes. *I could go to the mainland, buy a place*, she thought. Just as quickly, the thought died. Truth was, she wanted to be married, she wanted bairns, she didn't want to be a *spinster of the parish* pitied for her plainness and lack of family to take care of her in her old age and become a charity case.

She studied herself in the pock-marked mirror, reached behind her head and loosened her hair, letting it fall around her face. Her hair was thick and softly waved, dark with a hint of auburn, her best feature. She could brighten the dull pastiness of her skin with rouge, and she was sure she could lose weight now she didn't have to rely on bread and dripping as her main source of food.

But what was the use? With so many pretty, young girls who could laugh and flirt, unwed on the island, what chance did she have? Yet she did have something they didn't. She had a croft and a cottage and that was a fine start for any ambitious young man.

Her thoughts turned to Nick Sinclair. He had seemed interested and she wondered if he still was. The idea was taking hold. Nick was a good-looking man; the sun had both bleached his hair over the summer and tanned his skin to a deep golden brown, making his eyes appear bluer than ever.

And he owned one of the finest houses on the island.

Suddenly she reprimanded herself. What was she thinking?

His first wife, Bel, had been the complete opposite of Jeannie. She had been a gentle, trusting soul, but delicate, like a waif that would blow away in the wind. There was no way she could ever compete with that ghost. And then there was Annie Reid. Before he married, Nick had set his cap at her. The fact that she hated him did not necessarily mean his desire had lessened. But Annie and her parents were still bringing up Nick's daughter, keeping her promise to Bel and keeping a connection between her and Nick. She wondered if she married Nick, would she be expected to take the ailing bairn on?

Less than a week later, she still had no firm plan about what to do next. There came a quick rap, rap, rap on the door. Knowing that she was expected to be sad, she rearranged her face, opened the door and took a step back, shocked to see Nick Sinclair standing there, dressed in a black suit which had grown tight over the years and now strained across his shoulders.

'I've been thinking,' he said and hesitated.

With a pulse beating in her throat, she waited. What should she do? Should she ask him in? Offer him tea? She was so devoid of social graces she had no idea how to behave.

'About what your dad said...'

She drew her brows together, peered at him and swallowed.

He ran his hand over his head and studied his feet. 'Unless ye're sure ye're up to running the place yerself, like.'

'I'm perfectly capable, although he didn't want to give me the chance,' she said bitterly. A surge of bravado powered through her, something she'd never experienced before. She was no longer meek, downtrodden Jeannie MacKay. Not wanting to appear too keen, she lifted her head, jutted out her jaw and lied. 'Anyway, I do not even want to stay here.'

Nick looked surprised. 'I suppose it does need a fair bit o' work.'

'And,' she said mustering all her newly found confidence, 'according to the newspapers there are all sorts of opportunities for women nowadays. I was good at my lessons, and it's not too late for me to do something else.'

Nick met her gaze. There was a new look in his eyes. Surprise? Respect? Whatever it was it encouraged her.

'It'll not be easy to bring it back to full production, but that's not it.' The bitterness remained in her voice. 'Paw always led me to believe that the farm would be mine one day. Now it's full of bad memories for me.'

'I wanted to talk to ye about the croft.'

'Ye'd best come in,' she said, deciding this must be what people did. Her heartbeat raced. He was still interested.

'If ye still want a man…'

'Are ye offering me help?' she asked.

'We could help each other.'

'What are ye saying? Yer own croft needs work. What time will ye have to help me?'

He cleared his throat. 'If we pooled resources, if we worked together…' his voice trailed away and she realised that he, too, was unsure.

'Are ye saying ye want to marry me?'

For a moment he looked even more uncomfortable and shuffled his feet and she feared she might have been too forward — that she had scared him away. His next words relieved her.

'It would be a business proposal,' he said.

'I don't need a man to survive and I know it's only the croft ye're wanting.'

'I'll no deny it,' he said. 'But I do need a wife. And ye need a man to do the heavy work.' He glanced out of the window. 'There's no way ye'll bring this land back on yer own, it's been left too long.'

'I know ye'd never look at me in normal circumstances, and I'm not sure I want what ye're offering,' she said, hoping he would say something kind but that was not to be.

'Ye don't have the looks right enough,' he said, and held up his hand as she made to say more. 'Ye're young and strong and looks are no everything. And, if ye don't want to live here anymore, where would ye go? Aye, there may be more chances for women nowadays, but is that what ye really want? Marry me and ye can live in Scartongarth. We could rent out this place and, with all that land to manage, we could be well off. It makes sense, doesn't it?'

Stung by his directness, she wanted to tell him to get out, that she wanted a man who would see her as a woman, not a commodity, but confidence failed her and she remained silent. Best to say nothing than regret her words later, she reasoned, but things being what they were, she might never get another chance. Nick did own Scartongarth, a house she had always coveted.

Simultaneously feeling both hurt and excited, she studied the floor, hoping she could afford to take her time.

'A business proposition is it?' She raised her eyes.

'It may be a business proposition, but,' he hesitated, 'it's best to be honest at the off. I want a son.'

She forced herself to contain a smile. 'I would love a family,' she said, 'but I'll need to think on it.'

'I'll come back tomorrow, then?' he raised his eyebrows. 'Will that give ye enough time?'

'It might,' she said, silently pleading that he would not change his mind. She wanted him, but deep down she knew that, although he missed Bel, he had always desired Annie Reid, a woman who would have none of him.

She could not sleep that night. Nick Sinclair was the bonniest man on the island, and her bairns would surely be bonnier than she was. She had known she would accept his offer, even as she asked for more time.

Next morning she washed her hair and left it loose, dressed in her best clothes, did some baking and set the table. When Nick arrived, she invited him in.

He looked around the room as if surprised. 'Quite a difference from the last time I was here,' he said.

'When my father said I was a good worker, he was right. Ye'll have tea?'

'Aye,' he sat down at the table. 'Have ye thought any more about what I said?'

'Ye still want to go ahead?' she asked.

He looked around the room again. 'And get scones and a warm fire every day? Aye, I do.'

She held out her hand the way she had seen men clinch a deal. 'Then I accept.'

A smile spread across his face. 'Fine. We'll go to the mainland and get married in the registry office. I will not have any of Annie Reid's family near us and that rules the minister out.'

The mention of Annie Reid stung. 'I agree,' she said. She knew that if Annie Reid wanted him, he would go there in a shot, but Annie hated him with as much passion as he desired her.

'I'll need to get a new dress,' she said. 'I've nothing suitable.'

'What you're wearing will do. I've no the money for clothes.'

She had money, but something stopped her from disclosing it.

'A couple of things I want to get clear,' she said. 'I was downtrodden by my father all my life, and I'll no put up with it from another man. I have heard you can be handy with yer fists. I warn ye now, if ye ever lift a hand to me, ye'll not sleep easy in yer bed.' She trembled inside as she said the words, her mouth dry.

A muscle along his jawline twitched. 'I never lifted my hand to Bel and I'll no lift my hand to ye.'

'And Bel's baby, will you take her back from Annie Reid? I can bring her up now.'

'I wasn't planning on taking her back. It's because of her that Bel died and I can't even bring myself to look at her face. Annie Reid promised to look after her, and it's a promise I'll see she keeps.'

'But...she is yours.'

'I told you, woman, I do not want that child. In any case, she'll never make old bones.'

Less than a year later Nick's baby daughter had joined her mother in the graveyard. Jeannie was sorry for the child, but glad that the last link her man had with Annie Reid was severed. The news of Annie leaving the island to train for the nursing was yet a further boost to Jeannie's confidence, the more miles between Annie Reid and Nick Sinclair the better.

Now all she needed was to give him a son. She did not know then how many years it was to take before that happened.

Three years later, Annie Reid returned. By then, Jeannie had grown into her looks and learned which clothes best suited her shape. She knew she would never be beautiful; she was too much of everything, too tall, too broad, her features too irregular. Yet, to a stranger's eye, she might have been called handsome. But that had done nothing to make Nick Sinclair desire her. And she had already begun to despise him.

Chapter 17

Annie: Raumsey 1941.

'How is our boy today?' Annie asked as she entered the cottage.

Denis's mother, Brenda, stood over the range stirring something in a pot. 'He'll no get out o' bed.' Brenda turned to her with a despondent face. 'He's that low, Annie.' She seemed close to tears. 'He's only thirteen.'

'It's early days. Losing a limb is a bereavement in a way, especially for a boy who loved football. I'll go and see him shall I?'

'I'd be more than grateful if ye could get him moving,' said Brenda, her face a mask of concern. 'With his dad away at the war, I don't know what I would do if I lost him too.'

Annie opened the bedroom door. Denis was no more than a heap of blankets in the middle of the bed. She walked over and pulled them back. 'Denis, it's me, your friendly nurse. Let me look at your dressing.'

The boy turned to stare at her but said nothing. He lay placidly only flinching when she removed the bandage. 'A bit tender is it?' Although everything looked good from a medical point of view, something worried her. What Eliza with her tea leaves had predicted, made her extra concerned for her patients.

Denis nodded.

She couldn't afford to miss anything. 'Do you hurt

anywhere else?' she asked.

He shook his head and turned his face away.

'Doctor Anderson thinks you should try to take a few steps with your new crutches today. What do you say to that?'

Denis shook his head. 'Don't want to.'

Annie despaired. Lying in bed wasn't doing his overall health any good. 'It's been hard, but you're stronger than you think.'

'I'll fall.'

'Let me show you,' she said, crossing the room to lift the wooden crutches from where they sat, propped against the wall. She put one leather-padded support snugly under each armpit and grabbed the vertical shaft about halfway down. Bending a knee so that she balanced on one leg, she swung herself across the room. 'Look, it's fun. You'll be better than me because they're too short for me. There's a rubber tip so you won't slide. And in time, you'll manage with one. It's okay to be scared, Denis. Everybody feels like that when they're learning something new. But I'll be here with you, to catch you. This isn't about doing it perfectly, it's about taking that first step.'

His lip quivered. 'Everybody'll laugh at me. I'm not going back to school, I'm not.'

'You know, some clever people are working on artificial limbs that you can wear under your trousers and no one will ever know. Will I get some photos for you?'

He looked uncertain but nodded.

Encouraged, she forged on. 'I'll bring them next time, but until you're fit enough to go to hospital and have one fitted, this will get you moving.' She set her hand on the crutches. 'Will we try? If I can do it surely a strapping young lad like yourself can as well.'

At this, the beginning of a smile formed at the corner of his mouth. 'Come on, I'll help you.' She stopped at his bedside, lowered herself down and held out her hand to him. As she helped, she despaired at how light he'd gotten. Was losing this boy the disaster Eliza had spoken about?' She helped him place the crutches under his arms and held him as he stood upright.

'I'm all wobbly,' he said in panic.

'You've been lying in bed too long that's all. The muscles on your good leg are weak.'

'Will I be like the soldiers that get their legs blown off in the war?'

'Absolutely. A brave soldier. Now, try and get your balance and we'll give it a rest for today.'

He swung himself a few steps and she steadied him as he turned, encouraged by the light in his eyes. By the time she tucked him back into bed, she felt a lot more optimistic.

'Tell Mam I'm hungry,' he said.

With glistening eyes, his mother laid a hand on Annie's arm. 'This is the first time he's asked for food. Ye're a Godsend, so ye are.'

'If ye've any worries, any at all, come and get me,' said Annie.

Her next visit was to a new baby born just over a week ago. She was a healthy, thriving little girl and the mother was doing well. After six children she was an old hand.

'Ye're that good with her,' said Nancy. 'Ye'll maybe have more yerself when ye and Magnus get wed.'

'Magnus and I will not be getting wed. It's not like that.' Annie laughed.

'It's no natural, a bonny woman like yerself all alone.'

'I'm fine the way I am.' Why did women like Nancy think that having bairns was all there was to life?

Looking at the baby, she wondered if her lips looked slightly blue. She'd heard of healthy babies dying in their sleep.

'Is something wrong?' asked Nancy, sudden concern in her voice.

'No, not at all.' Annie gave herself a mental shake. Letting an old woman reading tealeaves spook her, she was really slipping.

'What about Jeannie Sinclair, then?' said Nancy as Annie packed away her things. 'She'll have to rely on ye for all sorts now.'

Annie shook her head. 'They don't want me. It's no more than I expected. I just hope she's getting regular checkups.'

'She's the daft one, then,' said Nancy. 'She'll no get better than ye. Ye've been there for my last three and although Alexina's a good howdie and all, she's getting on now and she's no got the new ideas like ye do.'

Annie shrugged. 'It's Jeannie's choice.' *Probably Nick Sinclair's choice*, she thought and wondered, not for the first time, if he had seen anything other than a free croft in Jeannie Sinclair all those years ago.

Chapter 18

Alexander: Singapore 1941

Wilbur's plantation was eight miles outside Singapore. Lush green avenues, trim lawns, bungalows with red-tiled roofs, and then the mansions of the rich plantation owners lined the roadside. Alexander tried not to gasp as the car swung into a driveway that appeared a mile long. Before him was an impressive display of wealth and influence, more than he had even imagined.

The white mansion in the distance, gleaming in the sun, sat at the end of a drive lined with palm trees. As they drew closer, he saw a tennis court with two white-clad girls playing. Beside a large swimming pool, a woman lay on a lounger sipping a drink. She stood up as the car drew to a standstill and came towards them. Tall and willowy, with deep golden hair swept up, and green eyes slightly slanted that captured Alexander's as she reached out a slender hand, she spoke in a voice as rich and golden as her hair. 'You must be the reporter from Scotland. I am Amelia, Wilbur's wife.'

Surprised, Alexander accepted the hand. This woman must be at least twenty years Wilbur's junior, and slim and attractive. He glanced towards the tennis court.

'Wilbur's twin daughters by a previous marriage.' She slipped her arm through his. 'Come inside and have a drink and I'll see if I can find Wilbur.'

She led him through sliding glass doors, into a large bright lounge area with a chandelier above their heads. Everything seemed to be made of glass and marble, with large leafy pot plants and oriental rugs on the floor. 'What are you drinking?' she asked opening a cabinet that seemed to be full of every kind of liquor one could name.

'Whisky and water,' he said.

'Glenmorangie? We have the best here.' She half-filled a glass and clunked some ice into it. 'Make yourself comfortable and I'll go to find my husband.' She handed the drink to him, her eyes never leaving his.

She had barely left the room when Wilbur entered. 'There you are, my boy.' His smile filled his face. 'I see my wife has already poured you a drink. Come along, come along, we'll sit on the terrace until dinner is served.' He led Alexander outside to where a few wicker chairs with chintzy cushions sat around a small table. 'What do you make of the situation in Singapore? A lot of noise about nothing, don't you say?'

'I don't think it's nothing,' said Alexander. 'Troops are pouring in from all over. I hear the Japs are sweeping down Malaysia.'

Wilbur mopped his brow. 'They might well be, but we are getting ready. I know the news from Europe isn't good, but the Japs will never capture Singapore.'

'You're still in the calm of a phoney war, as it's called. But don't be too relaxed. Women and children are already being evacuated. Have you any plans to go?' Alexander did not agree with Wilbur but didn't want to argue too much with his host.

Amelia returned at this point. 'Wilbur thinks it's all smoke and mirrors. The Japanese are only little men with bad eyesight. Isn't that so, darling?'

'Of course they are,' said Wilbur. 'They've never fought a serious war, just skirmishes with the Chinese and they are every bit as useless. They'll be no match for our boys.'

'I don't think we should underestimate them.' Alexander looked at Amelia. 'Aren't you scared?'

She shrugged and pouted. 'I leave all that to the men,' but he didn't miss the way her forehead crinkled with a worried frown. 'But dinner is ready. Let's not worry too much tonight and just have a nice time.'

The food was delicious, but despite Amelia trying to keep the conversation light, it inevitably strayed to talk of war.

'Singapore is well protected. The Brits have stationed troops and ships all along the coastline. The Japs would be brave indeed if they launched any attacks against British territories.' Wilbur spoke nonstop, sounding as if he was trying to convince himself as well as his audience.

Alexander believed from what he had heard that Singapore with its lack of heavy armour and air power was sadly unprepared but said nothing.

Wilbur blotted his lips with a napkin and reached for his box of cigars. 'A man can make a lot of money off the rubber.' He lit his cigar and drew deeply. The aroma of rich tobacco drifted into the room. 'I've worked hard for all this and I'm not giving it up without a fight. Pour me another whisky would you, Amelia?' He held out the box of cigars to Alexander.

He declined.

Amelia filled a cut crystal glass three-quarters the way up and handed it to her husband.' He drank the whisky in two mouthfuls and tapped the remnants of his cigar into an onyx ashtray. Leaning back in his chair, he closed his eyes. 'Another, Amelia,' he said. Once again she almost filled the glass and added ice.

'Here you are, darling.' She placed the glass in his hand.

He swallowed the whisky. 'Get one for our guest,' he slurred.

'Not for me,' said Alexander. 'I've still got this one.' By the time he'd ended his sentence, Wilbur had fallen asleep and was snoring loudly.

Alexander finished his drink and stood up. 'I'll need to go now,' he said.

'I'll walk you to the car.' Amelia came over to his side and slipped her arm through his.

Outside, the sky had plunged into inky blue, heralding the coming night. The song of the cicadas filled the air. Fireflies started to emerge, their tiny lights flickering like stars among the shadows of the trees.

'Don't you think it's beautiful here?' She hugged his arm so that he felt the pressure of her breast. 'Let's walk in the garden.'

Feeling uncomfortable but not knowing how to reject her without offending, he allowed her to lead him down the veranda steps. Fragrant frangipani trees, their waxy white and yellow blooms cascading down, lined the pathways, while vibrant bougainvillaea climbed up trellises, adding splashes of magenta to the scene.

'It is beautiful,' agreed Alexander.

'Wilbur won't wake until morning. I get lonely, you know?' She squeezed his arm gently.

He tensed. There was no way he misunderstood her meaning. 'I'd better get back,' he said.

'I'll call Zi Han if you want, but,' she increased the pressure on his arm, 'you could stay.'

Alexander hesitated. It had been a long time since he had been with a woman, and in this lush tropical paradise, the air thick with the scent of jasmine and the earthy aroma of damp soil, a reminder of the recent afternoon rain, he felt far removed from the threat of war or anything in his previous life. The alcohol he had consumed dulled his senses.

A narrow, cobblestone path led to a secluded corner of the garden, where a small wrought-iron table and two matching chairs sat beneath a large banyan tree.

'We could sit for a while,' she said in a breathless whisper.

The moment felt timeless, suspended between the beauty of nature and the uncertainty of the world beyond the garden's borders.

He looked at her in the moonlight, her lips curved up

slightly, almost pleadingly, and he was torn between his strict Catholic beliefs, his new-found friend sleeping on the veranda, and the offer that was difficult to refuse. The sudden thought of Wilbur jerked him into reality.

He lifted her hand from his arm and set it decisively by her side. 'You're a beautiful woman, but I've got to say no. Please don't be offended. I need to start early tomorrow.'

Her mouth turned down at the corners. 'I'll call your driver if you're sure.' She replaced her hand on his and raised her eyebrows. 'If you ever change your mind, no strings attached.'

'Call Zi Han. And thanks again for dinner.' He hurried away, suddenly sober, his heart thundering, horrified at what he had been tempted to do. There had been something so vulnerable and lonely about Amelia that it had transcended his distaste at her behaviour, and he surprised himself with a powerful urge to protect her.

Chapter 19

Jeannie: Raumsey 1941

In the kitchen of Scartongarth, Jeannie heaved her clumsy body towards the stove, where a pot of soup simmered, filling the room with a warm aroma. She stirred the contents of the pot and returned to the baking bowl on the table where she shaped the dough and set it aside to prove, cleaned the excess from her hands and waited. Nick would be home soon, but the bread still needed baking. She felt so tired these days that it took her all her time to get through the chores.

The sun was casting long shadows across the floor by the time the front door creaked on its hinges and then slammed. Jeannie tensed; Nick's mood was not good. She counted his steps, tacketty boots on the flagstone, closer and closer, and she held her breath.

Over the years, she had fought to be the strong woman Bel had never been, fought to hold her own against Nick's moods and demands, but she had grown tired. He would never give her the respect she deserved nor the love she craved. Now she existed, sunk in disappointment and regret. She loved this house, had made it her own: it was the anchor that bound her to Nick Sinclair.

He walked into the kitchen and slapped a small cod on the table, then stood for a minute, his eyes scanning the room. 'Ye've got the place spotless. There's no need. Not now.' he said and scowled. 'I told ye not to overtire yerself.'

‘I didn’t, I won’t.’ It was hard to know what to do for the best. The need to prove herself was always with her. All she did know was that she was too tired for an argument. ‘Was it a good catch today?’ She tried to change the subject, to find some common ground.

‘Fair. Are ye sure ye’re all right?’

She released a breath. This concern for her welfare was only because she was carrying his child and she knew it. But she’d had little enough kindness in her life and she revelled in any scrap that came her way.

‘I am a wee bit tired,’ she said with a martyred sigh. ‘But I’ll not see my man hungry.’

‘Ye’ll put the bairn first.’

He glanced at her swollen ankles and sucked a deep breath.

‘Is that normal?’

‘How do I know what’s normal? This is my first.’

His eyes opened as if startled at her sharp words. Then he nodded. ‘I’ll gut the fish.’

He doesn’t give a pig’s arse for ye, it’s just the bairn he wants. She imagined her father’s scornful voice and clenched her jaw.

‘*I don’t care,*’ she screamed silently. She would gladly fill the house with bairns if it meant Nick caring for her.

Stop trying. It’ll never work, ye’re a failure, always have been. The bairn doesn’t want to be born to a pig like you. She clutched her stomach, cradling the child within. ‘I’ll keep ye safe,’ she whispered.

‘What did ye say?’ Nick turned from where he was gutting the fish.

With her arms crossed over her stomach, Jeannie rocked slowly. ‘I said I’ll keep my bairn safe.’

Nick smiled. ‘Ye’re doing a grand job.’ He nodded in approval.

She wished she could tell him that she still imagined her father’s voice, that it wouldn’t leave her alone, she wished he would care if she did.

The barren years were still fresh in her memory. The recriminations. The blame. The guilt.

She had tried so hard to be everything he wanted. The house was always spotless and there were never better dinners in the whole of Raumsey, even on the meagre rations afforded since the war. There were not many that could catch and kill a crow and make a tasty pie from its flesh to supplement the diet of salt herring and smoked pork when the seas were too rough to fish, the rabbits became hard to catch, and the hens no longer laid. Jeannie had ways of making even the blandest of meals taste appetising.

Every day she fed the hens, collected the eggs, milked the cow, mucked out the byre, and worked as hard as any man in the harvest fields and at the lambing, all without a word of appreciation. The fact that every night he often came home, sat down, cleaned his plate, then rose to go out again to God knew where filled her with sorrow. Then she would hear her father in the shadows, his voice low and scathing, *He will never see ye as anything other than a servant and an unpaid one at that. Do ye know who he's with now? Someone a lot bonnier than ye.*

She tried to ignore it, tried to believe what Nick had told her, that there was still work to do, even in the moonlight, but the doubts grew and tortured her.

Every monthly that came upon her caused Nick's mood to sour, and his words to become cutting enough to flay the flesh from her bones. 'If only I'd known ye were barren.'

And then the miracle happened.

She hadn't told him at first, afraid that her body would once again let her down. But now she was seven months along and counting.

Chapter 20

Annie: Raumsey 1941

'The Japanese have bombed Pearl Harbour, it's on the wireless,' Isa said once Annie came through the door. 'If that doesn't bring the Americans to help us, I don't know what will.'

Annie sighed. She found it hard to get excited about anything these days. 'It may make matters worse,' she said. 'The world's on fire.'

'We've got to stay positive,' said Isa. 'Have a cup of tea and tell me all your news.'

Annie picked up her son and set him on her knee. 'And what has my brave boy been doing today?'

'He's been a wee angel,' said Isa. 'That pup is the best thing ever. He plays with it all the time.'

Isa poured the tea and set a slice of bread with home-churned butter and rhubarb jam before her. 'I couldn't get enough sugar, so the jam's a bit bitter. But the hens are laying well. We should have enough for an omelette for tonight's meal.'

Once she finished her tea, Annie pulled her coat over her shoulders. 'I'm going to see Eliza. I've not had time this last wee while and I need to check on her leg. It's not just her leg though. She's losing weight, and I'm a bit worried. She's that proud she'd never admit to feeling poorly.'

'Take as long as you need, lass,' said Isa.

Annie found Margaret in her grandmother's house, but not the usual smiling girl she'd come to know. Her eyes were red and puffy as if she'd been crying.

'What's wrong?' she asked. 'Where's Eliza?'

'Oh, Annie, I hate to burden ye.' Her cheeks flushed.

'Is it your gran?' Annie looked around the room alarmed. 'Where is she?'

Margaret shook her head. 'Gran's fine. Having a lie-down. She's awfully tired these days, fast asleep last time I looked.'

'How's her leg?' asked Annie.

'She's hirpling about on a walking stick,' said Margaret. 'But will she give in? Will she heck.'

'I was hoping to see her,' said Annie, 'I'm a bit concerned about her overall health.'

'She's no eating. I help Mam to keep an eye on her. It's just, well, she's no getting any younger as Mam keeps reminding me.'

Annie took a seat. 'Now that I'm here, you need to tell me what else is wrong.'

Margaret sniffed. 'Freddy's had his call-up papers. Oh Annie he's just turned eighteen. I wish we were married already, but Mam's so set on us waiting. What's the point? I won't love anyone else, I know I won't.'

'But your mam says you want to join the WVS while he's gone. I think that's a grand idea.'

'I did want to do that, but I can't. Everything's awful.' She sniffed again and wiped at her eyes.

'Why? Come on, love, it can't be that bad.' Annie remembered her time in Glasgow. The initial fear of leaving everything she knew, the later excitement of a different life. 'It'll do you good in the long run. You'll love it, you'll see.'

'Ye don't understand. I can't join anything. I've got to get married — now.'

A sinking feeling started in Annie's stomach. 'What is it?'

'Promise ye won't tell Mam?'

Annie felt sure she knew what was coming next. 'I

promise.'

'I'm having a bairn and I daren't let Mam know. Dad'll go berserk. I didn't mean it to happen. I'm no a bad lassie.'

Annie put an arm around the girl's shoulder. 'Come on, I'm the last person to judge you.' She thought for a moment. 'Tell yer mam that ye want to get married before Freddy goes to the forces and you've changed your mind about the WVS. That'll be a relief for her. She was worried about you going.'

'Ye don't know what like she is. She wants to give me a fine wedding one day, but not now. And with rationing and all it takes a fair bit of saving up.'

'Do you want me to speak to your mother? She's not that bad.'

'It won't do any good. I've tried. She just makes me feel guilty about denying her that special day. That's why I said about the WVF. I thought that would make her change her mind.'

'When does Freddy have to go?'

'Four weeks' time. Right after Christmas. Ye can't tell Mam I'm expecting, please.'

'I'll not tell her. I promise.' At the same time, Annie wondered if her friend would ever forgive her for plotting with Margaret behind her back.

'But it'll be different coming from me. I'll try to persuade her without saying anything about the bairn.'

'All right. But mind, ye promised.'

'I'll go round first thing tomorrow. Now is that a kettle I hear boiling?'

Margaret crossed to the stove. 'And then there's Dolly. She's being a right bitch. I think she's guessed. I just want her to shut up.'

'Have you told anyone else?'

'No, no one knows but you.'

'Then she can't possibly know.'

Margaret had calmed down. 'Thanks for listening,' she said.

'If I can get your mam to agree, I'll speak to Donald. I'll even use your gran's health. I mean you want her at yer wedding?'

'Of course I do. I didn't think of that. It just feels like, she'll be here forever.' Her face fell as if she only realised at this moment how frail Eliza had become.

'With any luck, we'll have the wedding as soon as possible. Speak to Dolly. Maybe she's hurt that you've gone quiet with her. You used to tell each other everything.'

'Maybe. But I think it's more because Rory's away at the war and he never asked her to get wed before he went. She'll have a field day if she finds out about me. The only reason she isn't expecting is sheer luck.'

'Don't be like that. You've been friends since school. Look, I'll tell you what, you ask Dolly to be your bridesmaid and I'll be your matron of honour.'

Margaret smiled. 'I will think about asking her and that.'

'But will ye do it?' Annie thought Margaret needed all her friends around her now and Dolly wasn't a bad sort. A bit too easily offended maybe.

'If ye can persuade Mam, maybe we'll see,' said Margaret.

Annie looked in on Eliza before she left. The old lady was awake, bright and glad to see her. She grabbed Annie's hand. 'Mind what I said, lassie. The tea leaves don't lie. There's stormy times ahead for ye.'

'There's stormy times ahead for all of us,' said Annie. 'But we'll weather through.' And the feeling of dread filled her once more.

Annie went round to Ada's house before her rounds the next morning. She found both Ada and her man in the kitchen, Sandy having returned from setting his creels, and Ada baking pancakes. Sandy sat at the table, packing the strands of tobacco into the chamber of his pipe with his thumb, the way Annie's father used to do.

'Annie, come in. How are ye? It's grand to see ye.'

'I want to speak to you about Margaret,' said Annie sitting down opposite Sandy. It was as well to find out what Sandy thought too. Most of the time he gave in to whatever Ada wanted.

'She'll be wanting you to speak to me about the wedding,' said Ada. 'We've both told her not yet and that's it.' Ada's face was set.

Annie knew just how determined her friend could be.

'She's really upset about Freddy getting called up,' said Annie. 'I hate seeing her like that.'

'Aye, it's no handy. I never know what's going on in that lassie's mind. All this about the WVS as well. Yer lucky ye only have a lad.'

'I'd love to have a lassie like Margaret. And what if Freddy doesn't come back?' Here she stopped for a beat. 'Heaven forbid, but we don't know what might happen.'

Ada banged the teapot down, suddenly angry. 'This blasted war. She's my only lassie. Anyway, she's far too young to get wed or leave home.'

Annie knew she wanted to add, *It's none of your business.* The unspoken words hung in the air.

'My mam was married at sixteen,' said Annie. 'My dad wasn't the catch my grandparents wanted, but she never regretted it.'

Ada spun round to face Annie. 'Has Margaret sent ye to persuade me to change my mind?'

'I shouldn't interfere, but I did promise to have a word. I'm worried. She's usually such a happy soul. I get the feeling she doesn't really want to join the voluntary service, and you don't want her to either. Maybe if you agreed to the wedding, she wouldn't go. They love each other and there are no guarantees in this war. She's worried sick about his going, and, I hate to say this, but your mother is failing. Margaret can see it and I'm sure she wants her gran at her wedding.' Annie suffered a pang of guilt for using Eliza, but there was truth in her words.

Ada gave a deep sigh. 'I can't deny my mam's going downhill. I've been trying not to admit it.'

'She's ninety-two,' said Sandy. 'She's a grand soul, and I'm that fond of her too, but ye're lucky to have had her this long.' Ada put her hand up to push the hair back off her forehead. 'Ye're right. I hadn't thought about it like that. Do ye think she's that bad?'

'There's nothing I can pinpoint. I'm going to speak to the doctor, but don't bury your head in the sand, Ada.'

'I'll need to face it, I will, but Margaret, I didn't manage a wedding for myself. The least she could do was let me enjoy the day. I've been dreaming of it since she was born. Ye should see the stuff in her bottom drawer.'

'I know what you mean, Ada, but the war has changed everything. Think of it, if, heaven forbid, something bad happened to Freddy, what if he never came home, would Margaret live with regret for the rest of her life? Would you? What if she holds it against you? What if she's so broken-hearted that she never gets wed? What if it drives a wedge between you?'

'Well, I never saw the sense in making them wait,' said Sandy. 'But ye know women.'

Ada shook her head. 'I have thought about it, lass, don't think I haven't, but I so wanted to give her the wedding I never had. Freddy doesn't have to go till after Christmas and then there's a six-week training program and he'll get leave before he's posted. That'll give me a bit of time to get used to the idea. I'll agree to that.' She stopped for a beat. 'How bad do ye think my mam is?'

'She's doing well for her age, but I'm just a bit concerned. A Christmas wedding would be grand, and just before Freddy goes. Think about it, maybe snow and bells. I want to help. You've been a good friend to me and she has asked me to be her maid of honour after all.' She reached over and covered Ada's hand with her own. 'She doesn't want to disappoint you, but they love each other. Let them have some time as man and wife without guilt. Margaret wants your blessing, but I've a feeling she'll do it anyway, with or without it. You were young and in love once yourself.'

'Aye, that's as maybe, but I grew out of it.'

'Come on, you're not telling me you have regrets, now?' said Annie, glancing at a bemused Sandy.

'Well, no, for I was lucky. I got a good man.' She stopped suddenly and looked at Annie as if the truth had dawned on her. 'Is there any other reason for the hurry?'

Annie felt that maybe she'd pushed it too far. 'It's that I understand, and, well, with the war nothing's certain. If there's a crisis he may not get leave. And,' Annie paused for effect, 'You do have the bottom drawer all ready.'

'Ye may be right,' Ada said her eyes still on her friend. 'Ye wouldn't keep anything back from me, would ye?'

Annie hated having to lie, so she tried to fudge the truth. 'This war has changed everything. All our dreams.'

'For goodness sake, Ada, let the girl get married. I want to walk her down the aisle, no have her running away to some registry office,' said Sandy.

Ada pursed her mouth. 'Seems like I've been outvoted,' she said, huffily

Annie breathed in relief. 'Can I tell her it's fine to go ahead?'

'Aye, I suppose so, but I'm still no best pleased — with either of ye.'

'I'll see my stepfather too, he can call the first banns this Sunday,' said Annie.

'Oh wait, that soon? I don't know.' Ada suddenly looked flustered.

'Ada, you know it's the right thing to do. Get it over with before Freddy leaves so that they can have some time together,' said Annie.

Ada nodded. 'It's just…she's still ma bairn, ye know? I'm so disappointed. '

‘I know,’ said Annie. ‘She always will be yer bairn and at least she won’t be joining the WVS.’

Ada followed Annie to the door and closed it behind her. In a low voice, she said, ‘She is expecting, isn’t she?’

Annie took a breath. ‘It’s not my place to tell you that.’

‘She made ye promise not to tell me. I’m not a fool, Annie.’

‘No, but if I break her trust, she’ll never confide in me again. So I’m telling you nothing.’

‘I knew it,’ snapped Ada. ‘All that butting yer nose in. Why couldn’t she come to me?’

‘She doesn’t want to disappoint you. Ye’ve been a good friend all these years and I’m right fond of Margaret and all. I don’t want anything to change.’

Ada did not look pleased, but she nodded. ‘It won’t,’ she said, but huffily.

Chapter 21

Alexander: Singapore 1941

Alexander found his surroundings pleasantly hot now that he had become accustomed to the climate. With nothing much to do, he wandered into the Chinese quarter and was amazed by the stalls heaving with snakes and eels and others full of fruit and vegetables of every kind, some of which he had never seen before. Eventually, he wandered into Central Area, Singapore and followed the sounds of music. He arrived at a dance hall where a live band was playing. Standing around the bar, he recognised many of the soldiers he had travelled with.

'Bertie,' he shouted to the young man he had grown particularly close to.

'Alex!' Bertie's face was flushed and he held a glass in his hand as he pushed his way through his pals. 'Bloody hell, man, just look at these dolls.' He waved a hand to encompass the room.

Sitting or standing around the perimeter were an array of very beautiful Chinese, Malay and Eurasian girls.

'I've found out how it works.' He leaned closer to Alexander and pulled a bunch of tickets from his pocket. 'I had to buy these. The girls are taxi dancers. For every dance, I have to give the girl a ticket. Are you a good dancer? Here, have one on me.'

Alexander shook his head. He felt strongly that the girls were prostitutes and the dance was only a prelude to what they offered later. 'As long as you only dance with them,' he said.

'Oh, we've been warned. You should have heard the pep talk we had before they let us leave the barracks.' Bertie pulled himself up to his full height and, mimicking his sergeant major's voice, he said, 'Any soldier who is found to have contracted venereal disease will be subject to the most severe of punishments. Make sure you stay away from the locals. And you do not leave the barracks without a full uniform. If you do, you will be picked up by the military police and there will be severe consequences.' He laughed. 'What's a red-blooded lad like myself supposed to do? We're thrown in here with all this temptation, and we may all be dead tomorrow if we listen to the warnings. I, for one, don't want to go to my bloody maker without sampling a few Eastern delights.'

'You have to fight it, my lad,' said Alexander with a laugh.

'For God's sake, I came to fight the Japs, not the girls,' said Bertie. 'There's damn all to worry about. I hear the Japs aren't good at fighting, no match for us.'

'I don't know about that. No one expected them to bomb Pearl Harbour. They seem pretty determined,' Alexander replied.

Bertie took a swig at his drink. 'Look on the bright side. Now the Americans are joining us, we'll be home before we know it.'

Alexander wasn't too sure. And he had not missed the tension beneath his friend's words.

'I hear the Russians have joined us as well. We'll drive the bastards back on all fronts,' Bertie continued as if trying to convince himself.

'Do we believe that? Or is it just rubbish to keep us from panicking?' asked Alexander. 'From what I see, Singapore lacks heavy armour and air power, which makes it sadly unprepared. We can only hope the Japanese are as useless as we've been told.' Somehow, he doubted that.

'Some life they have here, though. Dancing everywhere and the lassies, bloody beautiful, are they no? Maybe we should have a damn good time while we can.'

'I'm here to report on the war, not to spend time with the lassies,' said Alexander. 'But you're right about them being bonny. I've not seen an ugly one yet.'

Suddenly serious, Bertie studied his drink. He was obviously more worried than he was letting on. 'We've got a Tamil to help in the office. I don't trust him. There's something about him I can't put my finger on. He's a shifty wee bugger.' He swallowed his beer, looked around, and wiped his forehead. The beads of sweat gathered there were caused by more than the heat. The hand that clutched the pint glass before him trembled. 'I've not seen action before,' he said. 'I don't mind telling you, I'm fucking scared, man.'

'That's understandable,' said Alexander.

This is off the record,' Bertie said, lowering his voice and leaning forward. 'I shouldn't be telling you so no writing it in your newspaper.'

Alexander swore secrecy. 'I won't write a word... for now,' he added. 'What is it?'

'Matador.' Bertie took a swallow of his beer and wiped the froth from his mouth. 'A fellow in the signal department told me.'

'Matador?' asked Alexander.

'It's a code word. It'll be used when we know the Japs are coming.'

'We always knew they're coming, we just don't know when,' replied Alexander.

'But we have a plan,' the young soldier hurried on, 'They won't stand a chance in hell. The British, Australians, Indians, Gurkhas and the Malayans and surely soon the Americans will launch a defensive strike. We'll turn the bastards back at the beaches. We'll be fine.' He gave a laugh, but it was high-pitched, shaky, and uneven.

True to his word, Alexander had not written about Matador, which was just as well. He waited for it to be implemented. And he waited. And waited.

Chapter 22

Alexander: Singapore 1941

'Sorry, I can't stay. I've been invited to Wilbur's house. He's a plantation owner I met in the bar.' Alexander glanced at this watch. 'I'd better get back to the hotel. He's sending a car to pick me up at eight. Apparently, he's hosting a barbeque for other owners tonight.' Alexander would have preferred to stay with Bertie and the other soldiers, but it was too late to cancel now. Furthermore, he was interested in how the other plantation owners viewed the coming threat. Surely, they weren't all as nonchalant as Wilbur.

As before, in Wilbur's abode, the air of opulence dominated. The women wore gold jewellery and fabulous clothes that Alexander could only surmise cost a fortune; the men in white or cream-coloured tuxedos and watches that could have carried the brand name of *Vacheron Constantin.* He felt underdressed. Although Wilbur's home had previously dazzled him, being surrounded by these entitled millionaires made him feel alien and out of place.

It was a soft evening, the slight breeze like silk against his skin. Lanterns cast a golden glow on the scene, and the gentle hum of cicadas filled the air as the group gathered on the patio. Conversation flowed freely, although voices were low and serious, punctuated by the occasional clink of glasses and the sizzling of meat on the grill.

The whole set-up, the peace, the whisky and the pure

luxury made Alexander feel uncomfortable when the locals who worked for them had barely enough to eat.

In this idyllic place, it was hard to imagine that there was a war raging around them, that death and destruction waited just beyond the borders and it frustrated him that they would not listen.

'Ah, Alexander, my boy,' shouted Wilbur when he saw him. 'Come over here.' He had been in earnest conversation with his neighbours. Alexander guessed the discussion was war-related.

'Meet my friends, all plantation owners like myself.' There were introductions all around.

'What do you make of all this then?' asked one younger man. 'Are we safe? Surely all these troops pouring in from all over will defend us to the hilt.'

'If I'm honest, I think we're underprepared,' said Alexander. 'From what I've gathered, the Japanese are sweeping across Malaya, and I believe they are lethal.'

'Rubbish,' declared one portly gentleman. 'Singapore is the Gibraltar of the East. It's heavily fortified to withstand any attack. The Japanese are just little yellow bastards with bad eyesight, no match for our boys. I say we do nothing, just sit back and wait until it all blows over.'

'But we do have to worry about the economic impact on the rubber industry, with all this war stuff,' said another. He glanced at Alexander. 'Do you have news of the war in Europe?'

Alexander felt strongly that they invited him not for his input but because, as a journalist, he might have more information than what was readily available to them.

'The government is advising Europeans to get out now. I would listen. I have no more information than you do, but from what I see, the threat isn't being taken seriously enough.

That obviously wasn't what they wanted to hear, and Alexander drifted away from them, hoping to return to Singapore and join the soldiers in the dance hall.

‘Alexander, over here.’ Amelia lay back in her lounger, sipping her wine, looking golden and beautiful, her eyes subtly locked onto Alexander’s.

‘Actually,’ he said as he walked towards her, ‘I was going to go. I’ve a lot to write up tomorrow.’

But tonight, it seemed, Amelia was determined to draw more than a glance.

After setting her glass down, she pushed herself to her feet and positioned herself beside him, her proximity more intimate than he was comfortable with.

‘Need any help with that?’ she asked, taking the empty glass from his hand. ‘I’ll get you a refill, or perhaps you’d like to come with me?’ Her voice was low and inviting.

Alexander glanced at her briefly, a polite smile on his lips. ‘No, I’m fine, thanks. Just about done here.’

Amelia leaned in closer, her hand brushing against his arm. ‘You’re very attractive, you know. Wilbur is so caught up with work and the plantation and all this war talk. It’s incredibly boring.’

Alexander’s smile stiffened slightly, his eyes flicked to her hand. ‘It is Wilbur’s life. It’s the lifestyle you bought into.’ Then he stopped, imagining that he had sounded sharper than he had meant to.

Amelia laughed, the sound a bit too loud, a bit too forced. ‘True, but I didn’t know how lonely it could be.’

Alexander shifted his weight, subtly stepping away from her touch.

Amelia’s eyes narrowed slightly, her face hardened, the frustration bubbling beneath her flirtatious façade beginning to show. She moved in front of him, blocking his path. ‘You’re always so serious, Alexander. Don’t you ever just… relax?’ She ran her hand along his arm, and his gaze met hers.

‘I relax just fine, Amelia. Now, if you’ll excuse me—’

But Amelia wasn’t ready to give up. She placed a hand on his chest, her fingers lingering. ‘We’ve known each other for a short time, but you don’t have to be so distant.’

Involuntarily, his jaw tightened, and he gently but firmly removed her hand from his chest. 'Amelia, I respect you and Wilbur. Please, don't do this.'

'I get it, you aren't interested in what I have to offer.'

He stepped around her and made his way to the table, the tension in the air dissipating as he joined the others. 'Thanks for inviting me, Wilbur, but I need to go now.'

Amelia stood there for a moment, her cheeks flushed. She took a deep breath before joining the group, a forced smile on her lips.

'Alexander, I will get Zi Han to drive you home,' she said in an over-sweet voice.

She followed him towards the car and put her hand on his arm. 'Actually, I'm not interested in you, not in the way you might imagine. I'm scared. I want you to get me out. Wilbur and his friends will end up dead, and I don't want to be here.'

Alexander wasn't sure if she was serious or was this was another game she was playing.

'You should talk to your husband about it.' He nodded, turned away, and left her standing there.

Back at the hotel, he exited the car and bade Zi Han goodbye. He had almost reached the door when Zi Han shouted to him. 'Don't forget the case, sir.'

'What case?' He half-turned.

'The case Miss Amelia left in the trunk. I have instructions to give it to you.' He opened the boot and lifted out a large pink case.

'There must be some mistake. I know nothing of any case. Take it back with you.' But before he could make a move, Zi Han returned to the driver's seat and took off, leaving the case on the pavement.

Alexander cursed. He took the case upstairs to his room, where he opened it. It was full of women's clothes, makeup and feminine articles.

He sank onto the bed. What was this woman up to?

Chapter 23

Jeannie: Raumsey 1941

Meanwhile, on Raumsey, Jeannie Sinclair stood in the porch, her swollen belly brushing against the edge of the table as she washed the last of the dishes in the enamel basin. The house was quiet, only the ticking of the clock and the settling of the peat in the stove.

Then she heard Nick's boots on the flagstone outside, the creak as the door opened, the sharp snap as it shut. She heard him struggle out of his boots, clear his throat, and she tensed.

Breathing in slowly, she forced herself to relax. She set her hand on her belly and felt a soft kick. This bairn, her bairn was her reason for being.

She wondered what future could she ever give this child she carried. Wiping her hands, she glanced at the small kitchen clock.

Nick walked into the room filling the air with the stench of smoke, engine oil, fish and old sweaty socks. He took a seat on the rocking chair, his unshaven face slack and weathered, broken veins on his cheeks, pillows of fat beneath his eyes and she wondered why she had ever thought this man was handsome. For a moment, their eyes met and his slid away as if the sight of her was distasteful to him.

God knew she had tried and done everything she could to be a good wife, but she had come to the realisation that Nick would never love her.

'Is dinner ready?' he asked.

She rubbed her forehead, the headache she had been nursing all day suddenly worsening.

'It's ready.' She waddled to the dresser and retrieved two plates.

'Is everything all right? Is the bairn all right?'

See? It's all about the bairn. He cares nothing for ye, she imagined her father's words echoing down the years, still having the power to wound after all this time. Suddenly, it was all too much. Her body felt heavy and her legs pained her badly. 'I don't feel well. I'm tired.'

He sprung to his feet. 'Sit down then, sit down.'

He indicated the chair he had just vacated. 'Is this normal?'

'I don't know how I should feel. I need to get out of the house to speak to other women. I'm going to the sewing circle tonight.'

Nick screwed down his eyes. 'Ye're going out?' He stared at her, his jaw working, weighing the words. She could see the wheels turning behind his eyes, the calculation. Then he shrugged, feigning indifference. 'Good. That's good. Go out to yer sewing circle or whatever else the gossips do.'

He knows they'll all laugh at ye. That's what he wants. Gus's voice taunted her. 'Just go away,' she shouted. Her hand flew to her mouth when she realised she had spoken aloud.

'What?' asked Nick.

She put her hand to her forehead. ‘Nothing, it’s my head. I have a pain. I wish it would go away.’

‘Are ye sure ye should go out?’ There appeared to be concern in his voice but she couldn’t trust it.

‘Fresh air’ll do me good.’

‘Fine, then,’ he said, but there was irritation in his voice.

Tears sprung to her eyes. She wanted him to care, to care enough to listen to her, shc wanted to tell him that memories of her father’s words wouldn’t leave her alone, she wanted him to put his arms around her and keep her safe, but she knew that would never happen. She waited for him to speak again.

She wouldn’t go out. She knew she wouldn’t. At the lat minute, her confidence failed her.

Chapter 24

Alexander: Singapore 1941

The next day, after his shower, Alexander was getting ready for breakfast, when there was a sharp rap at the door and Amelia breezed in. Dressed in a yellow dress pinched at the waist and a large sunhat, she smiled up at him. 'I thought you might like company,' she said in a trilling voice.

'Amelia,' he replied, 'What can I do for you? I need to get my reports finished. And what in the name of hell am I doing with your luggage?' He was aware of her perfume and moved towards the desk where he picked up a sheet of paper for no reason other than his hands needed something to do.

'I'm not here to seduce you. I've been thinking about what you said.' She sat down on his bed and removed her hat and sunglasses. Her eyes were red and puffy. She looked like she'd been crying all night. 'Wilbur is so pig-headed. Do you really think the Japs will come here?'

'Of course I do. All the signs are there. You and the girls should go even if Wilbur refuses to.' He replaced the paper and turned his attention to organising the pile.

'I want to but he's so controlling. He handles the money. How would I afford to live if I went back to the UK? I've nowhere to go.'

'You've no relatives who would take you in?'

'No, none.' She shook her head. 'Could you help me? I'd

be so grateful.' She rose from the bed and walked over until there was no more than an inch between them. 'I seem to make you nervous, but there's no need.' She raised her hands as if to cup his face.

'Amelia, stop this.' Irritated, he grabbed her wrists and set her hands at her side. 'You are a very attractive woman, but you are married to a friend of mine.'

'It's not that. I know you are not interested in me in that way. Pity.' To his surprise, she burst into tears. 'I'm so frightened. Please help me.' She wiped at her cheeks.

Alexander could never cope with a woman's tears. He felt the instinct to comfort her by taking her in his arms and assuring her everything would be all right, but he knew she would misinterpret his actions. 'I'll talk to Wilbur again, but that's all I can do.' He turned away so that he didn't have to look at those desperate eyes.

'He won't listen. You could lend me money. I'd get it back to you somehow.' She choked out the words between sobs.

Alexander scratched the back of his neck. 'I'm not rich. And what about the twins?'

'They don't like me. They wouldn't come anyway. They believe their father. I feel like I'm in prison there. I've got to get away before the Japs come.'

Alexander thought it a strange kind of prison. Feeling the need to be away from her presence, he glanced at his watch. 'I have to get on now, but I will talk to Wilbur. I promise I'll make him see sense.'

'I'm not going back,' she said. 'I want to leave today and I need money.'

'Look, if I give you enough to buy a passage, a meal and a night in a hotel once you get to the UK, will you go? I don't want to be involved any further than that.'

Her lip quivered. 'And then what will I do?'

'Then you can sell some of that.' Alexander nodded at the bracelet on her wrist. 'And your rings. That should bring in enough to keep you going till you get a job.'

‘I suppose so,’ she said meekly, looking at the floor. She raised a shaking hand to her mouth. ‘Will you take me to the docks? I’m so useless.’

‘I really shouldn’t.’ This woman was making him very uncomfortable. It wasn’t his place to get involved, but if he didn’t, he had a horrid suspicion she would be the devil to get rid of, and she did seem genuinely scared. Against his better judgment, he decided to buy her a ticket, see her aboard the ship and then leave her to it.

‘Come on then. Wipe your eyes. I’ll buy you breakfast and we’ll go.’

With a further sniff, she turned towards the door.

‘Wait a minute.’ He crossed to his desk. picked up a letter he had written to Annie and handed it to Amelia. ‘If I help you, promise me you’ll post this as soon as you reach the UK.’

She nodded. ‘Anything,’ she whispered as she took it, studied the address and tucked it into her handbag.

After a breakfast of croissants and coffee, he called a taxi to take them to the docks.

The vehicle moved slowly through streets thick with traffic and worried pedestrians. With the threat of war looming ever closer, the docks were worse, a frenzy of activity—soldiers, civilians, crates of supplies, and military personnel clambering for space. The air was humid, filled with the acrid smell of fuel and the sea. Ships bobbed restlessly in the harbour. Above it all, the looming silhouette of a Royal Navy cruiser stood anchored, a stark reminder of the power that had once made this port safe. Now it, too, was preparing to leave, its decks already packed with evacuees.

Amidst the din, Alexander weaved his way through the crowd, his grip firm on Amelia’s arm. They fought their way to the shipping office, where he bought a ticket.

Amelia clutched her suitcase, her face a mix of fear and determination.

‘Come on,’ he said. ‘It looks like you’re getting out just in time. This is going to get worse.'

'I won't forget this.' She gave him a smile.

'This way,' he said.

Her smile suddenly froze as she looked past him. Her eyes widened with panic. 'Oh God, no,' she whispered.

Alexander turned to follow the direction of her gaze. A sleek Mercedes stopped and Wilbur exited, red-faced and glowering. He fought his way through the crowds towards them.

'Amelia,' he shouted. 'What the hell do you think you're doing?'

He turned to Alexander. 'You, I make you welcome, feed you…' Rage made him splutter. 'You take off with my wife.' His fat hands bunched into fists and Alexander stepped back, holding his hands, palms outward. A physical altercation with Wilbur was the last thing he needed.

'She asked for help. I tried to persuade her not to go,' he explained. 'I wanted to talk to you first but — '

Wilbur clenched his teeth. He turned on Amelia and slapped her so hard she fell over, staggering against a small Malay who cursed at her in his own language.

Shocked, Alexander couldn't believe that Wilbur could be violent. Reaching out to grab the other man's arm, he shouted above the surrounding noise. 'Look at this.' He waved his hand at the surging crowds. 'You need to follow her, get away from here, now.'

'Get out of my business!' yelled Wilbur. He turned and bent down, grabbed Amelia by the hand and jerked her to her feet. By now, a small crowd had gathered. Two soldiers who were trying to keep order elbowed their way over. 'I think you'd better let the lady go,' said one.

The other looked at Alexander. 'What's going on here?'

'She wants to leave. Her husband is preventing her,' he said.

Amelia's expression flickered with a mix of relief and terror. Wilbur's grip on her arm tightened.

The younger soldier looked confused as if he didn't know what to do.

'Do you want to go back with him?' asked Alexander, knowing the answer, but wanting the others now crowding around to know it, too. If it hadn't been for the slap, he would have walked away and left them to work it out themselves.

'No, I want to go back to England.' Her cheek was red where she'd been hit. Tears streamed down her face.

'It would be wise to let her go,' said the older soldier. 'And wiser still to go with her. The Japanese are at the gates.'

Alexander stepped forward. 'You want to stay and be a fool, fine. But let Amelia get on that ship. And I suggest you let your daughters go with her.'

Wilbur sneered and dragged Amelia closer. 'I'm her husband. They are my daughters. You don't get to decide. They stay with me.'

Amelia's eyes met Wilbur's— a silent plea.

'Please. It's not safe. I'm not sleeping. I have to go.'

Alexander reached into his trouser pocket. He pulled out a ship ticket and held it out to her. He had done all he could. 'Leave now, or don't leave at all. It's up to you. He won't hurt you, not while the soldiers are here.'

Amelia's eyes locked onto the ticket.

Wilbur tried to snatch it.

The older soldier stepped between them. 'Will I escort you to the ship, miss?' He took the ticket from Alexander's hand.

Wilbur no longer looked like a raging bull, but sad and defeated. 'I trusted you.' And he walked away, shaking his head.

'It's for the best, Wilbur. I don't want to go against you, but I can't stand men who hit women.' Alexander shouted after him, but Wilbur did not turn around.

A ship horn blared, signalling the last call. The crowd surged, and Alexander backed away, hoping he would never see the pair of them again.

Chapter 25

Alexander: Singapore 1941

The ceiling fan whirled above his head, the draught disturbing the papers on his desk. Alexander batted at a fly that would not leave him alone and ran his fingers over his head. He glanced at the clock. It was 10.00 p.m. Back home, it would be about 4.10 in the afternoon.

He meant to go downstairs and treat himself to a whisky before bed. Suddenly, the earth shook, and a deafening explosion shattered the tranquillity. The roar was unrelenting, like a freight train crashing through the night, disorienting him. The windows rattled and then burst inward, sending shards of glass flying in all directions like deadly confetti.

Alexander stumbled backwards, instinctively shielding his face with his arm as glass pieces rained down. He felt a sharp sting on his cheek; a sliver of glass had nicked him. His ears rang, muffling the sound of his ragged breathing.

The realisation dawned slowly, cutting through the haze. The first bomb had exploded on a tennis court beside the hotel. There had been no warning siren.

For a moment, he stood frozen in the chaos, staring at the gaping hole where the window used to be. Outside, the sky was alive with flashes of light, a macabre dance of shadows and flame. Plumes of smoke billowed upward, illuminated by the orange glow of burning debris. The once tranquil night was now a theatre of war.

The acrid smell of smoke and burning rubber filled the room, stinging his eyes. He could taste the bitterness of ash on his tongue. The dull thud of more bombs echoed in the distance.

Snapping out of his daze, adrenaline suddenly coursed through his veins. He needed to move. He needed to get out.

At the door, he hesitated, glancing back at the papers scattered on his desk — articles he had written, letters from home, reports that now seemed utterly meaningless. He cursed under his breath and grabbed his jacket, shoving a few of the more important articles into his pocket, though he knew deep down that nothing could shield him from what was coming.

The hallway outside was a scene of utter pandemonium. Hotel guests, some still in their evening attire, others half-dressed in nightclothes, were running, screaming, or crouched in corners, shielding their heads as if the walls could protect them. The chandeliers swung violently, casting eerie, flickering shadows that only heightened the sense of impending doom.

Alexander pushed through the crowd, his mind racing. He needed to find a shelter, the usual procedures felt useless now. He had always imagined there would be a warning, a chance to prepare. Instead, they had been caught off guard, like sitting ducks.

He made his way to the stairwell, gripping the railing as another explosion shook the building. His senses on high alert, he descended two steps at a time. The lobby was already filling with smoke, and the air was thick with the sounds of chaos—cries of panic, the crackling of fire, and the shouts of hotel staff desperately trying to maintain some semblance of order.

He reached the ground floor and spotted the bar, its polished mahogany counter now strewn with broken bottles and shards of glass. His gaze lingered for a moment on the spilt whisky, the golden liquid seeping into the carpet — a small, absurd tragedy amidst the larger catastrophe.

But there was no time to think. The city outside was ablaze, the once-familiar streets now unrecognisable under the orange glow of flames. Military trucks were speeding by, soldiers shouting orders, trying to direct terrified civilians to safety. The crackle of gunfire in the distance sent an added chill down his spine.

He turned and pushed his way through the crowd, his thoughts on the next step, the next move. Survival instincts had kicked in, but beneath it all, a nagging question gnawed at him: How had it come to this? The invincible fortress of Singapore, brought to its knees in a single, brutal night.

Amidst the pandemonium, he saw it — the Union Jack still flying defiantly above the hotel entrance, though tattered and scorched by the heat of the explosions. A symbol of a crumbling empire, a reminder of promises made and obvious failures.

The city might be falling, but he doubted if the British had finished fighting. Not yet.

'This is it, my man,' he told himself. 'It's war. You should have got out while you could.'

That damn Tamil. He's been a spy for the Japs. God knows what he's been smuggling out of the office, he thought, remembering Bertie's words.

Someone grabbed his arm. The commandant from the barracks pulled him aside. 'I've been looking for you. Come with me, back to Selerang,' he said. 'It isn't safe for you here anymore.'

They ran through the chaos to the waiting jeep.

For the next two days, the bombs continued to fall. No order had been given to blackout and those blazing street lights acted as a beacon for the enemy bombers. Within hours, a black pall of smoke hung over the city and rolled towards

Selerang. The smell of burning and smoke mixed with that of pulverised earth and shattered wood created a nauseating, acrid aroma.

Chapter 26

Annie: Raumsey 1941

After the heartening news that America had joined the war, Annie, Ada and Margaret went about planning the wedding with renewed energy. Seeing the happiness at her forthcoming marriage on her friend's face made Annie slightly envious. It would be good to feel like that. Then memories flew back to when she and Alexander decided to tie the knot and she imagined how different her life would have been if they had gone through with it. She wondered if that feeling of walking on air only came once in a lifetime. What she felt for Magnus was very different, but perhaps, in time, equally deep.

'Whoever got married on Christmas day?' Ada said, still a bit put out by her daughter's rushed wedding.

Margaret and Freddy's wedding took place the next week. Annie and her mother made sandwiches, cutting the loaves as thin as possible and spreading them with butter, boiled eggs, and some with salmon paste. Isa baked scones, queen cakes, and one large iced cake for the centre of the table.

Ada did her bit by providing baking and stovies. 'This is so good of ye all,' she said when she came up to the manse to help them carry the food to the newly built hall, erected before war was a rumour. 'I wanted to do it all myself, but....' And her voice trailed away as her lip wobbled.

There were no invitations sent out, as, with any wedding, it was a given that all were welcome. Even Eliza had managed, and friends had brought in a special chair for her to sit in. But every time her eyes met Annie's, her expression became worried, giving Annie that same uneasy feeling that she had the first time Eliza read her tea leaves.

Most of the islanders attended the wedding celebrations, but, Annie noticed that Jeannie and Nick were absent. She had hoped that they could put the past behind them, at least for the time being.

There was a certain sadness to the celebrations, though. Most of the lads who danced and flirted were waiting for their call-up papers, and many young men were already absent. Who knew what the future held?

Annie had approached Cecil Mackintosh, an elderly man with a bulbous nose, red cheeks, a snow-white beard that almost reached his stomach and the deepest voice she'd ever heard to dress up in a red costume and pretend to be Santa. Not that he fooled any of the children, for they all knew Cecil too well. But they were happy enough to believe that the real Santa was so busy this time of year, especially with the war and all, that Cecil had been called in to help. It would have been dangerous for the real gentleman to fly through the sky with the German planes in the area.

All Cecil had in his sack for the bairns were sweeties collected by the islanders over the year so that there was plenty to go around.

The island musicians, with the accordion, the fiddle and the mouth organ, provided entertainment.

Margaret, her cheeks glowing, clasped Annie's hands. 'I can't thank ye enough,' she said.' She looked beautiful in the gown her grandmother had worn at her wedding. Annie was especially pleased to see Denis walking with one crutch alongside his mother and younger brother.

'You seem to be managing well,' she said, and he gave her a smile that would light up any room, a smile that had been missing for too long.

'Aye, I'm getting better all the time and Dr Anderson says I can go for a fitting for a false leg as soon as the weather gets better. But he thinks it'd be better to wait a while as they're really heavy and they might hurt, and they're working on more lightweight ones all the time. I'm getting round good on the crutches, though.'

'Aye, he is, and it's all down to ye.' His mother beamed at Annie. 'He lives for yer visits.'

'I'll let you into a secret,' she leaned close to Denis's ear. 'I live for them, too. I've never met anyone with such a lovely smile.'

The boy's cheeks grew pink, and the edges of his lips twitched as if he were fighting the urge to smile again.

Dolly, her round face shining, kept pulling Magnus onto the dance floor. Margaret had relented and asked her to be a bridesmaid after all, and she glowed almost as much as the bride.

'I think she's got her eye on you,' said Annie after he returned from yet another dance.

He laughed awkwardly. 'She's too young for me, and all that energy. I'm done in.' His eyes turned to Annie, and the look in them tugged at her heart.

'Ye look lovely tonight, Annie.'

'Don't. You know I can't commit,' she said. 'Not yet.' It wasn't fair to keep him hanging on; marrying him made sense, but didn't he deserve a girl who could love him completely, not someone whose heart would always be elsewhere?

'You do like her, though?' she asked. 'Dolly?'

'Who wouldn't? She's bonny and fun, but if ye said the word, Annie…' He let his voice trail off.

Chapter 27

Alexander: Singapore 1941

Christmas day was like any other and in Singapore City, bombs were falling. Innocent men, women and children were dying. In the rest of Malaya, fighting was intense. There would be no Christmas celebrations for Alexander or the many soldiers stationed in Selerang. He thought of snowy Aberdeen and how it used to be. His cousins, aunts and uncles all in the wee kitchen gorging themselves on whatever the dinner was, then afterwards taking part in a sing-song around the piano. Britain, too, would be suffering with the war, and he wondered what dinner would consist of this year, but he dreamed of a blazing fire, snow outside, breath that feathered in the air.

He thought again of Annie Reid, thought of her sitting down with her husband and children and wondered what house she lived in now. He imagined her still in Raumsey, the tang of saltwater in the air, the mauve clouds promising snow. Perhaps she hadn't married after all but had grown tired of waiting for him. How could he ever move on with his life if he didn't know? He would find out if he ever got back home again, then he could put it to rest for good and all.

His poor parents had to be worried sick about him. The letters he had written to both them and Annie were possibly now at the bottom of the sea. Although he continued to write his daily reports, all systems were down and there was no way of getting them back to his newspaper.

As statements about barbaric massacres of civilians and allied prisoners filtered in, the fighting grew closer. The commandant drew Alexander aside. 'You'd better get out now,' he said. 'You're a civilian, you don't need to be here.'

Alexander was torn. There were still stories to write, but it looked increasingly as if these stories would never get back to the UK. Once the causeway that linked Malaya to Singapore was blown up they were truly on their own. The only fleet that could have come to save them was lying at the bottom of Pearl Harbour. The last message from the UK was for civilians to get out, now. Decision made, Alexander lifted his camera, reports, notepad and pen, and put them in his case.

The trip back through the bombed-out streets was very different than when he'd arrived. A blood-red sun shone through the acrid smoke from still-smouldering buildings and blazing fuel-storage tanks, adding to the searing heat. The fumes caught on his lungs, and the stench of death filled his nostrils. A brief thought that had he taken his parents' advice and gone back to teaching he would be in a far better position now flickered through his mind.

The driver took him directly to Singapore harbour, finding it in chaos. The terrified population surged towards the docks, desperate for a place on a liner.

'I'd better wait with you,' said the driver. 'looks like I'll be taking you back with me.'

Many deserters fought to board the ships sent to rescue women and children. The military police took to firing over their heads. A group of British soldiers stood nearby, rifles slung across their backs, their expressions a mix of helplessness and grim resolve. They had the task of maintaining order, but even they seemed overwhelmed by the sheer number of desperate people.

One soldier, barely out of his teens, leaned against a crate and lit a cigarette, his hands trembling slightly as he inhaled. 'Bloody mess, this,' he muttered to his comrade, who only nodded in agreement.

The looming silhouette of a Royal Navy cruiser stood anchored before him, a reminder of the power that had once made this port safe. A group of nurses, their white uniforms stark against the grime and smoke of the port, stood near the edge of the dock. A tall woman with a calm, determined expression, and who seemed to be in charge, caught Alexander's eye. She had been speaking softly to an elderly man, adjusting his makeshift bed to make him more comfortable before he was winched onto the deck.

'You didn't go with him?' asked Alexander, as the woman waved her patient goodbye.

'None of the nurses are going.' she replied. 'The hospital is full of those unfit to move. We can't leave them.'

Alexander watched as the nurses arranged their patients, ensuring everyone was as settled as possible.

An officer on board lifted a megaphone and shouted into it, his voice echoing over the harbour. 'We are full. No more boarding. We are full.'

Further down the dock, a young Indian couple struggled to hold onto their twin sons, who were crying and seemed terrified. The mother tried to soothe them. Her husband was frantically waving at the ship, shouting, 'Please! Just the children. Take the children.' But the ship was already moving, its crew too preoccupied with their own escape.

As the sun dipped lower, the sky turned a bruised shade of purple and the first stars blinked into existence. Somewhere in the distance, the low hum of an aeroplane engine could be heard, a poignant reminder of what was to come.

People continued to uselessly jostle and plead, clinging to the last threads of hope as the night slowly swallowed them. They were running out of time and they knew it.

Alexander remained on the crowded dock. It seemed the choice had been taken not only from him but from all the people huddled around him, parents soothing, children crying, and soldiers barking orders as they tried to maintain control amid the confusion.

As the last ship began to pull away, the gap between the dock and the vessel widening, Alexander felt a pang of despair. It was really happening. All these people were being left behind. He wanted to shout, to do something, but his voice caught in his throat.

Then, he heard it. A soft, trembling melody that grew stronger with each note. The nurses had linked their arms and formed a line along the shore, and they were singing. He recognised the hymn, one his mother used to sing during difficult times.

'Abide with me, fast falls the eventide; The darkness deepens; Lord, with me abide.'

Their voices were clear and unwavering, rising above the pandemonium on the dock. A lump formed in Alexander's throat as he listened. The sound was beautiful and haunting, a contrast to the fear and panic filling the port. It was a moment of pure beauty amid horror.

He looked at the faces of the nurses, their expressions serene and resolute. They chose to stay, to stand by their patients even as the world crumbled around them. Their bravery was a reminder that, even in the worst of times, there were those who would stand firm in their compassion and courage.

The ship grew smaller in the distance, the passengers waving and swaying as if also singing along as the music carried over the water. Alexander felt a tear slide down his cheek and did nothing to wipe it away.

The now sombre crowd stopped pushing and stood still as if accepting the inevitability of their fate. Many joined the nurses in song, a plea to whatever god they worshipped, as they watched their last chance of salvation disappear into the horizon.

The hymn ended, and the nurses turned back to resume

their duties. Alexander took a deep breath, sensing a calm among the crowd that had not been there before. 'Take me back to the barracks,' he said to his driver. He didn't know what the future held, but the strength he had witnessed in those nurses gave him the courage to face whatever came next.

Chapter 28

Nick: Raumsey 1942

On the island of Raumsey winter had set in with a vengeance. Despite the lashing rain, flames licked and crackled, igniting petrol, rubber tyres and old oil, highlighting yellow-clad figures with heads bowed, hands busy. Sinclair pulled his sou'wester hat further down on his head as the wind, sharp as gutting knives, drove freezing rain into his eyes all but blinding him. He put his back against his boat pushing it across the shingle and into the foaming surf.

'What the hell are ye doing, man?' shouted Danny, another fisherman. He cocked his head in the direction of the bonfire on the beach. 'No doctor'll come on a night like this. That's if he even sees the fire. And there's a war on. Do ye want to attract the bombers?'

'I have to get the doctor.' Sinclair wiped the rain from his eyes. 'I need another man on the boat. Can ye help me?'

'Don't be mad.' Danny continued to drag his own boat further up the beach, well out of harm's way. 'Nobody's going out in this weather. What's the emergency?'

Nick ignored him and pushed his yawl into the water. He jumped in and grabbed the oars. A large wave hit it broadside on and threw it back onto the shingle. He swore and leapt ashore. 'Will any of ye men come with me?' he shouted, but his voice was lost in the wind.

'The storm's going to get worse,' Danny shouted. 'Even if ye get over ye'll no get back.'

Sinclair looked up at the sky. 'I've crossed in worse weather than this,' he said. 'Aye, and came back.' Once more he ran with his boat into the surf and once more he was forced back to shore.

'I think auld Neptune's trying to tell ye something,' said Bill Mar, one of the best seamen in his day. Now in his eightieth year, he was still known to take chances where others did not. His own yawl was already secure and he came down the beach to put his hand on the prow of Sinclair's boat. 'If I was ye, I'd be inclined to listen.'

Chapter 29

Annie: Raumsey 1942

'Story, story, Mam,' said Dee as Annie tucked him up in bed, his dog sleeping on a rug on the floor.

'Just one more then and you'll promise to go to sleep?'

Dee clutched his teddy and nodded. 'Tell I 'bout Canada and Unci Dan,' he said.

'What, again?' asked Annie. She tucked the covers under his chin and began to tell him all about her brother in Canada.

Before Annie finished her story, Dee had drifted away. She rose, quietly tiptoed to the door, crept down the stairs and into the kitchen where Isa looked up from her knitting. 'A cup of tea? Donald and I were just going to have one.'

'Thanks, Mam.'

Donald folded his newspaper and set it by his side. 'It's getting wild out there,' he said, as the rain rattled against the window. 'You'd better hope no one needs your services this night, eh?' The fire settled, the clock continued its steady tick, the cat purred, and the wireless played music from the BBC home service. A sudden gust of wind blew the smoke down the chimney and out into the room.

'You'll have to do something about that chimney pot, Donald,' Isa sprang up and closed the range door trapping both smoke and the cheery glow of flames behind it.

'Aye, I'll see if the Church of Scotland will come up with the funds. I can get Bert Manson to take a look once the storm dies.'

Annie accepted her cup of tea and barely managed a sip before there was a wild knocking at the back door.

Rising to his feet, Donald threw the women a curious glance, looked at the clock and gave a deep sigh. 'Looks like it'll not be an early night for you, Annie,' he said.

As soon as he turned the knob, the door burst open. Red-faced and gasping, Alexina, the woman who had worked as the midwife long before Annie returned, blew into the kitchen, and leaned her full weight against the door, trapping the storm outside.

She pressed her hand to her throat. Her headscarf was sodden and water streamed down her face.

'Come away in, Alexina,' said Isa rising to cross over to the woman. 'You're soaking.'

Alexina gulped and shook her head, her eyes on Annie.

'Oh, lass, ye've to come. It's Jeannie Sinclair.' Alexina stopped and dragged in more air. 'The bairn'll no wait.'

Annie froze. 'Jeannie Sinclair? But surely she's not due yet.' Then another thought struck her. 'Where's Nick?'

'He's trying to get over for the doctor but little chance of that on a night like this. She's in a poor way. I know there's ill feeling between ye, but the man's no right to stop ye helping her.'

'You're a good howdie, Alexina. Nick won't want me there. Are you sure you can't manage?' With a sinking heart, she knew Alexina would not be here if she could.

'I've no got the strength I had as a young woman, and ye've got all that new-fangled training.'

'Does Nick know you're here?'

Alexina glanced at the window and shook her head. 'He'll never get over for the doctor in this weather, and even if he makes the mainland, he'll no be coming back.'

'How long do you think Jeannie has?' Annie hoped for respite. It had been on just such a night that Bel had given birth and died.

'She's in strong labour, but the bairn's bottom first.'

'She hates me as much as he does,' Annie said, remembering insults from Jeannie on the day they buried Bel's baby. 'Does she know you've come for me?'

'She's in no fit state to argue,' said Alexina without any affirmation.

Annie looked again at the window, listened to what the weather was doing outside, and her heart sank. She pulled in a deep sigh. Of course she would go. It was her job and she couldn't ignore a woman in labour any more than she could an injured animal. 'I'll do my best,' she said, already feeling her pulse beat in her throat. Glancing at her mother for approval, she saw her concern mirrored in the warm brown eyes.

'There's nothing else ye can do, lass.' Isa nodded her understanding.

Donald, who had been quiet until now, peered over his glasses. 'You're doing the right thing, Annie,' he said. 'They'll never get a boat over the firth in this weather. Good luck to you, pet. I'll say a prayer for you and Jeannie.'

'How early is she exactly?' asked Annie, as they stepped out, heads lowered against the wind, scarves wrapped around their faces.

'About six weeks,' Alexina shouted. 'Nick's wrong in the head. I told him to send for ye, but ye know how he is.'

'I do,' said Annie. She knew just how Nick Sinclair was. He would rather let his wife die than have anything to feel grateful to Annie for. She looked towards the firth, hoping to see the light of a small boat ploughing its way towards the shore, but there was nothing but angry waves, white-tipped in the sporadic moonlight.

Tightening her coat about her, Annie said a silent prayer that nothing would go wrong. She hoped against hope that the birth would be easy and everything would be over before Nick returned.

They reached the end of the house known as Scartongarth,

and Annie tried to ignore the suffocating memory of the last time she had been here. But despite her efforts, she was transported back through the years to when another woman struggled to give birth in this same cottage, and a finger of dread traced itself down her spine. So strong was the sensation of history repeating itself that it stole her breath. She gave herself a mental shake. No time to worry about Nick Sinclair now. With her heart in her mouth, she walked into the house that had once been her home and should have been still.

Chapter 30

Annie: Raumsey 1942

A glance was all it took for Annie to realise that nothing had changed since she had lived here. The pine dresser was still full of her grandparents' crockery, the table still draped with a faded, once-white tablecloth with flowers around the edges, now yellowed by age, and two brown leather chairs set at either side of the fireplace. But there was no time to think about that. Jeannie lay on the bed, her face red and wet with sweat. When she saw Annie, she gave a little gasp. 'I'm supposed to go to hospital, I have to go to hospital.'

'No one's crossing that sound tonight,' said Annie, her professional voice calm and reasonable, belying the tremble within. She stepped to the bedside and set a hand on Jeannie's stomach. 'It's me or nobody. Anyway, it's too late. The bairn is on its way. How long have you been having pains?'

'They came on sudden. Nick's been waiting for a break in the weather. He'll be furious that ye're here.' She gasped between each rush of words.

'I care little for what Nick Sinclair thinks. You are a patient and I am a nurse and a midwife. That's my job and I'm good at it. The bairn is six weeks early. Now, are you going to let me examine you?'

Jeannie didn't answer but turned her sweating face away. 'I'm sorry,' she whispered, 'about Bel.' Her lip trembled. A purple bruise stretched down one cheek.

Annie said nothing, but gently felt around the extended stomach. 'Although the bairn's early, it seems a good size, but it's lying the wrong way round. This isn't going to be easy, Jeannie, but I'm sure you'll both be just fine. Have you had regular check-ups?'

She shook her head. 'Other women have bairns so easy. Why would I be different?'

Because you're older and this is your first, Annie wanted to shout. Instead, she kept her voice steady. Recriminations would not help now.

'Ye'll no hold it against me?' Jeannie asked. 'The things I said to ye when ye buried Bel's bairn?'

'Of course I won't,' Annie snapped. horrified that Jeannie would think that for one minute.

'Annie's the best there is,' said Alexina, clasping Jeannie's hand. 'Ye'll be fine with her here.'

Annie nodded her thanks to the older woman, but something else worried her. The child's heartbeat was faint and irregular. The infant was in distress and needed to be born as soon as possible.

Annie thought of the bruise on Jeannie's face. 'Did anything happen to bring labour on early?' Despite her best intentions, the accusation was evident in her voice.

'No, no, nothing,' cried Jeannie.

'It's fine. Try to relax between pains.' She would have to do her best to keep the woman calm.

When Nick didn't return after half an hour, Annie hoped he had managed to get a boat across the firth. She was no stranger to problem births, but she had been in a hospital with backup always available.

The sweat beaded on Jeannie's lip and her screams had turned to moans. The birth was taking far too long and Jeannie was exhausted. What was more, Annie could no longer hear a heartbeat.

Her eyes met Alexina's and saw her worry reflected there.

'We'll have to get the bairn out.' She wanted to add, or

we'll lose them both.

Alexina nodded as if she understood. 'I know,' she said, so quietly that only Annie could hear.

Time became a brutal thing. Annie swam through it as carefully but quickly as she could. Words of encouragement came from her mouth as she fought down a surging panic.

Finally, a limp little body lay in her hands. Gently, she removed the cord from around the neck and rubbed the child with the towel set there in readiness, although it was obvious it was too late.

'Is it a boy?' asked a weak voice from the bed.

Annie didn't speak. She was too busy blowing into the child's mouth and rubbing the unresponsive chest. She knew the child was dead, had been dead in the womb, but she had to try anyway. Desperately.

'What's wrong?' Jeannie's voice became urgent, tearful. 'Please. Why isn't he crying?'

Annie could see her hands doing the work, but had she been asked later how long she had worked on the child, she would have been unable to say. Eventually, she heard Alexina's whispered voice at her shoulder. 'Annie, Annie, it's too late.'

Finally, realising her efforts were useless, Annie straightened up, tears blocking her throat.

'Why isn't he crying?' repeated Jeannie.

Knowing she was the one who was supposed to reply, Annie swallowed and forced the words out. 'I'm really sorry, Jeannie.'

'No, no, don't give up,' cried Jeannie. 'You've got to keep trying. Keep trying, please. Ye promised, ye said!'

Alexina laid the child in the basket and pulled the little blanket over his face. 'It's better not to look,' she said.

'I want my baby.' Jeannie reached out her arms.

The belief was that a mother would recover better from the loss of a child if she didn't have an image to carry in her mind. Annie didn't agree. She glanced at the distraught woman on the bed. 'Let us wash him, then I'll let you have him.'

'Him? So it's a boy. Nick wanted a boy. Save him, ye've got to save him.' She began to cry aloud. 'Nick'll never forgive me.'

A frisson of shock that the main concern at this time was Nick startled Annie but she had no time to dwell on that now.

Gently, she picked the bundle up and carried him to the table. 'Could you put clean, warm water in the basin?' she asked Alexina.

'It is clean.'

'But it'll be cold.'

Alexina gave her an odd look but complied.

Annie tore off a wad of cotton wool from the roll she carried in her bag and began to wash the infant as tenderly as if he could still feel the strokes, speaking to him all the time. 'There, there, little man. We'll make you bonny for your mammy.' Once he was clean, she patted the bluish skin with the towel. Just as gently, she wrapped him in the shawl set aside for that purpose, cradled him as if it still mattered, and laid him in Jeannie's arms.

'He's all right then, he's all right?' whispered Jeannie, grasping the infant to her chest. She lifted tragic, tear-filled eyes to Annie. 'He's sleeping, isn't he? He's only sleeping?'

'I'm sorry, there was nothing any of us could have done.' Annie stroked a forefinger along the soft cheek and sniffed back her tears. 'He's with the angels now. I'll clean you up and then make you some tea. You take as long as you need.'

Jeannie smiled. 'No, no. He's only sleeping. Such a good baby,' she whispered, her voice fraught with the urgency of hope. 'Nick will be pleased.'

'Na, Jeannie, lass.' Alexina put a hand on her shoulder. 'The bairn's gone.'

The door burst open and Nick Sinclair's heavy form filled the space. 'I tried to launch the boat. God knows, I tried. The seas are too heavy.' His eyes fell on the woman on the bed with the baby in her arms and the weird smile on her face. 'The child has come?' For a moment, his face relaxed, then he glanced at Annie and his expression changed. His eyes hardened and rounded in question. 'What are *you* doing here?'

'I needed help. We did everything we could,' said Alexina.

Two strides took Nick across the room. He knelt by his wife.

'I'm really, really, sorry. He was too early.' Annie fought to keep the tremble out of her voice.

Jeannie looked up at her husband and gave a guileless smile. 'Come and see him. He's so good. Look, he isn't even crying.' She parted the shawl.

Nick shook his head and sprung to his feet. It was not sorrow that gathered around him, but disbelief followed by black anger. He stared at his wife, his mouth worked as if he were searching for words he couldn't find.

'He? A lad? And he's dead? You useless bitch. I need a son — I needed an heir and you couldn't even get that right.'

Horrified at his tone and the cowering woman on the bed, Annie intervened. 'No, Nick. It's not her fault.'

He spun around, turning his fury on Annie. 'No, it's yours. What did you do to him? You want your son to be heir to Scartongarth, you always have.' He pointed at Alexina. 'Ye should have known better than to let her anywhere near them.'

'She did everything...' started Alexina, but Nick was beyond reason.

'Don't ye say a word. Ye brought her here.' He looked at Annie. 'I'll tell you one thing; your child will never have any claim to Scartongarth. I'll make sure of that. You haven't heard the end of this. Get out, *now*!'

'Your wife needs you,' said Annie, shocked. 'Stay with her.' Every word felt raw and forced and with trembling hands, she began gathering the tools of her trade. Annie had never hardened to the effect of losing a patient, especially a child. Each death affected her deeply and she had seen many reactions from loved ones. Anger, disbelief, non-acceptance, and total anguish. She didn't know what to expect from Nick Sinclair, other than blame. But right now, he was a bereaved father, the same as any other, and deserved all the sympathy and support she could give. 'I am really sorry,' she ventured. 'If there's anything—'

Her words were met by a bellow of rage, his fist came hard against the wall, making her jump.

'You… should have never have been near Jeannie. I should have known…'

'I did everything possible…' Annie fought to keep her voice steady, sympathetic, but she was shaking now.

'Nick, Nick, it was God's will.' Alexina laid a hand on his arm.

Nick threw her aside, knocking her against the wall. 'Why did ye let her in here? Stupid woman.'

'Your wife needed help,' said Annie. 'You could have lost them both.'

'Get out of my house. Both of you.' He glared at Annie and pointed to the outside door. 'Ye killed my son. ye'll pay for this, Annie Reid.'

Annie tried to explain again. 'Even if she'd been in hospital, it probably wouldn't have made any difference. Jeannie needs medical attention now, she needs — '

'She needs nothing from you,' snarled Nick. 'Now get out.'

From the bed, Jeannie was rocking the baby, singing a soft lullaby with a serene smile. Her plain face looked almost pretty. There was something surreal about the whole scene. The white-faced woman on the bed singing to a dead child, her eyes vacant, Nick, red-faced and pacing, Alexina wringing her hands, lip trembling. It was all Annie could do to hold herself together. What else could she have done? Even if she had been allowed to do regular checks, who knew what difference it might have made? Fighting the urge to run, she took a step backwards, hand fumbling at the doorknob, pulling it towards her, hand slipping, a nameless fear preventing her from turning her back on Nick Sinclair.

'You evil bitch.' In one stride, he reached the table, picked up the large, brass lamp and raised it above his head as if to throw it at her.

Annie knew enough about Nick's temper to believe he would do it and all.

'Get…get her a doctor as soon as possible,' she stammered, jerking the door open.

'I'll report you to the Medical Service. I'll make sure you never harm another bairn,' he screamed after her.

'You do what you feel you have to do,' said Annie, slipping through the doorway. Outside, she took a deep breath and welcomed the sharp, salt air, so different from the muggy, anguish-filled atmosphere in the house. She only hoped he wouldn't take his temper out on Alexina, or, God forbid, the poor, hapless Jeannie who appeared to have lost her mind.

A fierce wind whipped off the sea, thrashed her hair and cooled her cheeks, and she stood there for a time, too shaken to move.

Damn Nick Sinclair, she thought. She had never liked him or Jeannie, but she had done everything in her power for both mother and child. Why, oh, why, after all the bairns she had delivered safely since her return, had this child been her first tragedy? Nick hated her and blamed her, as he blamed all his misfortunes on her, but it was the memory of the small pathetic body that drove her to dissolve into tears, her legs growing weak so that she had to lean against the wall for support.

It took quite a while to pull herself together. She straightened up and wiped her face. As quickly as it had sprung alive, the storm was dying. Already the clouds were thinning showing patches of amber sky where the rising sun painted morning. A fading moon fought to be recognised, and the spotlights on Scapa once more strobed across the sky, searching for enemy planes. She pushed herself away from the wall and ran her hand along the uneven, white-washed surface.

'Oh, God, Bel, it's happened again.' She spoke to the brief memory of her cousin. This house had seen so much tragedy, and now even more. Had she believed in such things, Annie would have thought a curse lurked within its walls.

'Are ye all right, hen?' Alexina came up behind her, her voice filled with tears.

'I'll survive. How about you?' asked Annie. Alexina wasn't young and shouldn't have had to put up with Nick's temper. It wasn't the first bairn the howdie had lost, but Annie guessed it would be the last.

'It's a bad business. Get yerself home, now.' Alexina turned to go.

'Will I see you to your cottage?' asked Annie, noticing how unsteady the woman was on her feet. 'I honestly don't feel like going straight home myself.'

Alexina nodded. 'I'd like that. Thank ye.'

They walked along the road into the early morning.

Annie linked arms with her friend and together they hurried towards the cottage.

When they let themselves into the kitchen, Alexina lit the oil lamp, heaped peat on the fire and fanned it to life. Together they drank tea in silence, both needing the other's company but not words.

Chapter 31

Nick: Raumsey 1942

Back at Scartongarth, while the fire murmured its last in the grate, Nick Sinclair silently stared at his son for over an hour. Jeannie had fallen into an exhausted sleep. He saw her slack mouth, the line of dribble running onto the pillow, her stringy hair damp with sweat, the purple bruise that the stupid bitch had asked for one time too often, and felt a sense of revulsion. He rose and went outside.

The storm was over and the air felt fresh and new; the sky streaked with amber where the rising sun fought for dominance. Nick Sinclair stood at the end of the house, his head in his hands and railed at an unjust world. At last, after all these barren years, Jeannie had given him a child, and the stupid bitch couldn't even hold onto it till full term. What evil had he committed in his lifetime for fate to have treated him so unfairly? First, there was Bel, sweet, lovely Bel, and he had loved her in his way — the fact that she had come with a house and croft was a bonus. Then her cousin from Canada arrived, and his feelings turned on their heads. He had been young and stupid and headstrong. Bel was pretty in a fragile way, but Annie was beautiful with a wildfire in her eyes, and, surely, she too would own part of Scartongarth, or so he thought. Over the next few weeks, he had become obsessed with her, but she thought herself too good for the likes of him. Stuck up cow.

Why was he ever such a fool as to marry Jeannie? Stonehill had not turned out to be very profitable with stony ground and clay in the soil. It had only ever been suitable for hill sheep. He should have gone to the mainland to get a wife, fresh breeding stock to inject new blood into an island with too much inbreeding. But at the time he had found himself cold and lonely and still suffering the loss of Bel. God, he had missed Bel and not just for the creature comforts she afforded him. He cursed the fate that had taken her from him and could find no care in his heart for the sickly child who had caused her death.

He didn't shed a tear when the bairn, too, died. If it had been a healthy boy who would grow up to be his heir, he might have forgiven him, but it would be years before the girl would have been any good, even if it was only to do the housework and cooking. It was maybe just as well she didn't survive. He couldn't have looked after her. He could barely look after himself back then. It had suited him that, on her deathbed, Bel had extracted a promise from her cousin to take the child, another of his children Annie Reid had allowed to die. She would suffer for this, by hell, she would!

'Nick, Nick,' came the reed-thin voice from inside the cottage. 'I'm bleeding, help me.'

For a minute, he contemplated leaving her to bleed to death. Why should he care? She couldn't even deliver a live bairn. A brief vision of a cold empty house and no decent food flashed through his mind. She did have her uses. He returned indoors.

'Isn't that normal after a bairn?' he asked.

'I don't know. Not this much, I think. Get Annie.'

'I will do no such thing,' he yelled. 'How could you even suggest it?' He stormed out of the house and went to Alexina's. As he approached, Annie was coming out through the doorway. His hand closed into a tight fist and he thumped his forehead. Afraid that if he approached her, he would grab her by the throat and strangle the life from her, he remained in the shadows until she was far enough away, then he crossed to the cottage door and pushed it open. 'Alexina,' he shouted into the gloom.

From where she sat in her chair, Alexina started as if she'd been asleep. 'Nick, is something wrong?' she asked.

'Jeannie thinks she's losing too much blood.'

'Ye should have let us tend to her not sent us away.' She pushed herself to her feet. 'Annie has the learning; it's her ye should get.'

Nick ground his teeth. 'It'll be a cold day in hell before I let that bitch anywhere near my house. Come with me, woman, and do what ye can.'

Alexina glowered at him but went anyway.

With Nick's help, she raised the foot of the bed then shooed him out while she checked the afterbirth and examined his wife.

'It should be less now,' she explained after removing the wad of blood-soaked rags and washing Jeannie down. 'But ye stay in bed and lie still. It's what's best for ye. Ye need good feeding now to make up for the loss of blood.'

'Maybe it's best if I die,' Jeannie said miserably. 'What have I got to live for now?'

'Ye're young enough yet. Ye might have another bairn. Don't give up.' She patted Jeannie's hand. 'I'm going to give ye some milk laced with fennel seed and whisky, then I want ye to sleep. The storm has settled and I'll send Nick for the doctor. I'm sure ye'll be grand.' But as she left the room her weary face scrunched with worry.

Once more Nick walked to the beach, his mood low. Jeannie had done her best to be a good wife to him and a small frisson of guilt caught in his throat. Maybe he should have been more attentive, and he shouldn't have hit her. It was the first time he'd lifted his hand, but she had pushed him too damn far. Was it his fault that he preferred the banter and bawdy jokes of the men in the sailboat shed where they met of an evening to mend nets, make creels, build model yachts, and maybe sample a drop or two of the home brew? If she was going to start nagging, he had to nip it in the bud.

Then the anger enveloped him again. It was Annie's fault, all Annie's fault. If she hadn't rejected him all these years ago, he could have made her a good husband.

Back then he was well sought after by the young lassies, a steady worker too, but when he had set his cap at Annie Reid, she had spurned him, threatened him with a pitchfork, humiliated him, and he had never forgiven her. Too good for a mere crofter-fisherman she thought herself and instead had chased after the schoolteacher with the Spanish name, dark good looks, cultured voice and soft hands.

At least she'd never told anyone of his advances, but the knowledge lay between them. Whenever she looked his way, he fancied that her narrowed eyes smirked and laughed at him, and a new wave of hatred filled him. She had detested the fact that Bel had married him and that alone had given him a sense of pleasure.

He had tried to be a good husband to Bel, done everything right and yet she was so meek and had cowered away from him, but, luckily, not before she had signed the property to him. He would never have hurt her — she just didn't understand a man's needs.

Then there was Annie. She could have come back to Scartongarth after Bel died. He forgave her everything and made the offer. Once again she spurned him as if he were the dirt beneath her shoe and she even laughed. By God, he had wanted to kill her that night.

Jeannie had been different from the beginning. She always welcomed him to her bed and normally never reprimanded him for having a drink too many. She was no beauty, but she'd not once shirked her duties — except for one. Had he known back then that she would never give him a healthy bairn, would he still have married her? Probably not. If there was no heir, Scartongarth might once again revert to the Reid family one day, and he could not have that.

A fresh wave of pain swept over him when he remembered walking through the door and seeing that uppity, self-serving bitch standing over his wife.

He shook his head to clear it of the images of what should have been, of the little boy who would run after him, who would call him Dad and would adore him the way he had never adored his father, who would grow up to work beside him on the land, who would inherit Scartongarth.

All of a sudden, the drone of aeroplanes filled the sky, the distant wail of sirens travelled across the water, and gunfire and explosions erupted from Orkney's shores.

Jeannie always ran for the coal cellar. Nick didn't see what difference the coal cellar would make if stray bits of shrapnel rained down on them, something that happened from time to time.

He sat where he was, almost wishing a misplaced bomb would fall on his head.

Chapter 32

Annie: Raumsey 1942

Annie reread the letter from the Caithness Executive Council and let it fall from her hands. What had she expected? It should have been obvious by the smirk on Nick's face when she walked into the shop yesterday that the letter would be arriving.

The normal customers who seemed to come in to only pass the time of day lifted their eyes when she appeared and immediately fell silent. Obviously, she had been the topic of conversation. Nick Sinclair was standing at the counter. He turned, his eyes slitted as they met hers and he sneered, grabbed a wad of tobacco from the counter, threw down a few coins and, although she had stepped back giving him plenty of room, he shouldered her roughly on his way out, all but knocking her over.

With a communal gasp, the other women in the shop turned away, and Connie, the shopkeeper, lowered her eyes and wiped the counter. She cleared her throat and looked up as Annie righted herself.

'Did he hurt ye, lass?' she said, her voice embarrassed.

'No, I'm fine.' Annie smoothed her hands over her coat and straightened herself.

'He canna blame ye for the bairn,' Connie said. 'But he must be hurting something sore.'

Annie felt herself near to tears. 'Have you heard how

Jeannie's doing?' she asked.

'The doctor has been,' said Maggie. 'But you know Nick. He's not one for giving much away. Ach, but my heart's breaking for them, so it is. He's no had it easy losing his first wife and bairn and now this.'

'It's good the doctor's taking charge anyway,' said Annie, genuinely glad that at least the woman was being seen to. She didn't doubt that Jeannie's dislike of her had been fuelled by Nick.

'How is yer brother, Dan?' said Maggie. 'I remember when yer mam had him. He was an early bairn and all, but Chrissie and her granny were the best howdies we ever had. Aye, there's a lot to be said for the old howdies.'

'Dan's doing well,' said Annie, her voice tight. She hadn't missed the innuendo.

'Come on now,' said Connie. 'A fair number of bairns were lost back then and women, too.'

Maggie sniffed. The other two women looked embarrassed.

Annie felt sick. Did Maggie honestly think that the old howdies could have done better than a time-served nurse and midwife?' Why mention her brother who had grown into a fine young man now living in Canada? Imagining accusing eyes upon her, she had collected her shopping and left as quickly as possible.

With a heavy heart, she folded the letter and pushed it back into the envelope. She would break the news to her parents later, right now, there were patients who needed her at least until the replacement arrived.

She had been suspended pending an investigation. Her replacement would be arriving tomorrow afternoon. Annie was expected to vacate the cottage in the meantime. 'There is no problem there,' she said to the paper in her hand. 'I don't live there anyway.'

She started when the knock came to the door.

'Dr Anderson,' she said when she opened it. 'You've heard?'

He nodded.

'How is Jeannie?' She stepped back to allow him to enter.

He set his case on the floor and took a seat by the table. Annie sat opposite him.

'Physically she's mending, but she's in a state of deep melancholia.'

'I think he hit her, brought the birth on. There were bruises.'

'They both claim she fell.'

Silence reigned between them for a beat.

'On the other matter….'

'Yes.' Annie picked up the letter from where she had dropped it on the table. 'I should have known he would report me.'

'It's not an uncommon reaction with a bereavement. They want someone to blame. He is quite adamant…' he cleared his throat, 'In fact, they both are, that the child cried then made choking noises and you did nothing to resuscitate him.'

Her blood turned to ice, 'What? Nick wasn't even there. Have you spoken to Alexina?'

'Alexina backs up your story.'

'Then how can they do this to me?' Needing something to do with her hands, she picked up the letter and set it down again.

'Don't worry. The authorities have to follow up on any complaint, but it shouldn't take long. I doubt if you've anything to be concerned about. Now, did you say something about tea?'

She crossed to the stove and pulled the kettle over the hottest part. Nothing to worry about? No, she would be exonerated she was sure of that, but even in this place where she was respected, mud could stick. Oh, folk were nice enough to her face, but she could sense the shifting of mood when she walked into the shop or even visited her patients.

They looked at her with different eyes, and they spoke to her with careful voices. Trying to convince herself that it was all in her head didn't work, and since Maggie's remark about the skill of the howdies, she was even less sure.

She gave a little snort. 'Eliza saw it in the tea leaves. She said there was a black cloud around me, and I was in danger. I paid no attention of course. Pure coincidence.' Nevertheless, a cold chill had crawled up her spine. Was there worse to come?

'Eliza is very superstitious. A lot of the old folk are. Then something coincidental happens, and it strengthens their beliefs.'

Also, Nick's words still rang in her ears. 'Your son will never be heir to Scartongarth, I'll make sure of that.' What would his next step be? Surely he wouldn't hurt Dee? She set the tea and scones in front of the doctor.

'For your own sake, though, it might be worth talking to a lawyer,' he said.

'Why, what are you talking about?' She spun to face him. 'Is it that bad?'

'I believe there was ill feeling between yourself and the Sinclairs. He claims you feel he cheated you out of your inheritance. And,' he hesitated, 'Alexina is very upset and her memory is often hazy. A good lawyer would pull her apart. And… she did leave the room to get clean water.' He gave a deep sigh.

Annie felt her cheeks flame. 'He did cheat me out of my inheritance, but what's that got to do with this? I'd never let my personal feelings interfere with my work.'

'I believe you, Annie, but you must see how it might look. From what I know of Nick Sinclair, he's a very dangerous man if you get on his wrong side.'

'He hates me. And I do hate him for what happened to Bel. But I swear I did everything in my power to save the baby.' Her voice faded and died. When she swallowed, her mouth and throat were dry.

Doctor Anderson's next words stabbed at her ears. 'And he'll play on that. He might gain a lot of sympathy because he lost his first wife and child.'

'What should I do?'

'All I'm saying is, be prepared for the worst possible scenario.' He stood up. 'You're a strong woman. I have every faith in you.'

'He threatened Dee.'

'He actually threatened your child?' The doctor scowled.

'Not in so many words, but he implied as much.'

'Should I speak to the constable?'

'No, Nick'll only deny it. And it'll make things worse.'

'Try not to worry too much.' The doctor finished his tea. 'Now I'll need to go. Unless there's someone else you want me to take a look at, I'll catch the mail boat over. I'll let myself out.'

'Thanks, Doctor.'

After he had gone, Annie covered her face with her hands. She hated all this. It was bad enough to lose a patient without being blamed for the death.

Chapter 33

Alexander: Singapore 1942

On the 15th of February, in Singapore, Alexander and several servicemen clustered around the wireless as a ceasefire was proclaimed.

There had been a blessed silence the night before since the shelling had ceased, but Alexander had hardly slept a wink. He was keen to write down the events of the day while they were still fresh in his memory. On the 16th, he wrote up his report without knowing if he would ever be able to send it.

Unconditional Surrender.

On February 15, 1942, Lieutenant General Percival and a few senior British officers met with General Yamashita at the Ford Motor Factory in Bukit Timah, which had been converted into Yamashita's headquarters. There they negotiated a surrender.

'You'd better get back to Singapore,' MacLeod told him the next day as he sipped his tea in the canteen. 'There's an order out for all civilians to go to Raffles Hotel to be registered. If you're caught here, it won't be good for you.' MacLeod took a moment. There were loud crashes and stamping feet coming from the yard outside. 'I'll get one of the recruits to take you back to your hotel. Sneak out the side way. Quickly now, the Japs are already in the front compound.'

Alexander gathered his belongings and bade a sad but quick goodbye to his companions, wondering if they would ever meet again. He had no way of knowing if his hotel was even habitable, or where he would sleep that night. He and Bertie made a run for the jeep as the sound of pounding boots and shouted orders echoed behind them.

The Union Jack had been taken down from the Cathay building and the flag of the Rising Sun flew in its place.

'What are you going to do, go back?' he asked Bertie.

'What else can I do?' said Bertie, his face white. 'I'm in fucking uniform, man. They'll shoot me without a second thought.' He gave a bitter little laugh. 'We never thought it would come to this, eh? I expected to fight, but I expected to win.'

The last he saw of Bertie was the dust thrown up by the wheels of the jeep.

The stifling heat lay heavy over the tarmac of the Beach Road. All signs of colonial life had been wiped away.

The lobby of the Raffles Hotel had been transformed into a scene of strict regulation with armed Japanese soldiers at every entrance. The Singapore residents stood in a long, shuffling line that snaked through the expansive hall and approached the desk, one by one. Some were white-faced and sobbing, others, grim and determined, but every face bore the wear of recent sleepless nights and strain.

The Japanese military commandeered the front desk. Behind it, a stern-faced officer from Hirohito's army sat, pen in his hand, a ledger before him, and flanked by two soldiers, their expressions unreadable.

Alexander stood in line, his heart pounding, clutching his passport, the corners of the worn leather case digging into his palm.

With a deep breath, he tried to steady himself as the line moved forward. Each short step seemed to take forever as yet another resident completed their registration and turned to leave.

Finally, it was his turn. He approached the desk, feeling the hard eyes of the Japanese soldiers follow him. The officer did not look up immediately, instead, he finished the notes on the previous person. The short pause felt like an eternity. When the officer finally raised his head, Alexander met his gaze with as much composure as he could muster.

'Name?' the officer asked, his voice clipped.

'Alexander Garcia,' he replied, his mouth dry.

The officer jotted down the name in the ledger.

'Nationality?'

'British,' Alexander answered.

'Passport,' snapped the officer.

Alexander handed it over with concern. His nationality could be a double-edged sword in these circumstances.

The officer glanced at it, then at Alexander, as if suspicious of his words, then his pen moved swiftly, recording the information. He took a rubber stamp, dipped it in ink, pressed it onto a sheet of paper and handed Alexander a small card with the number 1583. Alexander coughed to relieve the dryness in his throat. His identity had been reduced to four digits.

'Next,' the officer called, already looking at the next in line.

Clutching the card, Alexander stepped aside, wiped the sweat from his brow and wondered how it was possible to feel both hot and cold at the same time. As he made his way out of the lobby, he glanced back at the queue, at the faces of so many nationalities, all wearing the same expression of fear.

Outside, the sun was setting. Alexander thought briefly of Wilbur and the nights in his garden, of the beauty and peace, of the evening sun casting long shadows over the scene, bathing the garden in a golden light, at stark odds with the devastation unfolding around him. He thought of Amelia and the fiery scene at the harbour and wondered where they all were now. Did the liner carrying her make it home? Did Wilbur and the girls get out? He hoped so.

Back in his hotel, Alexander found what was left of the staff doing their best to tidy up. Along with a few of the residents remaining, he was given another room at the back of the hotel one of the few still inhabitable.

'There may be a layer of dust over everything, but as you see we are busy,' explained a pretty, young Eurasian maid.

Alexander had barely unpacked when the sounds of shouting and screaming came from outside. From the window, he watched as Japanese soldiers rushed into buildings and dragged people into the street at gunpoint.

Suddenly two of the soldiers who looked very young, and dressed in oversized uniforms, burst into his room. Screeching orders in their own language, they prodded him with their bayonets. Expecting the worst, he placed his hands on his head and thought of the Alexandra Hospital which had been destroyed overnight and felt his insides tighten. They punched, slapped and pushed him outside.

In the main street of Singapore, a victory parade had been arranged and the residents were forced to stand for hours in the blazing sun to witness it.

As Alexander stood on the crowded pavement with the unrelenting sun beating on his head, the parade began. Thousands of tanks rolled in first, followed by Japanese soldiers marching through the streets triumphantly waving the flag of the rising sun and shouting, 'Banzai, Banzai' (*Long live the Emperor*.) From somewhere came the steady beat of a large drum.

Behind them came the allied soldiers, then the British, all four nations, English, Scottish, Irish and Welsh. As they marched past, their voices rose in unison, '*There'll always be an England*,' while women along the pavement cheered them on and made the Victory sign.

Despite the fear of the unknown, Alexander concentrated on taking mental notes. Maybe he would get the chance to type them up later. For now, it was important to commit them to memory. Dehydrated, exhausted and hungry, he was finally allowed to go back to his room to collect only what he could carry, then along with the other civilians, men, women and children, he was forced to follow the imprisoned soldiers on the long march into captivity.

Chapter 34

Annie: Raumsey 1942

On the island of Raumsey, Annie answered the sharp knock on the door. She knew it couldn't be a local as they would have walked in with a cheery, 'hello.'

The woman standing there was tall and thin with a narrow nose and greying hair cut just below her ears. She flashed a badge and said, 'Elizabeth Marshall. Caithness Executive Council Ruling Body for Everything Medical. Are you Nurse Anne Reid?'

'Come in. I've been expecting you.' Annie stood back to allow her to enter. 'My stepfather's out, so we can use his study for privacy.' Annie led her through.

'I've spoken to the Sinclairs and to the other midwife. Can you give me your side of the story?' Elizabeth Marshall said once they were both seated in the study. She removed a pen and pad from her folder.

'How is Jeannie?' asked Annie.

'She is very distressed, as you can imagine.'

'I did everything I could to resuscitate the child,' said Annie.

'I'm sure you did.'

Isa came in carrying a tray with a teapot, cups, milk and sugar. She set it on the desk. Once she had left, Annie poured the tea and began her story from the beginning. 'I swear I did nothing to harm the bairn,' she finished.

Elizabeth Marshall looked up from her pad on which she constantly wrote, her face betraying nothing of her feelings.

'I'm sure you didn't. But the parents, well, you understand...' She quickly closed her mouth as if she felt she'd already said too much. 'Just one point I need to clear up. You say the child was stillborn, yet you sent the other midwife away to get warm water. Why?'

'To wash the baby.'

'But if, as you say, he had been stillborn, why would it matter?'

Annie shook her head. 'I don't know. It just seemed right, you know, to treat him with the respect I would with any other child.'

Elizabeth Marshall scribbled some more on her pad. 'I see,' she said, then returned her gaze to Annie.

'They claim that through your mismanagement, the child failed to survive.'

Shock settled like a rock in her stomach. Of course they would. 'I expected nothing less.' She cleared her throat. 'So, what happens now?'

'Your suspension will stand until our investigation is complete. As you may imagine, we have had trouble finding a replacement with the war and all, but we do have a nice older lady who is on the verge of retiring. She's willing to take over for the time being.'

'How long will that take?' asked Annie.

'I'll write my report, but there might be other steps we need to take. I'll let you know.' She stood up. 'We will be as quick as possible. I can say no more than that at this time.'

'When will the new nurse be taking over?'

'Tomorrow. It helps that you are staying with your parents. Had you been in the nurse's house we provided, well, it would be more complicated.'

'What's going to happen then?'

'I expect there will be a second opinion, but it's very hard to prove how an infant died. Under normal circumstances a stillborn child is just that, but…' She shrugged. 'We'll get in touch with the matron of the hospital in Glasgow, and if her report of you is as glowing as we have had already, it will work in your favour. Of course, it will be up to the Procurator Fiscal to decide whether there is a case to answer. Given how determined the Sinclairs are, even if no blame is attached to you, they might well try to sue through the courts.'

Annie walked her to the door.

'Thank you for your time.' Elizabeth Marshall gave Annie a sympathetic smile, more than she had done throughout the entire interview. She hesitated, then said almost apologetically. 'You do understand we have to do this?'

Annie nodded. She blinked rapidly to stem the sudden surge of tears.

I don't have to stay here, she thought. *I was already a time-served nurse before my career was cut short by my pregnancy.* She gave a snort. *Heck, I might have been matron by now, if men didn't make the rules.*

If it hadn't been for the marriage ban she would have married Alexander Garcia, never met Simon, never had Dee. At this point, she stopped. How could she regret Dee? He was the one good thing to come out of the mess of her life.

If a male doctor had been present at the birth, Nick would have never dared to go to these lengths. All the indignation of the unfairness of rules set for men and by men rose anew. She loved it here, loved working with the good-hearted country folk, but for the first time, she had doubts about staying indefinitely.

'How did it go?'

She turned at the voice from the doorway. Her stepfather had come home, the question in his eyes.

Annie shrugged. 'Well enough, I suppose.' She relayed what Elizabeth Marshall had said. 'But that's not the worst of it,' she continued. 'Oh, Donald, Doctor Anderson suggested I should talk to a lawyer. Surely it will never come to that?' She desperately willed him to reassure her in his steady supportive manner.

'I'm sure it won't.' He tapped his fingers on the desk before adding, 'It did cross my mind, however. Remember my nephew, Henry?'

'Of course I remember Henry. We grew quite close during my time in Glasgow. Is he still a rebel?'

'No. In fact, he went into law. And I believe he's very good. I hope you don't mind, but I discussed your case with him.'

'No, I don't mind. What does he think?'

'He thinks you'll be just fine. Luckily, he is due some time off at the moment. I took the liberty of inviting him north for a wee break.'

'So…so you think I'll need a lawyer?'

'I don't think it'll come to that, neither does he, but he would like to see you again and get away from the rat race for a few days.'

'I'd like to see him again, too,' said Annie. But deep down she felt that her stepfather was playing down the danger of her situation. Why else would he have invited Henry?

Chapter 35

Alexander: Changi 1942

In the overcrowded prison camp in Changi, Alexander desperately searched for a space where he could at least sit down, but with so many people in the compound, it was standing room only. The press of bodies beneath a searing sun added to the heat making remaining upright unbearable. He was about to collapse when the guards began shouting, jabbering and slapping again.

They separated women and children from the men and marched them out through the gates. There were tears and sobbing as fathers, husbands and sweethearts were forced from their loved ones at bayonet point.

The heat and thirst was excruciating. A tall youth stood shaking at his side, prompting Alexander to put a protective arm around the boy. 'Hold on,' he whispered. When the boy crumbled against him, Alexander tried again. 'What's your name?' he said.

'T...Tommy,' the lad stammered, pulling himself upright. 'What's going to happen to us?'

'I don't know, son, but we'll get through this.'

The guards pushed and prodded them into line as they separated the soldiers from the civilians, and herded them, too, out through the gates.

A Japanese officer marched down the remaining row of men and boys, his uniform pristine, medals gleaming on his chest. With a scornful expression, he surveyed the prisoners, raised a gloved hand, and began to speak in clear, but accented English.

'Attention, prisoners. I am Rikugun Taisa Yamamoto of the Imperial Japanese Army. You are now in Camp 18, under my command. You have been brought here because you are enemies of the Empire of Japan.' His eyes swept around the compound. 'While you are here, you are expected to follow all rules and regulations of this camp. Any disobedience will be met with severe consequences. You will work, you will eat, and you will sleep according to the schedule we set. Cooperation will ensure survival.' The distant cawing of a crow and an occasional shuddering sob broke the silence. He paused, no doubt letting his words sink in.

'You may find your conditions here harsh,' Yamamoto continued, narrow eyes gleaming. 'But remember, this is a war and you are prisoners. We will treat you in accordance with the laws of war as long as you abide by our rules. Any attempt to escape will be punished by death.'

A murmur rippled through the crowd, quickly silenced by shouted commands from the guards. Alexander thought any attempt to escape would be foolhardy anyway. Barbed wire enclosed the camp, and the countryside beyond was empty fields and dense jungle. A man could die out there without ever knowing where he was going.

Yamamoto reiterated, 'I urge you to remember that cooperation is your best path to survival. Conduct yourselves accordingly and you may see the end of this war. Defy us, and you will face the consequences.

'In the morning, Tenko will be taken. Prisoners will call out their prisoner number in Japanese. You will learn or be severely beaten. Then you will go to work in the fields. You will choose a hut to sleep in. There will be four prisoners per hut. Officers will have superior huts according to their rank.'

With a final, sweeping glance over the prisoners, Yamamoto turned on his heel and walked away, his boots crunching on the gravel. The guards began to bark orders no one understood. They waved their arms in the direction of rows of wooden huts.

'I think they want us to choose one,' said Alexander. He looked around.

'Me and my friends, can we share with you?' asked Tommy.

'Where are your friends?'

After a few minutes, Tommy brought two other boys back and introduced them to Alexander as Alfie and Ian. All three were sons of rubber plantation owners, and all three had similar looks of fear on their faces.

If they expected any degree of comfort, they were to be disappointed. There was no furniture in the huts and they were given mats to sleep on but no blankets. Ian was the youngest at fifteen, and Alexander could see that he was desperately trying not to cry.

'Don't worry,' he said, in an effort to lift their spirits. 'There'll be Red Cross parcels coming our way soon. We'll survive this.'

If the Red Cross parcels ever did come, the prisoners never saw them.

Although the officers and warrant officers had their own huts, their lot wasn't much better. Apart from Captain MacLeod, they were strangers to Alexander.

'I did my best to get you in with us,' MacLeod told Alexander. 'I'm surprised they turned me down. I thought that as a correspondent, they would want you to give a favourable account of your time here one day.'

Alexander gave a derisive laugh. 'My impression of the camp isn't very favourable at the moment. Not even a blanket.'

'They don't see that as cruelty. Their own soldiers have little better — maybe a bit more food,' he added. 'But they know you are a correspondent, that might work in your favour.' He lifted his shoulders in a shrug.

The next morning, after an exhausting and uncomfortable night, the guards ordered them outside and another prisoner ladled rice and water into a tin dish for each man. 'If you lose that dish,' he told them, 'you will never get another.'

'Is this all we're getting?' asked Tommy.

'That's it,' said the prisoner. 'Welcome to Paradise.'

As they chewed on the rice, trying to make it last, Tommy whispered, 'This is going to be hell.'

Alexander nodded grimly. 'We just have to stick together and get through somehow.'

'I wish I knew where they'd taken my mum and dad.' Tommy sniffed.

Alexander gave a deep sigh. 'Nothing goes on forever,' he said softly and rubbed the lad's shoulder. 'If the Americans get involved, we might be rescued before long. Keep that thought.'

With stomachs still crying out for food, they were herded out through the gate.

He could only try to reinforce the boys' spirits as best he could. As they walked, he tried to engage them in conversation. 'What were you doing before the Japs came?'

'I was studying science.'

Alexander nodded. 'We will get out. Make no mistake. You'll study science again.'

Once they reached the fields they were allowed to rest for a few minutes. The air was thick with the scent of freshly turned earth, the distant hum of cicadas, and the oppressive summer heat. Rows of crops — corn, wheat, and potatoes grew in regimented lines.

For hours, the group of prisoners worked, bent over the soil, planting and weeding under the watchful eyes of armed guards. Sweat glistened on their foreheads and stained their shirts, but every time fatigue got the better of a man he was punished with kicks, shouts and prods by a bayonet. They soon learned that steady labour was a means of survival.

Chapter 36

Annie: Raumsey 1942

A week passed, and then another. Still, there was no word from the Caithness Executive Council Ruling Body. The stress made Annie irritable and she found herself snapping at Dee for the slightest thing. 'I'm sorry,' she said, hugging him to her after her latest outburst brought tears to his eyes. 'It's not your fault.'

'No, it isn't,' said her mother, coming through the doorway. 'You've been like a bear with a sore head lately. I know you've been under a lot of stress, we all have. But this isn't like you.'

'I'm sorry, I really am. But I need to know whether I'm going to have any future in nursing. I wish I could knock the smirk off Nick Sinclair's ugly face.'

'Annie, he's just lost a bairn.'

She sank into the nearest chair. 'I am sorry about the bairn, and I'm sorry for Jeannie, but I didn't do anything wrong, so why am I being punished like this?' She pulled Dee onto her knee and he didn't protest. 'I'm sorry, little man,' she murmured into his hair.

Her stepfather came into the room and picked up his newspaper. 'No word yet?' he asked.

Annie shook her head. 'When is Henry coming?' Perhaps he could look into things and get events moving.'

'The last word I got was that he still had a few loose ends to tie up. But he is looking forward to the break. And to help you of course.'

'I hope he can do something. I need to be working. I love nursing. It's my life. But whatever happens, I think leaving the island is the only way.'

'Surely not,' said Isa. 'Dee loves it here. And the folk love you. I'm sure everything will be fine.'

Annie shrugged. 'But there's always gossip, you know how it is. And because there was a feud between me and Nick, there will be doubts.'

'Come on, no one would believe you would harm a baby.'

'Maybe I should speak to Jeannie.'

'No, Annie, that's not a good idea.'

'Nick's a hard man. I think she's ruled by him. Scared of him even. I need to know whether she blames me too. She's claiming she heard the baby cry, but that's not possible.'

'In that case, Rose Pennington can find out what's going on in her mind.'

'I can't just sit back and do nothing. I'm not like that. I'm sure Nick hit her. Maybe she won't back him up if I confront her.'

'You just said she's ruled by Nick. She won't go against him, you know that,' said Isa.

'But she's lying. Maybe she'll tell the truth if Nick isn't there. And, to be honest, I want her to understand how this is affecting me, too.'

‘Promise me you won’t go near them,’ said Isa.

‘I don’t know what I’m going to do,’ said Annie. No, she would make no promises. Even if she left the island, she would not go with a cloud hanging over her head.

Isa crossed over to the window. ‘It’s a nice day,’ she said. ‘Why don’t we take Dee for a picnic? And we’ll have no more negative talk.’

‘Might as well,’ said Annie, ‘I’m doing nothing else anyway.’

Isa took a loaf out of the pantry and began to slice it. ‘Put some eggs on to boil, Annie,’ she said. ‘We’ll make sandwiches. While I’m doing that, why don’t you go and invite Magnus too? I’m sure he could do with a break; he works too hard that lad.’

Annie reluctantly agreed. Not that she didn’t want Magnus’s company, but she wished her mother would stop throwing them together.

The picnic had been a good idea. Annie lay back on the soft grass and listened to the birdsong and the murmur of the waves flirting with the shore in the distance. Closing her eyes, she let the sun warm her skin. She didn’t go near the beach anymore, not since a body had been washed up the week before. Magnus sat beside her, his arms around his knees.

‘We should do this more often,’ he said, trailing the feathery head of a grass down her arm.

She batted it away. ‘Why did you never marry, Magnus?’ she asked.

‘After the war, I wasn’t much use to myself let alone anyone else for a long time. Then ye came back and I got to know ye better.’

‘You’re a good man, any woman would be lucky to have you,’ she said.

‘But not you.’ There was a note of sadness in his voice.

They both looked skyward as several planes flew north.

‘When will this end?’ she said.

‘It will end. We have to believe that.’

They sat in companionable silence as Isa and Dee played with the puppy further down the hill.

Chapter 37

Annie: Raumsey 1942

Annie had been in the Nurse's cottage since early in the morning making sure it was clean and aired for the replacement nurse. When she saw the boat sailing into the harbour, she filled the kettle and set out tea cups and bannock in preparation. As the truck spluttered to a halt outside, she opened the door and waited as Magnus helped an elderly, slightly overweight woman from the passenger's seat. He picked up her kist and carried it into the house. 'I'll leave you now. You'll find Annie very welcoming.' He nodded to the woman and winked at Annie.

Annie approached the new nurse with an outstretched hand. 'It's good to meet you.'

'Thank you for staying on to greet me, darling.' Nurse Pennington smiled at Annie. 'That nice young man told me all about it on the way here. I must say I didn't know what to expect, as I was simply told the circumstances. I wasn't sure if you'd resent my coming. I do hope I'm not putting you out of your home.'

'Not at all. I stay with my parents up at the manse.' Annie waved her hand in the direction of the kirk.

Rose Pennington had a round, kind face and Annie liked her immediately.

'It's not your fault or mine,' she said. 'I want you to know I did everything in my power to save that baby.' She felt her lip tremble and fought the moment down.

'It's not my place to judge, darling, and do call me Rose. Since I got on that boat, all I've heard is people singing your praises. If you're so highly thought of, you must be innocent. I'm sure when it's proved, you'll be reinstated and I'll have to leave.' She made the last statement rather sadly. 'Such a pity, it does seem to be a lovely place to stay.'

Annie nodded. 'It is. Come in, I have the kettle on.'

'Good, good, and we'll have a cup of tea while you bring me up to date on my patients.'

Annie relaxed and complied.

'You would think all the islanders would be on my side,' she said over the tea, 'but in small communities, the locals love nothing better than a bit of gossip. I have to be honest, there's a lot of bad feeling between me and Nick Sinclair and however nice they are to my face, some folk will always have doubts. But, my God, I would never harm a baby!' The pain began to rise again with a sense of indignation that it had even come to this.

'I believe you, darling.' Nurse Pennington patted Annie's hand. 'No nurse would.'

'And, furthermore,' continued Annie, 'after completing my training, I blotted my reputation by returning to the island with an illegitimate child. That's a talking point, especially for a daughter of the kirk. Oh, they forgave me in time and the talk died down, but one slip and they won't forget.'

'What is this feud you have with the Sinclairs?' asked Nurse Pennington. 'Maybe I should know all about it from yourself if I'm to hear conflicting tales.'

'It's a long story,' Annie said miserably.

'I'm sorry, it's none of my business. But if you want to talk about it, I have time,' said Rose. 'Any more tea in that pot?'

Annie went to top up their cups. Something about the woman's calm, kindly voice made her want to open up. She sat back down, held her cup between her hands and began.

‘I never liked Nick Sinclair. You know how you get an instinct about someone? He was smarmy and too full of his own importance. But my cousin Bel was mesmerised by him. She was head over heels.’

‘What happened to Bel?’ asked Rose.

Annie swallowed. ‘Bel was the sweetest, kindest soul who ever lived. But I think Nick wanted Scartongarth more than her. She did start to see through him for herself, though, and I was so glad. Then one day I found her broken and crying. She wanted to wait for marriage but he forced her. She was in an awful state, but at least by then she knew the brute he could be, and that romance was over.’ Annie took a deep breath and bit her lip, composing herself before continuing. ‘When she found out she was having his bairn, she returned to him. I tried everything to stop her, but you had to know Bel. She would never subject her child to the disgrace of being a bastard.’ Annie thought of her own child. ‘I’m afraid I was more selfish.’

Rose nodded and squeezed her hand. ‘I’m not here to judge. Go on,’ she said, softly.

‘I was living in Scartongarth then, with Bel. Our great-grandfather built the house with his own hands.

‘All three sons were dead so it should have gone to Bel’s brother, Jimmy, but he went to the mainland and didn’t want it. That’s why Bel took it over, but there was no will and nothing legal was done. When they married, Nick moved in and I went to stay with my mother and stepfather.

‘Anyway, he treated her badly. He didn’t like me visiting, and I could see how unhappy she was, how thin and ill she looked. She kept saying he would change once the baby was born, but near the end, she must have known because she made me promise that should anything happen to her, I would take the child and bring it up. I was only seventeen, but I promised anyway.

‘When she went into labour early, I was there despite Nick’s objections.’ Annie stopped and stared through the window. She wiped an errant tear from her cheek. Her voice broke when she next spoke. 'Bel died that night. Without our knowledge, Nick had somehow persuaded her to sign the property over to him, but I don't believe it was legal. We didn't have the money for a lawyer to fight him.'

Rose got up and crossed to the stove. 'I think we need more tea.' She made the tea and filled the cups. 'What happened to the baby?'

'Little Sina. Nick didn't want a girl and how could he care for a child anyway? We did our best, my mam and me. I didn't know it then, but cow's milk was too strong for her. She was sick a lot and failed to thrive. She was also asthmatic. I was devastated when she died in my arms. We'd so little money, and Nick wouldn't pay for medicine for her. It was only then that we found out he owned Scartongarth or thought he did. I felt so helpless. I couldn't save Bel or her child. That is when I decided to go into nursing. When I came back to the island with my own illegitimate child, Nick was so nasty, so gloating, I hated him more than ever. And his new wife was as bad as him at the time.'

'His first child also died under your care? How awful for you.' By now there was a tear in Rose's eye.

'Yes. So you see,' continued Annie, 'He's going to bring that up as well, casting more doubt on me.'

'I was told that he hadn't wanted you at the birth, but I didn't know the ins and outs of it.'

'What could I do?' asked Annie. 'I couldn't leave Alexina on her own with a problem birth.'

'I understand, darling. I do hope it will all be sorted out for you.'

'The truth is, I don't know if I want to stay here after this. The heart's gone out of me.'

'Another cup of tea?'

'No, for heaven's sake, I'm drowning in the stuff.'

'All right, darling, put on your coat and take me round, introduce me to my patients.'

Together they walked along the road. 'You will need to see Jeannie. I'm afraid she needs medical care, and of course…' Annie gestured hopelessly with her hands.

'Is this Nick a really bad person, then?'

Annie sighed. 'He was always a bit rough, sure of himself, thought he was God's gift to the lassies of Raumsey and a few on the mainland too. We've fallen out over the years, it's true, and the ownership of Scartongarth is a sore point.' Annie hesitated for a beat. 'We'll start at the Post Office and then go to the school. The children will love meeting you. They are pleasant bairns, very biddable.'

Chapter 38

Alexander: Changi 1942

Alexander, his hands now calloused and dirt-encrusted from fieldwork, glanced up briefly, wiping sweat from his brow with the back of his hand. The sight of the endless fields was both comforting and disheartening. It was a far cry from the life he once knew, but this was life now, and he had to make the best of it. He felt an enormous responsibility for the boys, and they looked to him for comfort and leadership.

Beside him, Tommy struggled with a particularly stubborn weed. He grunted in frustration, his face contorted with the effort. Alexander put a hand on his shoulder and offered a quiet word of encouragement.

'Take it slow, Tommy,' he said. 'We've all day.'

Tommy nodded, his grip on the weed tightening. 'I just want to get it right, Alex. I don't want to give them any reason to beat me. I'm still sore from the last time.'

A heartsore Alexander understood the lad's anxiety, hopelessness washing over him at his inability to protect the younger lads. They were no more than boys, their futures stretching out before them. They should be swimming, kicking a football about, chasing girls, thinking of their careers, anything but this.

The Japanese watched for any sign of laziness, and responded swiftly and brutally to any perceived slacking. All around the edge of the field, the guards stood, rifles slung over their shoulders, eyes scanning the workers with a mixture of boredom and suspicion.

As the day wore on, the sun climbed higher, and the heat became nearly unbearable. The prisoners paused occasionally to take sips of water from a shared canteen. Despite the harsh conditions, there was a silent understanding that they were all in this together.

In the distance, the sound of a gong rang out, one single tone, signalling the midday break. The prisoners straightened up, stretched their aching muscles and gathered in small groups to eat their meagre rations. More rice and water. Alexander and Tommy found a shady spot under a large oak tree, the coolness of the shade a welcome relief.

As they ate, Alexander found himself lost in thought, his mind drifting back to his family and then to Annie and her child. He wondered how they were coping, whether they were safe. What was going on in the UK now? They could already be under German rule for all he knew. The uncertainty was a constant ache, an added pain to the physical labour.

The guard struck the gong again. The break was over. The prisoners struggled to their feet, returning to the fields and more back-breaking work. Above them, the sun continued its relentless march across the sky, a silent witness to their struggle.

'You were a teacher,' said Tommy.

'I was,' replied Alexander.

'When we get out of here, I don't want to be stupid. Would you teach me?'

Alexander adjusted his tattered hat, delighted at Tommy's suggestion. It was something he had thought about but, expected to work twelve hours a day, could he commit another couple of hours to the boys?

‘If you have enough energy at the end of the day, we could give it a try,’ he said. It was a goal. And a goal was something that was needed, not only for himself but the boys as well. A new determination filled him up. ‘If you can get the rest of the boys to agree, we’ll do it.’

Chapter 39

Annie: Raumsey 1942.

Annie gasped when she opened the door. The man standing there grinned, and the years fell away.

He had generous slashes of grey at his temples, and his eyes had deeper lines around them than she remembered, but she could not fail to recognise the young man who had shown her around Glasgow, who had offered to marry her to save her from disgrace when she fell pregnant with Dee, the lawyer Donald had promised would help her, and her heart filled with hope. 'Henry,' she exclaimed.

He hugged her and then held her at arm's length. 'Annie, you look marvellous. What have you been up to, my girl?'

'It's so good to see you, Henry. You look well. I imagine Donald has told you what happened?'

'Yes. And more.'

She led him into the kitchen where the sun streamed through the windows, highlighting dust particles in the air.

'You know,' he said, 'I've always wanted to see this island of yours. Maybe not in those circumstances though.'

'I'm so happy you're here, Henry, after all this time.' Tears suddenly swelled as she filled with emotion. Henry had been a good friend to her back in her training days. After she returned to Raumsey, they had written occasionally, but the letters had been few and far between and eventually stopped.

He looked around. 'Where is my dear uncle and his lovely

wife?’

‘They’re in the kirk getting everything ready for tomorrow’s service. You’ll take tea, surely?’

‘I’d be delighted.’

She lifted the caddy from the mantlepiece. ‘I…I did hear you had taken a law degree. A lawyer, imagine that.’

‘And a very successful one. And I’m happy to be your legal representative,’ he said.

‘So you didn’t follow your father into banking?’ It didn’t surprise her. Back in the heady days of their youth, he rebelled against everything his father stood for.

He spread his hands, ‘As you see.’

‘I’ve not got a lot of money,’ she began. How could she even afford a successful lawyer?

‘Your stepfather is very worried about you. As soon as I heard, I dropped everything. I’m due time off from my firm, so it’s a holiday for me. *You* don’t have to worry about money.’

He reached over and clasped her hand. ‘I’ve heard your charges, now I want to hear the story from your own lips.’

Wiping a tear from her cheek, she began. She told him as much as she could.

‘I hope Dee copes well with all this.’

Henry nodded. ‘I believe he’s a fine boy. I can’t wait to meet him.’

‘Do you ever see Simon?’ she asked after Dee’s father, although she couldn’t care less, but did wonder if he ever thought about his child.

‘After he let you down the way he did, I dropped him. I believe he’s a gambler like his father and a womaniser. You are well out of that relationship. Anyway, we’ll have enough time to reminisce. Right now, getting you out of trouble is my number one priority. I don’t think they have enough to charge you. You’ll be pleading not guilty I assume?’

‘I am definitely not guilty,’ she said. ‘I did everything I could. Nick Sinclair won’t let it rest though. He’s determined to destroy my life. What will happen?'

'Several factors will be considered. If the Sinclairs continue to swear that they heard the baby cry, well…' he shrugged. 'A thorough examination will be conducted to look for any signs of trauma, congenital defects, or other causes. Maybe an autopsy will be performed to determine the cause of death.'

'He was early and the birth took too long,' said Annie. 'I swear I did everything to save his life.'

'They'll look into the mother's health records to check for any complications during pregnancy that might have contributed to the stillbirth.'

'She didn't have any checks as far as I know.'

'Then they'll look at your records, including your notes from the delivery. Your professional history and experience will also be scrutinised to assess if there have been previous complaints or issues.'

'There never have been.'

'Any other individuals present during the delivery will be interviewed.'

'Alexina. She's already spoken to the police and the medical examiner.'

'Her statement will be crucial. Does she back you up?'

'Yes, of course she does, except…she did leave to get warm water.'

'Why did you want warm water?'

'To wash the baby.'

He gave her a slightly bemused look, then cleared his throat. 'Don't worry too much. The burden of proof is on the parents to demonstrate that your actions caused the stillbirth. This requires clear evidence of negligence or malpractice.'

'Nick wasn't even there. But Jeannie claims she heard the baby cry after I sent Alexina from the room.'

'I'm sure you'll be exonerated. What kind of person is Jeannie?'

'Fragile. But even if I get off, it's so awful to be accused of something like that.'

'I could do with some of that tea, and I want to see my Uncle Donald again and meet his lovely wife and, of course, your child.'

Annie poured the tea and brought out some oat biscuits. As he ate, Donald and Isa followed by Dee and the pup, came into the kitchen.

'Henry,' cried Donald. 'So good to see you. I didn't know you'd arrived.' They shook hands, and Henry's eyes flitted to Isa. 'This must be your wife. She's as charming as I've been led to believe.' He clasped Isa's hand in turn. 'And this little chap,' he hunched down so that he was level with Dee. 'What's your name?'

'Dee,' he said, slinking behind his grandmother's skirt and sticking a finger in his mouth.

Henry stood up and turned to Annie.

'We'll talk more tonight. And tomorrow, I will go to Wick and find out what I can. Right now, I have to catch up with my uncle and the rest of the family. My father will pump me for news when I return home.

Chapter 40

Alexander: Changi 1942

Wilbur sat on the dry ground, his back against the rough, splintered wood of the hut. Although it was late in the day, the air was still thick with humidity and insects. Low now, the relentless sun hung like a red-hot eye, turning the camp into a cooker that sapped every ounce of strength from the worn-out prisoners.

Alexander looked once and then twice. He was sure. It was Wilbur. The man looked confused, a large bruise stretching up one side of his face, his eye blued and swollen. He had grown thinner, his jowls slack his skin burned and peeling with unprotected exposure to the elements, eyes blood-shot and shadowed. He sagged where he sat as if he had no more strength. A Japanese guard stood over him screaming and prodding him with his bayonet. Wilbur lurched to his feet and staggered forward supporting himself with the fence.

Alexander watched him from a distance, waited until the guards lost interest and then crossed the compound to offer Wilbur what was left of his water.

Wilbur stopped and stared at him, took a shuddering breath, and then recognition slowly filled his eyes. His voice stuttered, he fell silent and gulped the meagre drop of water like a dying man. 'Alexander Garcia. Is it really you?'

'It is. What happened to you?' Alexander asked.

A sob caught in his throat and he wiped his eyes with his forearm. 'I couldn't believe my eyes when I first saw them. Scruffy little men with trainers on their feet cycling into Singapore. I thought, we were conquered by that? We tried to hide out at the plantation.' He shuddered. 'That made it worse.'

'Your girls. What about them?'

'Patricia and Beatrice. My baby girls. They're somewhere out there — taken to another camp. I don't know where, or if they're safe, or if they even have enough food to survive.' He stared at the ground, his focus on the patch of dirt beneath his feet where ants marched in single file, oblivious to the human misery surrounding them. 'You told me to get out. You told me we needed to leave. I… I didn't listen.'

Alexander sighed, running a hand through his hair, feeling the grime cling to his fingers. The boys were waiting for him by the fence. He shouted to them. 'Get your rest, lads. We'll talk about school tomorrow.'

He turned to Wilbur. 'Keep walking,' he whispered. 'Where is your hut?'

'I thought I was doing the right thing. For the girls, for everyone.' His voice was cracked. Deep lines of worry etched into his face, the haunted look in his eyes was never there before.

Alexander read the man's anguish, the regret of every wrong decision tearing him apart.

'Wilbur,' he said quietly, his voice as soft as he could make it. 'You did what you thought was right. We all did what we had to do.' There was no point in I told you so, the time was way beyond that. He continued, his tone firmer, more resolute. 'But now… all we can do is survive. That's it. We get through this and we find them. We'll find Patricia and Beatrice.'

Wilbur nodded, but his eyes were wet, tears finally spilling over. 'I keep seeing their faces,' he said, his voice breaking. 'They were crying when they took them. I couldn't… I couldn't do anything.' His hands trembled as he covered his face.

'We're not dead yet.' Alexander's grip tightened on Wilbur's arm. 'You'll get out of this. You'll get back to them. Keep believing that.'

'I'm sorry,' Wilbur whispered. 'Sorry for what I said. At least you tried to get Amelia out, although I hear her ship was torpedoed not long after it left. I've no way of knowing whether she survived.'

Alexander gave a gasp. He knew there was always that risk, but knowing it had happened sent him into a new low. He had to believe that she was one of the lucky ones, otherwise his efforts had been in vain. 'We're in the same boat now,' he said, his voice steady. 'We'll do what we have to do, and we'll get through this.' But deep down, he feared that Wilbur, with his pampered lifestyle and flabby muscles, his soft bed and scented baths would be no match for the strict regime imposed on the prisoners. He was already breathing heavily.

'I haven't eaten,' said Wilbur.

'They'll give us a cup of rice soon. The chef here came out of Raffles, would you believe? He tries all sorts of tricks to make the rice taste better.'

'How does he do that?' asked Wilbur dolefully.

'We're rarely given fat in our diet. But we survive on rice, barley, green stew, meat or fish once a month and seaweed. You get used to it.'

'What about Red Cross parcels? Surely we get them?'

Alexander shook his head. 'If any arrive, it's a fair bet that the Japanese keep them for themselves. This is your life for the foreseeable future, my man.'

In truth, food haunted their dreams and thoughts. Hunger turned into starvation. Taste faded into memory.

The jungle pressed in around them, hot and unyielding. The two men sat in silence for a long moment, waiting for the tin spoon against the container that would signify what was humorously known as the evening meal.

Alexander had decided to hold the lessons at dusk after their working day was over when the guards were less vigilant. Only Alfie had complained. 'I never liked school. I was never very good at it, and I'm so tired.'

'We're all tired, Alfie. But we will be rescued. When we are, you don't want to be behind in your lessons, do you?' Alexander replied, 'Tell me what you were learning before the Japs came.'

'But we don't have any books,' complained Alfie.

'True we don't have books, but I can tell you what I know — anything I can, so you won't be too far behind when we go home.' Alexander needed to get them motivated.

'Come on.' Tommy put his arm around the younger boy. 'I'll help you.'

Alfie sniffed and wiped his eyes. 'I'm hungry. I want to go home.'

Alexander hugged him and stroked his hair. 'Think about your mum and dad. Think about when you meet them again.' He looked at the worried faces, the shadowed eyes. 'If you have a sweetheart or a girl you like, think about her, it helps.'

'Who do you think about?' Tommy asked. The other boys watched him with interest and Alexander searched his mind for a suitable answer. He closed his eyes, tilted his head back and let his memories take him through the years and over the miles. 'There's an island in Scotland where the wind smells of salt and the sea birds shriek and the seals, there are hundreds of them, and they cry like banshees in the night.' Recollections rushed at him: of cool air, the murmuring voices in the classroom, the young, eager faces of the children waiting to hear from their new tutor, and the way time had stopped the first time he had seen Annie Reid.

'Banshees,' said Tommy in an almost reverent whisper. 'Ghosts.'

Children always had a fascination with scary stories, and this was a good way to take their minds off their present situation, at least for a short time, Alexander realised.

'Tell us a ghost story,' said Ian.

'Once we start the school, I'll tell you lots of stories,' he said. The boys paid attention, eyes filled with interest, momentarily forgetting their circumstances.

'We'll do it then?' he asked.

'Yes, sir,' said Alfie.

A young Japanese guard stood nearby, watching them with curious eyes.

It was with the blessing of the more senior prisoners and under the wary eyes of their captors, that Alexander Garcia's impromptu school had been born. They gathered in a corner of the camp, using makeshift chalkboards made from scraps of wood and charcoal and often just writing in the dust beneath their feet. Because of the hunger, exhaustion, and the constant threat of violence, the school became a sanctuary. In Alexander's tales, the boys' eyes often lit up with a light that had been absent for too long. They shared their knowledge, their stories, and, most importantly, their hope.

One thing Alexander insisted on was that the boys washed regularly. The difficulty was that the shower facilities were based in a concrete building and the cold water was on briefly for about an hour each day. The only way to brush teeth was with water and a finger. There were no razors, so the men grew full beards. Therefore, cleanliness became a problem and body lice and hair lice soon affected them.

Although the officers didn't normally mix with the men, they often came to see what was going on and how the prisoners were holding up. The men looked to them for leadership and they did their best to keep morale up.

'I'm glad to see you've started a school,' MacLeod said to Alexander. 'I've managed to get permission to set up a hospital in an empty hut. We have a couple of doctors and some male nurses in the camp. They'll do what they can. A lot of the men are going down with fevers and who knows how long we'll be here.'

'Will they give us any medical supplies?' asked Alexander with little hope.

MacLeod shook his head. 'We're lucky to get this much. If we act subservient and do everything they ask, I'll maybe ask for something else, like blankets. But there's a lot of depression in the camp. I wondered if you could organise a concert, something to lift their spirits. I'm sure some of the men could do a turn.'

'That's a good idea. That's if they have any strength left at the end of the day.' Alexander wondered how he could find the energy to organise that and teach the boys.

Somehow, between him and Tommy, they managed to whip up enough enthusiasm to put on a concert, aware that at any moment, the Japs could put a stop to it. As it was, they just watched with interest, especially the young guard who it seemed was never far away.

The concert did seem to lift the men's spirits to a certain degree, and Alexander began to think that if they didn't starve to death, they could survive this hell after all.

The empty hut used as a hospital doubled as a church led by a Church of Scotland minister whenever prayer was possible. The Japanese did not allow any kind of religious worship, and no doubt there would have been severe repercussions if they were discovered. Alexander organised a choir and they would go in to sing to the patients. At first, the guards watched them, then appeared bored and drifted away. Undoubtedly when they occasionally heard the rendering of hymns, they thought it was just another song and left them alone.

Although he looked, Alexander never saw Wilbur again.

Chapter 41

Annie: Raumsey 1942

Annie was frying oatmeal and onions, and she hoped to add some chunks of cod or whatever fish her stepfather returned with after his visit to the pier. Isa was pounding the dough she was kneading to make bread when Henry tapped on the door and entered.

'That smells good. I hope there's enough for me.'

Annie set down her spatula and ran to give him a quick hug. 'How did you get on?'

He smiled and kissed her cheek. 'Very well. It seems like there's no case to answer.' He took a seat at the table.

'We'll always make enough for you,' said Isa, 'Annie, watch the skirlie. Don't let the oatmeal burn.'

Henry nodded and began. 'The other midwife gave a detailed description of how you fought to save the baby. Jeannie herself is unreliable as she seems confused. They have other character witnesses from your hospital days, and I must say, you have glowing testimonials.'

'Will they do a postmortem?'

'It may not be necessary. I believe they did a detailed examination of the baby's body and could find no sign of trauma other than that of the birth. They might still do a postmortem if the Sinclairs insist on it.'

'They will, knowing Nick,' said Annie.

'What I've learned is that it's very difficult to pinpoint

why a stillborn baby died. The authorities seem reluctant to move forward.'

'The thing is, if she'd had a caesarean the baby may have lived.'

Henry put his arms around her and hugged her. 'You don't know that. But what could you do in the circumstances?'

'Nothing, but if she'd had regular checks, the doctor would have known the bairn was the wrong way round. They might have taken her into hospital sooner given the time of year and her age.'

'None of it's your fault, Annie.' Henry rubbed her back and looked down into her face. 'You know that, don't you?'

'Of course I do. But I keep thinking whether there was anything else I could have done, you know. Spoken to her when she came to the sewing circle, tried to make her see…but you're right. What's done is done.' She wiped her eyes. 'Maybe that's why I feel I need to speak to her now.'

'Absolutely not,' said Hendry.

'It's a hard thing to lose a baby,' said Isa. 'And she didn't have the easiest of lives. But Henry's right, Annie. Stay away.'

Annie remembered Bel's baby, Sina, how hard she had fought to keep her alive, the pain both she and her parents had gone through then, and she remembered, too, Nick Sinclair's indifference. 'Jeannie'll need medical treatment. Rose is good but she doesn't know Nick Sinclair like I do. He's a hard, cruel man.' Despite everything, her heart went out to Jeannie.

'Don't go near her or Sinclair.' Henry reiterated. 'It's a nice night. Come on, show me this island of yours. Let's take a walk until the food's ready.'

'Aye, off you go but take your gasmasks,' said Isa, 'You're aye going out without it.'

Annie sighed and slung the strap of the mask over her arm.

The sun hung low in the sky, but not yet touching the horizon. The tide was high and flirting with the shore.

‘Do the birds always make such a noise?’ Henry looked up at the sky where angry terns swooped and threatened.

‘It’s nesting season. They quieten down once the young have gone. Anyway, I’d rather the birds than the bombs and guns over Scapa.’ She indicated northwards and the barrage balloons that filled the landscape of the islands to the north.

Henry looked around. ‘It’s so peaceful right now. I can imagine that it’s a great place to live when there is no war.’

‘The Germans aren’t interested in our wee island,’ she said, but occasionally, an unexploded shell or bits of shrapnel find their way here. A couple of times a mine has washed up on the shore. The home guard clears the area until they manage to make it safe.’

They walked on in silence for a beat. ‘That house over there, surrounded by buildings. It seems a lot grander than the others,’ said Henry.

‘The Mains. Many a good dance we've had in the loft before the hall was built.’

‘And the other big one, by the shore?’ He pointed.

Annie’s breath caught. ‘Aye,’ she said bitterly. ‘That’s Scartongarth. When I first came here, it was whitewashed and glistened in the sun. Look how grey it is now. You can just tell it’s an unhappy place.’

Henry fell silent again.

‘I still wish I could talk to Jeannie,’ said Annie.

‘No.’ Henry’s voice was sharp. ‘That is not advisable.’

Deep down, Annie knew what he said was true, but she could imagine the woman’s deep unhappiness, imagine, too, how little support she would get from her husband. She quickly changed the subject. ‘How is Glasgow faring with the war and all?’

‘The Clydebank bombing was bad, but apart from that we suffer from shortages, same as everywhere else.’

‘Is a lawyer a reserved occupation, then?’ she asked.

He winked. ‘Only for those advising on legal matters crucial to wartime governance.’

'And you — '

He held up his hand to stop her. 'That's all I can say.' He gave her a knowing look and she fell silent.

There were raised heads and questioning glances as they walked along the road. Annie understood her neighbours' curiosity. Margaret was emptying a bucket of water by the side of her grandmother's cottage when they drew near. She stood up and waved when she saw Annie.

Annie pulled Henry to a stop. 'My friend's daughter,' she explained, as the girl hurried towards them. She quickly introduced Henry. Within an hour or two everyone would know who he was.

'I hope ye get Annie off,' said Margaret in her breathy voice. 'I'm right glad that ye've come.' She rubbed her back and then turned her attention to Annie. 'I know ye would never hurt a bairn and I want ye to deliver mine.'

'Until I hear officially that they have cleared my name, I don't think I'll be allowed.' She leaned forward and looked at Margaret's face and then her ankles. They were slightly puffy. 'I think you should go to hospital. It's your first bairn.'

'Rose said that, but I really wanted ye there. I don't know if Freddy will get leave. I don't even know where he is.' Her eyes grew moist.

'If you agree to go to hospital, I'll come over with you. I'll be in the waiting room with your mam.'

'But aren't they dropping bombs on Wick?' she asked.

'The maternity hospital's a fair bit away from the harbour or the airport,' Annie said.

'Then I suppose that'll have to do.' Margaret still looked uneasy. 'I wanted ye to know I trust ye.'

'I know that, love.' Annie gave Margaret's arm a slight squeeze.

'Is this really what you want?' said Henry as they walked further. 'It is beautiful here, peaceful and you are thought well of and all, but isn't it a bit boring after Glasgow?'

'Of course it is. I've got a child and it's safer here than the city. And I'm a country girl at heart.' She gave a laugh but there was truth in his words.

'I'm going to miss you,' she said honestly. 'When do you have to go back?'

'I'll make sure everything is all right for you, then I should go. But I will return, next time you're in trouble.'

'Don't say that, not even in a joke.'

He squeezed her hand. 'I'm sure I won't be needed.'

She remembered Eliza's prediction and shivered. At least that's it over, she thought and wondered why the icy finger still traced its way down her spine.

Chapter 42

Alexander: Changi 1942

In the camp amid the Changi jungle, Alexander taught history, weaving tales of ancient civilisations and great leaders. He told the boys about the war in Spain and the politics that led to it. One of the lads, who had a knack for drawing, gave art lessons, sketching in the dust and on the walls of their huts. Another lad, James, who had been a science student, explained the mysteries of the natural world. Alexander had eight students, and as time passed, a few of the adults joined in, possibly to alleviate the boredom rather than any desire to learn.

The young guard who always seemed to be around began to take an interest in what Alexander was doing, and rather than stand stiff and straight, rifle at the ready, he watched intently.

One day, Alexander stood, dusting off his hands, and approached the guard slowly, careful to keep his movements non-threatening. His students glanced up, some with curiosity, others with a hint of fear. No one spoke to the guards; the risk was too high. The guard looked even younger in the soft evening light, barely older than Tommy.

By now Alexander had managed to pick up a smattering of Japanese. He had tried to get the guard on his side and gave him a smile and a nod whenever they met. When the guard nodded back, Alexander decided to take it a step further and began to speak to him. He would say something like, 'Nice night,' or 'hello,' and, when they left, it was 'goodbye.' The guard began to reply with similar phrases. He had to be careful, but the quiet tonight and the absence of other guards, seemed to invite a moment of connection. They eyed each other warily, but there was no immediate sign of hostility.

Carefully, he chose his words. 'Alexander,' he said, pointing to himself.

The guard stared at him, his expression inscrutable. After a long pause, he nodded slowly, a slight tilt of his head that suggested he was processing the moment. He hesitated before speaking, his voice soft and clipped. '*Yoshio,*' he replied, nodding and setting his hand on his chest. Then he pointed to the boys.

'Tell him your names,' Alexander said.

'He's the enemy,' Tommy whispered.

'Life might be easier if we can communicate with them,' said Alexander.

The lads obeyed. Tommy, Alfie, Ian, William, and John. It went on until all had complied.

Yoshio nodded and fumbled in his pocket, pulled out a worn envelope and extracted a few photographs. He held them out to Alexander.

'*Musuko, Hiroshi,*' he said, nodding and smiling.

Alexander took the photos and examined them. Two young boys gazed up at him.

'Your sons?'

'*Musuko*,' he said, nodding and pointing to himself and then the photo.

Alexander lifted another photo this time of a beautiful Japanese woman.

'*Tsuma*,' said Yoshio

'*Tsuma*,' repeated Alexander, not knowing if this was the word for wife or her name. 'Beautiful.'

Yoshio nodded, his pride evident despite the language barrier.

'Engrish?' said Yoshio.

'English,' repeated Alexander.

'Waar... bad.... famiry... good,'

'Yes, war is bad, family is good. Maybe one day, we won't have to fight.'

'Arigatou.' Yoshio tucked the photographs back in his pocket, but he didn't take his habitual stance. Instead, he watched with interest as Alexander gave the boys their lesson. The next evening, Yoshio stood behind the boys, watching them. Now and again, he repeated a word and the boys did the same in Japanese. Eventually, with at least a basic understanding of the language, it was easier to grasp orders, which helped to avoid beatings.

One night Tommy ran into camp. He had removed his tattered shirt and held it bunched up in his hands. 'Look what I've got,' he shouted. He slowly opened the bundle and there lay six gleaming eggs.

The eggs were like manna from Heaven. Nevertheless, the lad had put his life in danger in order to get them.

'Where did you find these?' asked Alexander, desperately afraid for the boy.

'I found a gap in the fence,' he whispered. 'The Japanese have chickens.'

‘For God’s sake, don’t you realise that if they catch you, they’ll kill you? What if one of them saw you?’ He wanted to shake the boy. The only thing that stopped him was the fear of losing the precious eggs.

‘I’m careful. Anyway, Yoshio saw me. He pointed the gap out. He even kept an eye out for other guards.’

‘Yoshio would have been killed, too. Promise me you won’t do it again, you young idiot.’

Tommy promised, but he held his hands behind his back and Alexander guessed he had his fingers crossed. ‘Go and get a shower. It’s a wonder they didn’t smell you. You must be crawling.’

Tommy pulled a face. The boys often had to be pushed into entering the stinking cubicle.

Alexander carried the eggs into the kitchen space and gave them to the chef whose eyes lit up when he saw them but didn’t ask any questions. ‘I’ll do my best to share them out,’ he said.

‘As always,’ answered Alexander.

Chapter 43

Annie: Raumsey 1942

Annie lay awake all last night. Despite Henry's advice, she wondered how to approach Jeannie. She needed to convince her that she had done nothing to harm the baby and, apart from anything else, there was no doubt that Jeannie had suffered living with Nick and now was a woman in mourning with little or no support.

She had finished her rounds, the Germans were quiet, and the boats were in the bay. The men were still at sea. Then, against her better judgement, she took a deep breath and, summoning all her courage, she turned towards Scartongarth. It started to rain, a pathetic drizzle that threatened to become worse.

Teddy was still there. an old horse now, but he seemed to know her and ambled up to the gate. She rubbed the soft muzzle. 'You remember me, boy, don't you?' She laid her head against his and breathed in the heady equine scent of him. Back in the days when she had lived in Scartongarth, she had ridden him often. Having grown up around horses, she missed them, especially this big, gentle soul. Closing her eyes, she allowed her memory to take her back to the day Bel told her she was going to marry Nick Sinclair. She saw again his grinning face, the handsome mask hiding his true nature.

He stood across the yard from her that day and waited

until she dismounted. Without uttering a word, she led Teddy towards the stable.

With a few quick strides, Nick was beside her. 'Ye'll not be happy that Bel's agreed to marry me, then,' he said with his mocking grin.

Her temper rose. 'I don't want to talk to you.' She pushed open the stable door.

'That's a shame. We both want ye to be a bridesmaid. Would ye no do that for a girl ye claim to be fond of?' His voice had been as smooth as treacle and just as dark.

Annie dampened her lips. 'If you ever hurt Bel again, I'll —'

His hand shot out and he grabbed the harness. 'Ye'll do what?'

Annie wished she owned a horsewhip. She wished she had the means to wipe the smug look from his handsome face. 'Let go of my horse and get out of my way.'

He released the reins and laughed. 'Your horse? In a couple of weeks, he'll be my horse. Be nice to me and I might let you carry on riding him. In the meantime, take good care of him. Oh, and that bicycle you use to get around, I'll have that back as well.' He walked away, his cruel laugh echoing behind him.

The rain was coming down like stair rods by now, driving into her face, jerking her into the present, and the horse was shivering. 'You poor old boy,' she said. 'They shouldn't leave you out in this.' She looked towards Scartongarth, but there was no one to be seen. The stable wasn't too far away and she wondered if she should risk putting him in. Looking at the bowed head, she came to a decision. She would put the horse inside and use that as her excuse to visit Jeannie; she would have to tell her what she'd done.

After leading the horse into the stable, she tied him in the stall and turned to leave. The air moved around her, full of musty, dank smells.

Shadows shifted.

Something blocked the light from the door.

She spun around to see the cold glitter of hard eyes and bared teeth.

'What the hell are you doing here?' Nick Sinclair bellowed.

'I…what…' she stammered, shrinking back in shock, then filled with rage, she pulled herself to her full height.

'You hate me, but there's no reason to make the animal suffer. He's an old horse and he shouldn't be out all winter. He'll die. I was trying to help, not you, but an innocent animal.'

Nick took a step towards her. 'And what business is it of yours? The horse is no use anyway. If I had a gun he'd have had a bullet before now.'

'I've put him in now. I'll go.' She couldn't let him see how afraid she was and shuffled sideways in an effort to get around him, but he moved to block her until their movements became a macabre dance.

'Let me go,' said Annie, fighting to keep her voice steady.

'Or what?' With one quick movement, he lunged forward and grabbed her arms. The heat of his body enveloped her, as did the force of his anger.

She whimpered with fear. He twisted her arm behind her and pressed himself against her, forcing her backwards until the wall stopped them.

'Maybe it wasn't the horse you came for,' he said with a suggestive grin twisting his lips. His forearm pressed against her windpipe, forcing her to stop struggling.

Fighting him off was useless; he was all muscle. With his free hand, he ripped the front of her blouse and grasped her breast until she cried out. He reached down and pulled her skirt up around her waist. 'I should have done this years ago.' His breath came fast and heavy. 'Showed you what a real man can do. Showed you what it was that took Bel back to me despite all yer efforts to break us up.'

Bel's name on his foul lips gave her an added strength and she tried to twist her head away, but it was to no avail. He was too strong for her. He reached to unbutton his fly. Screaming now, hysterically, she knew that the only person within earshot would be Jeannie.

Chapter 44

Jeannie: Raumsey 1942

Inside the house, Jeannie sat scrunched up in the rocking chair. Unable to face the present and what her life had become, she stared into the distance but saw nothing. Outside the wind whistled eerily in the eaves, rain splattered against the pane, the fire sparked then settled, the clock ticked steadily on. Everything was so familiar, so much the same, but nothing would ever be the same again. The one thing that gave her a reason to exist was gone, taken from her. As her breasts grew heavy and the ache in her heart grew even heavier, she asked herself how had she even come to this.

Her future stretched before her like a black tunnel of misery. Was this how her mother had felt the day she walked into the sea?

If Nick had not struck her that night knocking her to the floor, she believed she would not have gone into early labour. For that brief moment, when his temper overcame his desire to protect the child, she had felt real fear for her life. Now there was no reason for him to be kind. All her life, her father had treated her like the dirt beneath his shoe but she still suffered the pangs of guilt for taking his life. His voice still came to her on the wind, still berating her, still sucking the confidence out of her.

Nick was another matter altogether. Once upon a time, she believed that she might win his heart, or at least his respect, but in his desire for a child, he had treated her no better than a broodmare. What was it about her that made men treat her so badly? Annie Reid would never have put up with it. She had it all: looks, career, popularity, a child, and, undoubtedly, she still believed she owned Scartongarth.

Jeannie realised long ago that part of Nick's hatred of Annie Reid was because she had rejected him.

At the exact moment that she heard Annie's scream, she was contemplating ending her life. Her breath quickened. Someone was in the outhouses. Nick hadn't gone to sea today, he told her he was taking the boat into Laries Geo to tar the keel. Had he returned? Or was it an intruder?

Her heart beating unsteadily, she walked into the pantry and found the mallet Nick used to knock in stabs. Hiding it behind her back, she crept up to the stable and pushed open the door. What she saw froze her.

Nick had Annie Reid on the floor and it was all too obvious what was going on. She had to stop him any way she could.

Suddenly, just as Annie thought all was lost, Nick went limp and crumbled on top of her. She pushed him off and heard the thud as his head hit the flagstone floor. After struggling to her feet, she steadied herself against the stall and adjusted her clothes, shaking so hard she could barely stand.

Jeannie faced her, blank-eyed, panting, with a bloody mallet in her hand.

Annie glanced at Nick. He lay, eyes open, staring, sightless.

'Oh, God,' cried Annie, dropped to her knees beside him and felt his neck for a pulse. It was fluttering and weak. Then there was none.

Struggling to compose herself, she rose to her feet, took the mallet from Jeannie's hand and set it to one side. 'Jeannie,' she said, 'Jeannie.' She gave her a gentle shake.

Jeannie slowly turned to look at her and then down to the

body at her feet. 'Oh, my Sweet Jesus. I've killed him. I'll hang.'

'No, no,' said Annie. 'You did it to save me, you saved me.'

But Jeannie didn't seem to hear her. 'After everything I've been through, I can't end up at the end of a rope. Ye've made my life hell, Annie Reid. Why did ye ever come back to this island? It was always ye he wanted.'

Shocked, Annie grabbed both of Jeannie's arms. 'Listen to me, Jeannie, I want to help you.'

Jeannie suddenly began to scream hysterically, her whole body shaking.

Annie grabbed her by the shoulders. 'Stop it, stop it,' she shouted, but Jeannie didn't seem to be able to catch her breath between screams.

Annie slapped her, hard. It was the only way to stop someone in a state of panic.

Jeannie gasped, her eyes opened wide and she raised her hand to her cheek, but she did get control of herself. Covering her face with her hands, she began to sob.

'Come on.' Annie took her arm. 'I'll get you indoors. You're in shock.'

Jeannie tore away from Annie's grasp and looked wildly around her. 'We have to hide the body. We have to — '

'Jeannie, we have to tell the truth. I'll help you — '

'No,' Jeannie backed away from her. 'I'll deny I was here. They'll blame ye. That's what'll happen. I will not hang for ye!'

Annie gasped. She had more reason than most to kill Nick Sinclair, and she had bruises on her back where he had pushed her against the wall. Her fingerprints were also on the mallet.

If Jeannie blamed her, who would the authorities believe? It was possible that one of them, or maybe both of them, would end up in prison.

'It'll be fine,' she said as gently as she could.

'He was never going to change, ye know it and so do I. Why should either of us have to pay for this?' Tears still streamed down Jeannie's cheeks and she spoke in a broken voice.

'You had no other choice.' Annie tried once more. She had to tell the truth, but if Jeannie was less than honest, who knew what the outcome would be? What would happen to Dee if she was sent to prison? And even if they did believe her, did Jeannie deserve punishment for saving her? From what she had heard, women still had a very hard time with the courts.

Jeannie spun around, her eyes everywhere. 'I know,' she whispered frantically, 'We'll blame the horse. He reared up and— '

'Kicked him in the back of the head? No one will believe that.' Annie swallowed with nothing but dryness to swallow. 'I'll ask my stepfather…he'll help, he'll know what to do.'

'No,' shouted Jeannie. 'He's a minister. He'll want to go to the law.'

Annie knew it was true. But going to the law was the only option. She shouldn't involve anyone else in this but she had to make Jeannie see sense. If only Henry hadn't gone home.

'We have to go to the law. You acted to save me. You'll get off. Honestly, it will be fine.'

Jeannie stared at her and then at the mallet. There was a gleam in her eyes that verged on madness.

Suddenly afraid, Annie stepped sideways so that she was between the weapon and Jeannie. 'You didn't do anything wrong, Jeannie,' she said in the most persuasive voice she could muster. 'Come on, I'll take you into the house. We need tea with lots of sugar.' She glanced back at the body and bile rose, burning her throat.

Subdued now, Jeannie allowed herself to be led towards the house. Once they were inside, she lifted her eyes to Annie's. 'Ye'd best call the constable then, hadn't ye?' Her voice was flat and dry as if facing the inevitable.

'And you'll tell the truth?'

'I'll tell it all,' said Jeannie, gazing at the floor, her voice a monotone.

'I'll get you the tea, then I'll go and see Nurse Pennington. I'll phone from there. She'll come and give you something to help you sleep.'

Jeannie drank the tea with lots of sugar that Annie gave her. She hadn't loved Nick, that was a fact, but she hadn't meant to kill him. It came as a surprise that Annie seemed kind. Although panicky herself, she had settled Jeannie into bed with a hot water bottle and stoked up the fire. For the first time Jeannie thought that, under different circumstances, she could have liked this woman, they might have even been friends. At that thought a laugh bubbled up in her throat.

'I have to leave you now. I need to phone. Nothing will happen tonight, so try and get some sleep,' said Annie. 'I'll phone from Nurse Pennington's, and I'll ask her to come and stay with you.'

'There's no need for that,' said Jeannie. 'I'll sleep now.'

'Are you sure?'

'Please. I don't want anyone else here. Just go.' Jeannie had no intention of sleeping. She had to think of a way to make sure she was safe because she didn't believe Annie when she said it would be all right. When had anything ever been all right in her life? There was always the possibility that she would be charged with murder and hanged. She couldn't let that happen.

There would be questions asked and she would have to have her answers ready. Since she lost the baby, she had been studying her doctor's book desperately seeking answers. Now she needed to acquaint herself with the facts of postpartum complications, a condition she had come across while leafing through the pages. Even if her body had healed, they could not examine her mind and she had every reason to suffer acutely after the death of her bairn. Would that be enough to get her off? Somehow, she doubted it. Then she gave a little laugh as an idea formed in her mind. Nick had gone, and now she saw a way to get rid of Annie as well. Scartongarth would be hers.

The minute Annie left the house, Jeannie rose and took the heavy book from the shelf. She settled by the kitchen table and, by the soft flame from the paraffin lamp, she began to read.

Chapter 45

Annie: Raumsey 1942

The rain had stopped, but the wind was still high. The moon sailed through tattered clouds, glinting off the pale caps of billows in the firth and providing enough light for her to see her way along the road. There was no way of knowing whether Rose Pennington was still awake, the blackout blinds were effective. Annie knocked on the door. When there was no answer, she thumped loudly with her fists, all her pent-up panic suddenly released.

'I'm coming,' came the sleepy voice from inside. Eventually, Rose opened the door, holding a paraffin lamp in one hand, a shawl over her shoulders and her hair in disarray, her face an eery mask of light and shadow in the flickering flame.

'Annie, what is it?' She seized Annie's arm with her free hand and pulled her inside, leaning against the door to shut it. In the kitchen, she set the lamp on the table, grabbed Annie's arms and forced her to sit. 'Deep breaths,' she said, and breathed deeply along with her until she calmed down.

'What's happened? Is it Dee?'

Still unable to speak, Annie shook her head.

'Sit for a minute,' said Rose. She stirred the embers in the stove and added some peat from a bucket that sat to one side, then took a seat across from Annie. 'Now, take your time, what is it?'

'It's Nick Sinclair,' stammered Annie, surprising herself

at how she managed to get the words out at all, it was almost as if she didn't inhabit her own body, as if she were a clockwork toy functioning on a tightly wound spring slowly unravelling. 'Jeannie killed him. We need to phone the police.'

Shock registered on Rose's face. She turned up the flame on the lamp and peered closely at Annie. Then, as if she saw the truth there, she got up and began to make the tea. 'What happened?' she said, almost as if she still didn't believe what she was hearing.

The vision of Nick's shattered head and lifeless eyes stayed with Annie as she recounted the story.

'Oh, darling, how awful! I think we need something a wee bit stronger than tea.' Nurse Pennington, her voice shaking now, went into her cupboard and brought out two glasses and a bottle of whisky.

She handed a glass to Annie and set the other on the table. 'Pour them,' she ordered and went into the passageway where she phoned the police station on the mainland.

Annie hardly heard the voice from behind the door. After pouring the whisky with a shaking hand, she swallowed hers in one mouthful.

Rose returned. 'I've explained what happened. They agreed that no one's crossing that sound tonight. I have instructions to confirm death and let no one else near the body. I'll get dressed and go up to Scartongarth. You'd best be off home. You've had a nasty shock.'

Annie nodded. The power of speech had left her once more. Her legs were soft, no longer able to bear her weight, and her head felt as if it contained a strange substance that swelled and pressed against her skull until she wanted to scream. She fought to contain that scream otherwise she would never be able to stop. but fall into a pit filled with her own screaming.

Rose Pennington looked at her. 'Oh, my goodness, don't you pass out on me, darling. You just sit there. Take your time.'

Annie struggled to pull herself together and as soon as she felt strong enough, she pushed herself to her feet. 'I'm fine now. I'll go.' She wanted her mother and the calm reassurance of her stepfather.

Outside nothing moved not even the faint ghostly shapes of sheep. Not a light seeped from a window. But she knew her mother and Donald, steeped in worry, would be waiting for her return. Exhausted, both mentally and physically, all she wanted to do was return to the warmth of their love, kiss the innocent cheek of her sleeping son, bury under her blankets and shut out the world. She gasped in the pure fresh air and forced her jelly legs to carry her forward.

'What is it? What's wrong?' asked Isa, the minute Annie entered.

'Nick,' was all she could say as she grabbed hold of the back of a chair and swung it round so that she could collapse into it.

Isa rushed forward and grabbed both her daughter's shoulders. 'What has he done?'

Annie shook her head. 'He…he attacked me. Jeannie…she…she killed him.'

'What?' Isa sank into the opposite chair. For a moment Annie was faced with the same disbelief she had encountered from Rose.

'He's dead. I was there.' And then she finally, gave way to great hiccupy tears.

'Nick's dead?' Isa rose.

Donald came into the room in time to hear what she said. Without speaking, he paced to the window, his face grim. 'Are you sure?'

'I'm a nurse. I know when someone is dead.'

'What exactly happened?' Isa, her voice high with concern, 'For God's sake, what were you doing there?'

Gulping between words, Annie recounted the events. 'I phoned the police station. No. No not me. Rose Pennington did.'

Donald set his hand on her bowed head. 'You've done nothing wrong,' he said grimly. 'It'll all be sorted out. Jeannie has serious problems, they'll see that soon enough. Have you got anything to calm yourself down?'

'I'm not taking anything,' said Annie. 'I need a clear head.'

'You'd best go to bed. Try to get some sleep.' He rubbed his forehead.

'I'll never sleep.' Annie stared at the floor. She couldn't believe this had happened. Any minute now she would wake up and find that it was all a dream.

Donald picked up the phone. 'I'd better contact Henry again, hadn't I?' he said grimly.

Chapter 46

Jeannie: Raumsey 1942

When the knock came in the early morning, she hadn't slept at all. She returned the book she'd been studying all night to the shelf in the back of the cupboard and made her way slowly to the door. With one hand clutching her shawl to her throat, she edged it open, peering around. Two men stood there. One was middle-aged, heavily built, with fleshy lips and pouches under his eyes. The other was younger, taller than average, fresh-faced and quite handsome. He looked too young to be a policeman.

'I'm Detective Inspector Rodger Hammond.' The elder of the two flashed his badge. 'And this is Police Constable William Begg. You are Jean Amelia Sinclair?'

She nodded. Beyond them, she saw Doctor Anderson and two other men enter the barn.

The inspector followed her gaze. 'Once the experts are finished, we'll take the body away. Do you mind if we come in?'

She shook her head, wondering what they would do if she refused and stepped back, opening the door just wide enough to let them enter, one at a time.

In the kitchen, they took a seat without being asked.

'I know this is very upsetting, but we have to ask some

questions. Are you well enough to proceed or would you like someone with you? A friend perhaps or a family member?'

She pursed her lips and looked down at her hands. There was no need to pretend, they were visibly shaking. 'I have no one,' she said, miserably.

'We can give you more time if you'd prefer to have the doctor here,' said Hammond.

'No, I want it over with.'

Hammond adjusted himself on the chair and leaned towards her. 'Can you talk us through the events of last night?' His voice was soft. He was sympathetic, she thought, and that was a good sign.

'I was here.' Her throat was so dry the words came out as a rasp. 'I was in bed.' After a minute of silence, she spoke again. 'I heard footsteps outside.'

She hunched her shoulders and rubbed her head. 'I thought it was Nick returning, but no one came to the door.'

'And what happened then?'

There was a moment's hesitation. 'I looked out of the window and I saw Annie Reid going into the stable.' At her lie, something inside recoiled, but then she imagined her father's voice. *They want to see ye hang. Ye'll be with me in hell.* She waved her hand as if that would get rid of the false words. 'I have to stop for a wee while.'

'Understandable,' said Hammond. 'Take your time.'

They gave her a minute to compose herself.

'Where was Mr Sinclair at this time?' asked Hammond.

'I didn't see him.'

'What happened next?'

'I heard a scream.'

'A woman's scream?'

'I... don't know. It could have been Nick.' She was suddenly unsure. She hadn't expected this question. Her mind raced. 'I wasn't well, but I got the strength from somewhere. I went out to the stable.'

'And what did you see then?'

'Nick was lying on the ground and Annie was standing over him. She had the mallet in her hand and there was blood on it. Then I screamed, and she turned and saw me.' The words fell from her lips almost unbidden.

'And?'

'She shouted, and she just kept shouting that he had attacked her. Then she said that we'd have to hide the body. I told her we couldn't do that and she said that if I didn't help her, she'd blame me.' Jeannie was on a roll and there was no stopping her. 'She always hated him, you see. She hated us both. She let our baby die, but that wasn't enough.' Jeannie wiped the flecks of spittle from her lips. 'Annie Reid had no reason to come here, none at all.'

Looking beyond them, through the window, Jeannie wondered what was taking the doctor and the other two men so long.

'And how did you feel about her?'

'I didn't know her. Of course I knew who she was, it's a small community, but I never met her face to face before she came to deliver the bairn. I just knew what Nick told me.'

'Are you saying that Nick was already on the ground when you entered the barn?'

She nodded. 'He was, he was,' and she began to cry covering her face with her hands.

'Where is the mallet normally kept?' asked Hammond.

Flustered, Jeannie couldn't think for a moment. 'In the barn,' she hurriedly said, her eyes flitting from left to right.

'All right. Don't upset yourself. We'll talk to the doctor now, then he'll come and see you,' said the detective.

Hammond smiled but his smile was as thin as morning haar. 'You've been very helpful. Thank you.' His eyes flitted to his colleague who did not react. They rose to their feet and nodded at her.

'We'll be in touch,' he said, and they left her alone. As soon as the door closed, she sat upright and watched them through the window, hoping they believed her. They stopped a little way down the path and for a moment, were engaged in deep conversation.

The doctor left the barn and the stretcher-bearers loaded the undertaker's cart. They were taking Nick away and she was glad.

She hadn't meant to kill Nick and she regretted having to blame Annie, but it was necessary for her survival. Annie wouldn't hang, her kind never did. But now, Jeannie thought, she could be somebody at last, the owner of the largest farm next to the Mains in her own right. The sooner she had it transferred into her name the better. Her father had always been a stickler for doing things through lawyers. 'Get it on paper,' he used to say, 'Then none can go against ye.' There was no room for guilt. She deserved it after all she'd been through.

Let Annie Reid try to get it back, she would fail. She had been kind, but that could be all show, to ensure that Jeannie took the blame, then she would turn her back, just like everyone else. In any case, Annie Reid already had everything she needed and that fancy lawyer, he would find a way to get her off, just like he did when the bairn died.

Chapter 47

Annie: Raumsey 1942

Sometime after dawn, Annie had slipped into a fitful sleep, only to be wakened by the harsh banging at the door. She blinked herself fully awake and looked at the clock on the bedside table. Half the morning had gone.

'Annie,' came her mother's voice from below. 'There are two constables here to see you.'

'I'll be a minute.' She dragged herself out of bed, struggled into her clothes and hurried downstairs.

'We thought it best to let you sleep,' said Isa. Dark circles ringed her eyes, sad testament that she'd had little sleep herself the night before. 'I'll make tea.' She left them alone.

Annie smiled weakly at the two men on the doorstep. 'I'm Detective Inspector Rodger Hammond.' The elder of the two introduced himself. 'And this is Police Constable William Begg. You are Nurse Anne Reid?'

Annie nodded. 'Yes. Won't you come in?' Aware of how she must look with her uncombed hair and heavy eyes and how strained her voice sounded and not caring, she stepped back to allow them to enter, then ushered them into the sitting room.

The officers exchanged a glance, which unnerved Annie. She swallowed with difficulty.

'I believe you know what this is about?' said Hammond. Annie fought down a sudden, mad desire to giggle.

She nodded.

At that moment Isa appeared in the doorway. ‘How do you take your tea?’ She looked at the policemen.

‘Thank you. Milk and two sugars, twice,’ said Hammond as he took a seat and turned his eyes to Annie. ‘We’ve already spoken to Mrs Sinclair.’

‘And?’

‘You know her husband is dead?’

‘Of course I do. Nurse Pennington phoned you last night.’

‘Miss Reid, am I right in saying you were at Scartongarth yesterday evening?’

Annie’s breath caught in her throat. ‘You already know this. It was me who reported it to Nurse Pennington.’

They accepted the tea tray Isa brought, then waited until she left.

‘Could you tell us about the altercation between you and Nick Sinclair?’

‘Altercation? He attacked me. What did Jeannie say?’ More in control now, she told herself she was a professional. She could not show them how shaken she was.

‘Just answer the questions.’

‘I was there. I believe he was going to rape me. Jeannie came in and struck him with a mallet. She saved me. There was nothing I could do.’

‘Well, you see, there we have a problem. Mrs Sinclair claims she only heard the altercation and came out after her husband was dead,’ said DI Hammond.

‘What? I don’t understand.’ A confused Annie looked from one to the other. Jeannie had done what she threatened. She was blaming Annie.

‘Why didn’t you phone us right away?’ asked the constable.

‘Jeannie almost collapsed. I had to get her into bed. She was…we both were….in a state.’

‘Did you check that he was dead?’

‘Of course I did.’

‘And had he still been alive you would have helped him?’

'Yes, of course.'

'Even if you hated him?'

'As a nurse, I do not judge.'

The officers exchanged another look. 'But that's not what Mrs Sinclair says.'

'What? But…I don't understand.' Annie's voice ran out as the full realisation of what was happening struck her. They believed Jeannie. 'She's lying.'

'Why did you go to Scartongarth?' asked Hammond, setting down his cup.

Annie left her tea untouched, to eat or drink anything now would choke her. 'I wanted to talk to Jeannie alone. She's a sick woman who lost a baby. I wanted to explain, to help her in some way maybe.'

'Why would you want to help a woman who was trying to destroy your career?'

'I know what Nick Sinclair is like…was like. She wouldn't have any say in the matter. I wanted to explain that I didn't harm the child, that I was not the enemy.'

'And persuade her to change her story about the death of her child?' said Hammond.

Annie took a breath. Yes, there had been an element of that. 'Not to persuade her, no. To see what she really remembered perhaps,' she admitted.

'But you didn't go up to the house, did you?'

'The horse had been left out. He was an old horse and he was shivering. I intended to put him in the stable and go and see Jeannie.'

'It wasn't that you saw Nick Sinclair go into the stable and saw your chance for revenge? You see, we know all about his case against you.'

Words failed Annie.

A silence stretched as Hammond helped himself to a second cup of tea. 'I believe there was some history between you and Sinclair even before that,' he said at last.

'But…yes, he was a terrible man, but ….' Her voice ran

out.

'Is it correct to say that you hated him?'

'I won't deny I disliked him, but I didn't kill him. I don't think Jeannie did either — well she did but not on purpose. It was an accident.'

'You killed him by accident?'

'No… I. Did. Not. Kill him.'

PC Begg scribbled in a notebook.

D.I Hammond studied his thumbnail. 'And what time would that have been?'

'I'm not sure — it was late,' Annie said without thinking.

'And yet you didn't see fit to report directly to us?'

'I've already explained. Jeannie was in shock. As soon as I felt it was safe to leave her, I went to the nurse's house.'

'Mrs Sinclair was still suffering from complications caused by the birth of her child, yet you claim she had the strength to get out of bed and kill her husband — a big, robust man like him?' said DI Hammond.

'She was physically well. I believe she was suffering from deep melancholia. Ask Doctor Anderson.'

'Your friend, Doctor Anderson? Oh, we will.' Hammond opened his briefcase. 'We need your fingerprints. You can give them now, or drop into the police station in Wick within the next few days.'

'Let's get it over with,' she said. 'You will find my prints on the mallet. I took it from Jeannie's hand. I won't deny that.'

After the prints had been taken, Hammond closed his briefcase.

'That'll be all for now,' he said. 'But we'll be back. Don't leave Caithness. We'll see ourselves out.'

Annie sank into the chair and covered her face with her hands. Even the tears were trapped behind her eyes. This couldn't be happening.

As her mother entered the room, she shot to her feet and ran outside where she vomited among the bushes.

Chapter 48

Annie: Raumsey 1942

Later that afternoon, Annie opened the door to find Rose standing there, an anxious expression on her face. 'I came to make sure you were all right, darling,' She took a step back. 'Oh my goodness, you look a sight.'

'I've not slept much,' admitted Annie. She gave an unhappy little laugh. 'I've not even brushed my hair today, so I can imagine how I look. Come on in. I am glad to see you.' She ushered Rose into the kitchen where the ever-ready kettle simmered on the range.

'My parents are both out visiting elderly parishioners,' said Annie as she made tea. 'They took Dee with them as I'm not the best mother today.'

'I had to come and see how you are. That there are no hard feelings,' said Rose.

'Why should there be any hard feelings?'

Rose looked uncomfortable. 'My statement mightn't be helpful to you. I hope I've said nothing wrong.'

'To the police, you mean?' A shiver of apprehension ran down Annie's spine.

Rose chewed the inside of her lip and nodded.

'I suppose you've heard Jeannie's side?' said Annie. 'What's she saying?'

'With the symptoms she's complaining about, she really should go to the hospital. She doesn't sound at all well. I can imagine that she would have difficulty getting out of bed, let alone going outside to the stable.'

Annie gasped. The shiver turned icy. 'Let me guess, you told the police this? The inspector said as much, but I thought it was just her word. Are you saying you believe her?'

'I'm not saying that at all, darling. In moments of stress, we can gain amazing abilities. But with hindsight, I should have insisted she let me examine her.'

'You didn't examine her?'

Rose squirmed in her seat. Her eyes slid down to her cup. 'She wouldn't have it.'

'Then how can you be sure she's telling the truth about her symptoms?' Her voice rose a notch.

'That's the thing. No layperson would be able to make these symptoms up unless they experienced them. And she did look bad. She was as white as burnt-out ashes.'

'Jeannie isn't stupid.' Annie spoke patiently while holding onto her temper. How could a nurse give a diagnosis without checking the facts? 'You saw the bruises and marks on my back. I hope you told them about that, too.'

'Oh yes, I really did. But I couldn't swear to when they were inflicted.'

'You can only tell the truth, as you see it.' Annie said, her voice sharp now.

'I was honest. She was white and sweating. I haven't known Jeannie very long, but she was in a dreadful state.'

'As she would be after killing her husband,' said Annie bitterly.

'I wanted to help you, but I'm afraid I couldn't say anything for definite.'

'Then maybe you should go back and tell the police that you never examined her.'

'I'll do that. Is there anything else I can do? Do you want something to help you sleep?'

'No, I'll do without.' Annie suddenly wanted rid of her. She tried to make her words soft, but inside she felt all sharp and jagged edges. She only hoped that Doctor Anderson's statement would be more favourable, but he wasn't first on the scene. Rose was.

'I have to be somewhere now, Rose, if you don't mind.' She opened the door, stood back and waited as the other woman left.

She had to get out of the house, to breathe clean air. Her feet took her down to Larie's Geo, the place where she had first had a conversation with Alexander Garcia.

Despite warnings to stay clear of the coast, she climbed down the slope and sat on a rock, closing her eyes and listening to the steady whoosh of the sea. How had it all come to this?

'Annie.'

The voice startled her. Turning round she saw Magnus sliding down the slope. He lowered himself beside her. Without speaking, he put an arm around her shoulders and she leaned into him.

'I saw you come down here. Your ma told me what happened. Oh, Annie, what a terrible thing.'

'Thank you, Magnus,' she said. 'How has it come to this? I thought I had my life planned. I wish I'd never gone to that birth.'

'You had to. You'd never have forgiven yourself if you didn't. And then you would have been blamed for refusing to go. Ye know I would do anything I could to help ye. Whatever you want just say the word. I could say I saw Jeannie go into the byre with the mallet in her hand that night.'

A sudden bolt of hope made Annie straighten her shoulders. 'Did you?' she asked.

He shook his head. 'No, but I'm willing to swear under oath that I did.'

'You can't.' Annie shook her head. 'You can't lie for me.'

'Why not? Ye don't deserve to lose everything for that man.'

‘I didn’t do it! Surely the police will see that? You believe me, don’t you?’

He hesitated that moment too long before saying, ‘Of course I believe ye. But even if ye did, no one would blame ye.’

‘Is that what they think? The islanders?’

‘He attacked ye. But if ye tell me ye didn’t retaliate, I believe ye.’

Annie stood up. The police, Nurse Pennington, Magnus, hell, maybe her own parents, although they wouldn’t voice their suspicions. They knew her as feisty, ambitious, never scared to speak up for herself, they also knew Jeannie as meek, retiring, unable to fight her battles. Yes, she could see how it would look. Would her character witnesses even do her any good? Could she have killed him? If she were in Jeannie’s position, absolutely. If she had been the one with the mallet in her hand, who knew?

‘Thanks for the offer, Magnus, but I’ll fight my own battles,’ she said coldly and rose to her feet.

Suddenly, the sky filled with the buzz of planes. Gunfire started from Scapa. More planes took to the air. ‘Our boys,’ said Magnus. ‘A dog fight.’

He took Annie’s hand and she was glad of the warmth as they watched the battle in the sky. Suddenly a German plane plunged downward trailing smoke and crashed into the sea.

‘Got one,’ she shouted and immediately felt guilty. The pilot was some mother’s son, some girl's sweetheart, or even some child’s father. ‘Seems I do have evil in me,’ she said.

Magnus squeezed her hand. ‘I felt it too.’

They watched in a more sombre mood, as the fighting continued for some time before the German planes turned towards Norway.

It was two days later when she saw them coming over the brae. Annie knew that it wasn’t going to be good news. They walked with a determined stride, DI Hammond with his arms swinging, PC Begg looking more subdued, slinking rather than walking. They came right up to where she was standing at the manse door.

'Hammond took a deep breath. 'Anne Reid,' he said. 'I am arresting you for the unlawful killing of Nicholas Sinclair.'

'Don't come into the house,' she said. 'Let me tell my mother, then I'll come with you. My son is having breakfast and I don't want to alarm him.'

Hammond nodded. 'Take your time,' he said, his voice gruff. Annie had the impression that he wasn't enjoying this any more than she was.

'Don't worry,' said Isa, 'They'll find out the truth. Henry's on his way back up,'

'Of course, they'll find out the truth,' said Annie, although she wasn't sure at all. She grabbed her coat from the hooks behind the door and followed the policemen down the drive.

Chapter 49

Jeannie: Raumsey 1942

'Go away!' Jeannie tried to slam the door when she saw who was outside.

'I've come to offer comfort, Jeannie,' said Reverend Donald Charleston. 'Nothing else. I'm here as your minister, not Annie's stepfather.'

Jeannie didn't budge. His voice was soft and kind and she couldn't risk him making her feel guilty. 'I've done nothing wrong,' she shouted, and tried to shut the door again but Donald's foot was firmly lodged in the doorway.

'I'm here to help,' he tried again. 'Perhaps I could say a prayer? You must be in so much pain.'

'Go away.' Jeannie was getting agitated. He was in danger of suffering the same fate as Nick if he didn't go. 'Please, go away,' she said more softly, her voice becoming pleading. 'Please.'

Donald took his foot from the door. 'I'm not your enemy,' he said. 'Anything I can do, let me know.' He turned and walked down the path, taking his time. For a moment, she almost called him back. He had sounded kind, yet kindness was a trap that would lower her defences.

The voice of Nick Sinclair came into her head.

Don't listen to him. He knows ye're simple. He only wants to get Annie Reid off. They're in it together. They want to see ye hang.

'Shut up,' she shouted into the empty room, 'Just shut up.'

Over an hour later, Jeannie watched the two detectives and Annie walk down the metalled road and she smiled. Thank God she hadn't given in and spoken to the minister. Despite everything, Nick was looking out for her, even from the grave. She congratulated herself on studying the doctor's book so that she could describe her symptoms accurately. A woman suffering as much as she was would hardly have had the strength to rise from bed, let alone wield a mallet with enough force to bring down a large man like Nick. It was not yet over though. It would not be over until Annie was found guilty. There was a moment of hesitation, a moment where something tugged at her conscience. And then the voice of her mother banished all doubts. *Ye've got it, pet. Ye've got Scartongarth and ye've made them suffer, all them who did ye wrong. I'm proud of ye.*

Yes, she had Scartongarth and she could work as hard as any man to make sure it was a success. Farming was a hard reality, her life with her father had taught her that much, but she had done it before and she could do it again. It was made even harder with the young men away fighting. Those who were left needed all their time to keep their own farms producing, let alone help a widow. But what if Annie got off? And there was still that child who might well grow up to try and claim it back. In spite of him being a bastard, he was well-liked with his wide grin and pleasant nature. More than one person remarked how like he was to his granddad, Davie

Reid, and she was well aware that many believed Nick had no right to the farm or house. Any sideways glance in her direction, and hushed conversation as she drew near, heightened her paranoia. The thought of being banished back to the dilapidated house where she was brought up horrified her.

She would make her mam proud despite the many sideways glances as she walked up to the shop. She felt it every time she went out. Murder did not happen on Raumsey, had never happened in all the years she could remember or even all the years her parents could remember. If it had she would have heard it discussed.

It was Annie Reid's fault in the first place, all her fault. She led Nick on with her flashing eyes and her shapely figure. Anything that happened to her now was her own fault.

Chapter 50

Annie: Raumsey 1942

In the police station in Wick, Annie repeated her story several times. Henry sat beside her. 'My client has told you all she knows. You have no evidence against her and no reason to keep her here. So, with your permission, I shall take her home, unless, of course, you're going to charge her.' He raised his eyebrows. When Hammond gave a deep sigh, Henry stood up. 'Come on, Annie.'

The two police officers looked unhappy. 'You can go for now, pending further investigation,' Detective Inspector Rodger Hammond said, 'but remain at your address. We will want to speak to you again. And I advise you not to approach Jean Sinclair under any circumstances.'

Outside, Annie sagged against Henry and clutched his arm to prevent falling over. 'Can I be charged?' she asked.

'Let's go and grab a coffee somewhere.' Henry steered her along the street towards the Central Café. It was thankfully quiet at this time of day and they found a table in a corner. Henry ordered two coffees without asking her what she wanted. Annie didn't like coffee that much but what did it matter?

'What's going to happen?' she asked.

He leaned towards her and in a low voice began. 'The law follows the principle of *in dubio pro reo.* That's Latin for *when in doubt, rule for the accused.*

‘What?’ Annie swallowed a mouthful of the bitter, hot liquid.

‘It means that the burden of proof in a criminal case lies with the prosecution. Since it’s your word against hers, they must prove guilt beyond reasonable doubt. If it’s impossible to determine which of the two people committed the murder because both have reasonable explanations for their fingerprints being on the murder weapon, and there is no other conclusive evidence pointing to one over the other, it would be very difficult to secure a conviction against either of you.’

‘They must believe her. They arrested me.’

‘You had no reason to go there in their eyes. It doesn’t matter what they believe, it’s what they can prove.’

Annie blinked. ‘But…but,’ she faltered, her head still spinning.

‘Stick to your story.’

‘It’s the truth.’

‘Of course it is. And you’re a much more credible witness than Jeannie. Her only defence is that she was unable to get out of bed; she claims to be unfit to walk more than a few feet and then very slowly. Doctor Anderson could find no medical reason to support this, so no one is guaranteeing that either. The court cannot convict someone unless there’s clear evidence that points to them.’

‘Are you saying neither of us will be convicted?’

‘The police have their hands full right now between looters and deserters. I think they’d be happy if this would just go away. To charge either of you or both would result in a not-proven verdict. I know it, they know it, and the Procurator Fiscal knows it. The investigation will no doubt continue as it’s a serious crime. This could go on for many months. Whether or not you’ll be charged is up to the Procurator.’

‘So, the accusation will still hang over me. Even if I’m never charged, Dee will grow up thinking his mam could be a murderer.'

'Unless Jeannie changes her story or they find more evidence against her, it's the best we can hope for.'

'It's not enough. I need to be cleared,' said Annie.

The café began to fill up. Henry got to his feet. Let's find a phone box. I'll let Vera know you're on your way home and she'll send Hughie for you. I've parked my car by the harbour.'

'Who knows,' he said, as they walked along the street, 'this might be the push you need to come back to Glasgow. After the war, of course.'

Annie said nothing. The thought had been in her mind.

'You'll be fine in the bus?'

'Aren't you coming with me?' she asked.

'I have to make sure all the loose ends are tied up,' he replied. 'I'll see you, probably tomorrow.'

Next day Henry came back from Wick in good spirits. 'It's almost over,' he said.

'What, why?' Annie could hardly believe what he was saying.

'Even if Jeannie confessed, if she were to be diagnosed with postpartum psychosis as a mitigating factor, it has been recognised in Scottish law since 1922 in the context of infanticide cases. However, it has since been extended in various ways to other areas of law, especially when considering the impact of mental health in criminal defence.'

Relief flowed through Annie and almost lifted. 'But the doubt will still linger in many minds,' she said.

'It's a positive result. Given the apathy of the Procurator Fiscal and the worries about the war, I think they're happy for it to go away. I mean another bomb just dropped on Wick. That's all people are talking about right now.'

'But that won't stop the whispers or the assumptions.' She sank into the chair.

'I could ask you to come back with me. With injured men

coming home from the war and nurses volunteering to work in France, your skills are needed more than ever. You could stay with my parents, they missed you after you left.' Henry took a seat beside her.

'It's tempting, it is, but don't forget I've got a child,' she replied. 'And I wouldn't want to put your parents to any bother. Furthermore, what will the accusation do to my nursing career? I might not be allowed to continue.'

'Even if your nursing career is over, there are many other areas where you can help. I always liked you, Annie, you know that.' His voice was low and full of meaning.

'I like you too, like a brother.'

He took a moment. 'Is it still Garcia?'

'I don't know how I'd feel if I ever saw him again, but anyway, he's married, so no, it's not Garcia.' She wouldn't admit that the memory of him still stirred her blood. She wondered if it always would.

'I suppose this is goodbye, then.' Henry held out his hand.

'For now.' She reached up to kiss his cheek. 'I can never thank you enough for what you've done for me. And who knows, I might take you up on the offer to come to Glasgow, once the war is over.'

He picked up his case. 'I'll just give your parents a call, then maybe you'll all walk me to the haven.'

They linked arms and walked down the road.

Henry jumped aboard the mail boat and found a place beside a couple of new conscripts. The lads looked white-faced and scared, not eager for adventure as the first recruits had been. Too many devastating telegrams had already arrived on the island.

Annie stood on the shore among the other women who waved them goodbye, wondering how many would ever see Raumsey again. As she watched the boat sail away, she thought once more about Alexander. What was he doing now?

Margaret slipped her arm through Annie's, her other hand

on the pram handle. Her new baby girl, Betty, was a thriving, happy bairn who made a swift and easy appearance into the world over a month ago. Along with her mother, Margaret watched her younger brother go to war, his initial training over.

'Come back with me for a cup of tea. I don't want to return to a house with just my granny.' Margaret leaned on Annie's shoulder. 'Mam has to get home for the other bairns.'

'Would ye go with her, Annie? I feel like I'm being pulled in all directions right now,' said Ada.

'Mam,' Annie shouted over to Isa. 'Would you watch Dee? Margaret needs me.'

'Of course I will. You just spend as long as you like. We love to have the wee man, you know that. And Margaret looks as if she could do with the support.'

Margaret wiped the tears from her eyes. 'I'm missing Freddy so much,' she said. 'What if he doesn't come back?'

'Now, now,' said Isa, 'We can't think like that, love. You come round to our house whenever you want. And you've got your mam and dad. There's plenty of shoulders to cry on, and broad ones at that. Annie will go with you now for a wee while.'

'I can't thank you enough for all the help with the wedding and with my mam. At least I'll always have that couple of weeks with Freddy…' She covered her face, her shoulders shaking.

Eliza was delighted to see them. Her legs had let her down and her mind wandered, but her memories of long ago were sharp and she loved to tell stories. 'Have ye come to fix my ulcers?' she said from the bed in the corner when the two women entered.

'No, Nurse Pennington will do that,' said Annie. 'I've come for a cup of tea.'

'Then get the kettle on, Margaret. Where's Freddy?'

'I told you, Granny, Freddy's off to the army.'

'The army, is it? I remember fine when my Albert joined

up. Left me with three bairns to bring up by myself. But then all the women on the island were the same. Your granddad went with him, Annie. A fine figure of a man he was, too.' Her eyes became dreamy and she had slipped down the tunnel of the past.

'Come on,' said Margaret, 'she'll probably sleep now. We can sit by the window. 'I'm so glad for ye that that business with Jeannie has been sorted out. No one believed that ye were guilty, although I wouldn't have blamed ye. Nick Sinclair always gave me the creeps. Will ye get Scartongarth back now?'

The question took Annie by surprise. 'I haven't thought about it,' she said, 'But you're right, Jeannie will have no claim to it. But I wouldn't go into that right now.' No, she could hardly throw the woman out no matter what she'd done. But she would make sure that Jeannie knew whose house it was. Then, once again, her thoughts flew to Alexander and she wondered what he was doing. Probably living in neutral Spain with his wife, safe from the conflict. He might even have a few children playing in a sun-filled garden.

'I've had a letter telling me that if I want my job back, I have to be cleared of suspicion,' she said to her mother later that day.

'That's as expected,' said Isa. 'But I'm sure it'll all work out in the end.'

'I also had a letter from Tess. Nurses are needed more than ever now, what with so many leaving to go overseas, and so many wounded soldiers returning from the war and filling the hospital beds. Even if I can't work as a nurse, I feel I should be doing something more. Rose loves it here and the residents like her.' She shrugged. 'I don't feel I fit in anymore.'

'You can't leave. What about Dee?'

'That's the only drawback. I know he'd be fine with you and Donald, but it would be unfair of me to expect it of you.'

She would have loved to have gone abroad with the forces,

but becoming a mother had changed her outlook. The risk of leaving her son both motherless and fatherless was something she could never contemplate.

She glanced again through the window. 'Henry said I should get the legalities of Scartongarth sorted.'

'Do you intend to?'

A minute stretched before Annie answered. Jeannie would have happily seen her hang. Any sympathy she had had for that woman should be no longer there, yet, increasingly convinced that Jeannie was ill in the head, she couldn't see her homeless.

Annie gazed at Scartongarth and the expanse of land that should have been hers. It had been her dad's home, her grandparents' home and her great-grandparents' home. Yet now, it belonged to a stranger. Unsettling thoughts gnawed at her. Although she would never put Jeannie out, she had to make sure the farm reverted to the Reids one day.

'Don't worry,' she said to her son, stroking his hair, 'Scartongarth will be yours when the time comes.' She turned to her mother. 'I intend to get the legalities sorted and I've got a meeting with the lawyer soon, but Jeannie can live out her life there. I'll need to speak to her to explain that. I feel sorry for her. She's got no one now, not even one friend. Anyway, I couldn't run a farm and I don't want to.'

Chapter 51

Alexander: Changi 1942

Across the world, in Changi, the prisoners, riddled with dysentery, malaria, beriberi, tropical ulcers and disease, returned from the fields exhausted. The doctors and nurses did their utmost to help them but, without medical supplies, their efforts were often useless. The best they could do was claim a man was unfit to work and needed to rest up and hope the guards accepted that. Mostly they did, as a sick man was little good to them.

In the darkness of the tropical night when the rhythmic chirping of crickets and the high-pitched trill of tree frogs were outdone by moans, coughs and cries from the others in his hut, and when the air was too thick to breathe, Alexander found escape by allowing his mind to take him to the green dampness of Scotland, of the camaraderie of his parents' kitchen and the aroma of good Scotch broth. But more often his memories transported him to Raumsey and the young girl with fire in her eyes who had stolen his heart. Inside his head, he smelled the salt on the wind, heard the rattle of pebbles as the sea rushed over them, heard the yelps of the sea birds and the barks of the seals, and gazed at the endless expanse of sky. He saw again the row of cottages along the high rise, the road that led to the lighthouse, lit up windows giving the appearance of land-locked stars. Beyond that, he saw the hills of Hoy and the green undulating fields of mainland Orkney. He walked down the cart track to the horse-shoe shape of Laries Geo, and there she was, sitting on a rock, her feet half-buried in the sand. She threw her head back so that her black hair tumbled across her shoulders and down her back and red highlights caught the sun.

'Annie,' he whispered through dry lips, trying to hold onto the dream. Just as she turned to smile up at him, the rattle of a large spoon on tin jolted him back into hell and the dream disappeared. It was the signal that breakfast was ready. Still heavy with a sensation of having had no sleep at all, Alexander struggled to rise with aching, weakened limbs. He joined the queue for rice full of maggots and a cup of lukewarm water. At first, they had separated the maggots from the rice, but now the squirming creatures were a much-needed source of protein. By 7 a.m., they had to be ready for the work party. This was the daily routine of the camp.

One day, a British officer's runner came to Alexander and said, 'You're to report to Captain MacLeod's office.'

'Why?' he asked.

'Seems like some of your boys are going to a holiday camp.' And those words sent a shiver of unease along Alexander's spine.

In the hut that was the officer's headquarters, Captain MacLeod looked at him with defeat in his eyes. 'Some of the lads have been selected to go on a draft up country. Get them organised for tomorrow morning.' He handed over a sheet of paper.

'What is this for?' Alexander asked, the grim look on the Captain's face sending shafts of worry through his body. He read the list of names. Three of his most promising young students. 'But you can't send them, they're too young.'

MacLeod shrugged and shook his head. 'The Japanese give us orders; we pass them on. The boys are strong enough. I'm sorry, I did try to argue the case of them being so young but it fell on deaf ears.'

Tommy, Alfie and John were called aside along with many more of the fitter prisoners.

'Apparently, you're going to the holiday camp,' Alexander said with a wry grin.

'Are you coming, sir?' asked John, the fear in his eyes was heartbreaking.

'Doesn't seem like it,' said Alexander. He had become a father figure to them and the parting was going to be hard.

They looked at each other with dread.

'What do you think will happen to us?' asked Alfie, and bit on his bottom lip.

'I'm sure there will be an officer to look after you. It's a work detail. Don't worry, it can't be worse than here. But if you can, keep up the learning.' Alexander wished he was going too; he had grown very fond of *his laddies* as he thought of them.

'They are just boys,' Alexander said to Yoshio, knowing it was useless. The young guard had no power and was as afraid of his superiors as the prisoners were.

'I answer orders,' he said, avoiding Alexander's eyes.

'No longer boys,' said another guard, who prodded them into line with his bayonet.

As Alexander said goodbye to his friends, it felt like losing members of his family, especially Tommy. There would have been tears in his eyes had he any left to cry.

'I'll be fine,' said Tommy, as Alexander clutched his hand, but everything about him betrayed his fear. 'See you later, mucker.'

'Stay strong.' Overcome with emotion, Alexander grasped him in a brief hug. His hands closed into tight fists as he watched half the camp being herded away.

Sleep evaded him that night. No matter how he tried to travel outside himself, his mind was too full of apprehension to leave him in peace. He lay with his eyes scrunched shut to block out horrible visions of the boys being taken away to perhaps be executed. His only hope was that, as younger, fitter men, they were of more use to the Japanese alive than dead. Little did he know then that the prisoners selected were to work on the notorious Death Railway, so called because they were literally worked to death. Something he only learned about many years later.

Chapter 52

Annie: Raumsey 1942

Being unable to return to nursing, Annie upped her efforts in organising entertainment and evening classes for the islanders. She often spent time with Magnus, helping with the lambs and the harvesting.

'Ye know, it could always be like this,' said Magnus. 'The two of us together. I was a bit worried ye seemed so close to that lawyer guy.'

'You needn't have been. Henry is a very dear friend, nothing more.' At that moment, she realised that that was all Magnus would ever be as well. It wasn't fair to keep him hoping.

His expression was patient but knowing. He leant slightly forward, his fingers tracing her bare arm.

'I've been thinking a lot lately about us. About everything. If it's a definite no, please tell me now, and I'll try to move on. I want to get married, have bairns while I'm still young — well, youngish. Dolly's interested in me, don't ask me why, but I like her as well.'

'Dolly? I thought as much. What do you feel for her?'

He shrugged. 'I find her attractive and I like her well enough, but I've got to know, Annie, say ye'll marry me now or set me free.'

'I can't marry you. You must know that.' She was quiet for a beat.

He watched her, waiting for her next words.

'You mean so much to me, Magnus. You've always been there — since the beginning. I don't even know where I'd be without you.'

His mouth twitched. 'But…?'

'You've done more for me than anyone else ever has. You've been my rock. And... I love you. I really do. As a friend.'

'We could still make it work,' he insisted.

Annie's gaze dropped to her hands. She drew in a shaky breath. 'I can't feel what you want me to. I wish I could. You deserve that—more than anyone. You deserve everything.'

She looked up at him. 'My heart… it's with someone else and always will be.'

Magnus exhaled slowly, but he didn't flinch. 'I know that fine, but hearing it still hurts.' He took a long pause as if gathering himself. 'It's Garcia, isn't it?'

Annie nodded. 'I could be content with you, but it wouldn't be fair to you or to me if I tried to force my heart somewhere it just isn't.'

A sinking sun bathed the fields in its warm glow, spilling over crops still to be harvested. Soft murmurs of waves kissed the shore and constant cries of seabirds filled the air.

Magnus nodded slowly, his fingers curling into a fist before he relaxed them. His gaze drifted out to sea for a moment, his jaw tense. But when he looked back at her, his eyes were steady — filled with a deep, quiet sadness.

'Maybe I didn't want to accept it, but... I knew it.'

Annie reached across; her hand rested on his. He stared at it for a moment, then turned his palm up to hold hers. His grip was firm as if he was anchoring himself.

'But I'm not going to lie. Hope dies hard, but I'll be okay. Eventually.'

'With Dolly?'

A fond smile flirted with his lips. 'Maybe. But I'll be honest with her. I'm still in pain.'

For a minute, they stood there, the evening light casting soft shadows on their faces. Neither of them needed to speak. They'd said everything that mattered.

'Still friends?' He held out his hand.

'Always,' she replied. Memories of their time together rushed at her and she tried to ignore the doubts they brought with them. Had she done the right thing?

Three months later, Annie watched Hughie the Post cycling over the hill. He usually came here with mail for the minister and occasionally for herself. Her thoughts were still with Magnus and how bad she felt having hurt him.

Hughie turned into the drive and she opened the door to greet him. 'What have you got for me today?' she said.

'Looks official.' He handed her a brown envelope.

Finally, Annie had received the letter that lifted the cloud hanging over her head. However, it did not clear her, but a lesser cloud would remain. She read the letter several times before setting it to one side.

Crown Office and Procurator Fiscal Service

1st November 1942

Anne Reid

The Manse
Raumsey Island

Dear Miss Reid

RE: Investigation into the Death of Nicholas Sinclair

Following the recent investigation into the tragic death of Nicholas Sinclair which occurred on 08/05/1942, I write to inform you of the current standing of the case.

After thorough consideration of the facts presented by the police and a comprehensive review of all available evidence, it is my duty to inform you that at present, there is insufficient evidence to justify proceeding with criminal charges against you or Jean Sinclair.

There are no independent witnesses to the incident, nor is there forensic or other corroborative material which would allow us to establish a sufficient case before the courts. Therefore, it is not possible to proceed to trial at this time.

However, it must be clearly understood that this decision does not constitute a finding of innocence, nor does it imply that the matter is permanently closed. Should new evidence come to light, the case will be revisited and reconsidered in full.

I trust you will comprehend the gravity of this communication and the reasons for our decision. Should you require further clarification on this matter, you may contact my office at your convenience.

Yours faithfully,

John Robson
Procurator Fiscal
Crown Office

Chapter 53

Jeannie: Raumsey 1942

The wind howled outside, rattling the windows of Scartongarth. Inside, Jeannie paced the shining flagstone floor of the kitchen, her steps quick and frantic. The shadows from the flickering oil lamp danced across the faded wallpaper, casting an eerie glow in the corners where the ghosts of the past lingered.

She clutched a letter in her trembling hand, its edges crumpled from the grip of her fingers. The words on the page swam before her eyes, but she didn't need to read them again — every line burned into her memory.

Annie Reid had won again. Not enough evidence, they said. In other words, no one believed it was her.

Now that that fancy lawyer had been, would Annie start looking into the ownership of Scartongarth again? What if she came after it and threw Jeannie out? She couldn't blame Annie for wanting revenge on the woman who would see her hang.

Staring out the window as if she might find the answer to all her problems out there, she considered all the work needed to keep the farm going, too much for a woman alone. If it hadn't been for the war, there would have been more men around to give a hand to a grieving widow. The islanders were like that, always willing to help, but since so many young men had been conscripted, many more women were struggling to keep their land producing, but, she thought, many had young sons to help, or fathers too old to go to war but fit to fish and sow crops.

She had nobody. And the boat, it lay there with not a man to sail it. Her heart filled with self-pity. It wasn't her fault she was born ugly or had a brute of a father and had no child. She deserved better. And she would have better. '*You can shut up*,' she said to the memory of her father and his harsh words. But he didn't.

'*Annie Reid is fine and dandy in the manse with a bairn, the love of two parents, and that Magnus running after her like a dog in heat. She's going to claim Scartongarth, too. Then where will ye be?*'

She clapped her hands over her ears. 'Ye're no real,' she shouted into the air, 'I got rid of ye and I got rid of him and I can get rid of Annie Reid, too.' She gasped when she realised what she had said. Could she get away with it again?

She stared up the hill to where the steeple of the church poked above the greenery and her wrath gathered around her like a black cloud as she settled back to plan her next move. If another move was needed, once Scartongarth was in her name, Annie Reid could do nothing.

Jeannie searched the house but she found no title deeds. What she did find was the title deeds to Stonehill and a sheet of handwritten paper signed by Bel transferring everything she owned to Nick. Then it struck her, the lawyer must have the title deeds. Yes, that's where they would be. Nick might have even left a will. Once she got it sorted, it would all be legal, then she would feel secure.

She finished tidying the house. Knowing she would have to go to town and get the legalities sorted scared her, but now she was a free woman, she would have to do these things.

It was best to get it done now before Annie got any ideas. She put on her best coat and hat and keeping a wary eye out for Rose Pennington, after all, she was still meant to be a sick woman, she walked to the Post Office.

'Jeannie, lass, are ye feeling better? Come in, sit yerself down. I can't believe either ye or Annie are guilty of anything. It must have been a dreadful accident, but at least it's sorted now,' said Vera.

Warmed by the welcome, Jeannie moistened her lips. 'Thank ye, Vera.' She hesitated. 'I have to go to town.' She thought it better not to explain her reasons. 'What time does the post boat go?'

'Ye've an hour to wait. I'll make us tea,' said Vera. 'How are ye doing? Ye know ye only have to come here any time ye need company. Ye don't have to sit up there all on yer own. Doesn't do a buddy any good that, ye ken.'

Jeannie couldn't be bothered with niceties. 'I'm perfectly fine. I need to speak to a lawyer. Nick dealt with Pattersons. Will I need to tell them I'm coming?'

Vera looked taken aback at her sharp tone. 'Ye will need an appointment. Wait a wee while till I get the number. Ye can phone from here,' she said with a sniff.

'I've never had to deal with that stuff,' said Jeannie. 'I don't know what to do.' She was suddenly unsure of herself, and even more nervous than she had been this morning. Vera had always been kind to her. This woman was one of the few islanders she felt she could turn to. 'I'm sorry if I sounded sharp, I'm so nervous.'

Vera's face softened. 'We'll get ye an appointment. When ye get to Huna, wait for the bus into Wick. They'll let ye off in Bridge Street. Ask the driver for directions.'

Jeannie sipped her tea slowly as Vera made the phone call.

Why had she been so stupid that she thought she could just walk into a lawyer's office and be seen right away? She knew all about sheep and cows and when to plant hay, but this was a whole new experience. Her father had known about such things, so had Nick, but it was not a woman's place. *Well, it has to be now*, she told herself firmly. If she wanted to be her own master, she would have to learn.

'You're in luck,' said Vera coming into the room. 'He can see ye this afternoon. Ye'll get on fine with Mr Patterson. He's my lawyer and he's a lovely old man. Ye don't need to be so nervous.' She leaned forward and patted Jeannie's knee. 'It's an awful business all this. I'm no one to judge, but ye haven't been lucky with the men in your life. We all knew yer dad was a hard man, and Nick…' Her hand flew to her mouth. 'Sorry, I shouldn't speak ill of the dead.'

Jeannie sipped her tea. 'Nick wasn't easy to live with,' she said. 'But he was all I had,' she added quickly. 'I can't speak about it.' She tried to force a tear to her eye. Vera was fishing for information no doubt, something to gossip with when her customers came in.

'Ye'll feel better once the lawyer sorts everything out for ye. Is there a problem with Scartongarth?'

'Bel signed it over to Nick, fair and square.' She felt defiant as if she was being accused of something.

'Then ye'll be fine,' Vera said.

'Aye, I'm sure.' Jeannie softened her voice. 'Ye've been very kind, Vera. I'm just on edge. I didn't mean to snap at ye. Could ye no tell anybody that I've been here? I don't want the gossips prying into my business, it's been hard enough.'

'Of course, pet. I'll no tell a soul. But I can't speak for the boatmen.'

Jeannie didn't doubt that it would soon be all around the island, but the gossips would assume that her trip had to do with the death and wouldn't make too much of it. 'Can I wait here for the boat? I don't feel strong enough to go home,' she said. The truth was that, after all the lies about her health, she didn't want to be seen by Rose Pennington.

'Of course ye can, pet. Have another cup o' tea.'

The afternoon sun filtered through the large windows of the law office, casting a warm glow over the polished oak desk where Jeannie Sinclair sat, clutching her handbag tightly. The office, with its shelves lined with law books and certificates, projected an air of authority that made Jeannie feel small and insignificant. Her heart beat like a frightened bird trapped in her chest. Her mouth was dry.

Charles Patterson, a portly man with greying hair and a kind face, offered a reassuring smile. 'Ah, Mrs Sinclair. How can I assist you today?'

She wanted to ask for a drink of water but instead took a deep breath, her eyes briefly darting to the framed photograph of a woman with two young girls on the desk.

'I've come to transfer my late husband's property into my name. I can't find the title deeds. I was hoping ye might have them.'

Mr Patterson's expression softened with sympathy. 'I understand. Losing a loved one is hard enough without the added stress of legal matters. May I offer you my sincere condolences? Now, the name of your late husband is?'

After she explained the situation, he steepled his fingers. 'And you say you can't find the title?'

'No, I can't.'

The lawyer went to the door of his office and called. 'Moira, do we have any files on Nicholas Sinclair?'

'The name is unfamiliar to me,' he said as he returned to his seat. 'But best to be sure. I have so many clients.'

After what seemed like an age, the door opened and Moira popped her head around it. 'We have. But only when Angus MacKay gifted the property of Stonehill to him. Since then, nothing.'

Patterson spread his hands. 'It seems, Mrs Sinclair, that we did not represent your late husband. But he will have used someone else. I'm sure the deeds will be with them. You'll need to give me time to do a search. Can you come back next week? Make an appointment with Moira on the way out.'

Jeannie wasn't too happy with the situation, but what did she know about the wheels of the law? She nodded reluctantly and went to catch the next bus to Huna, trying to ignore the mocking laughter of her father.

A week later, she sat once more in the offices of Charles Patterson and Sons. Although she had been here before, she was still nervous.

'Thank you for seeing me again, Mr Patterson,' she said, her voice tinged with anxiety.

He opened a paper folder on his desk. Jeannie watched him, the silence in the room amplifying the sounds from the street outside. After a few moments, Mr Patterson looked up, his brow furrowed.

'Mrs Sinclair, I did a thorough search and I have to tell you, it appears that your late husband was never the legal owner of Scartongarth.'

Jeannie gasped. 'What? That can't be right. He always said it was his. He lived there for years. He inherited it from his first wife.'

Mr Patterson regarded her sadly and steepled his fingers. 'It doesn't look like your husband made a will with any law firms that I can find. Since you don't have a copy either, it appears no will was ever made.'

'But surely as his wife, I will inherit everything anyway?' she said, a sudden cold dread creeping into her bones.

'All we can find regarding the property known as Scartongarth is that the owner was a Daniel Donald Reid. It seems that nothing legally was done at the death of Mr Reid. Since all three of his sons are also deceased, I'm afraid we would have to search for the legal heir or heirs. Those are most likely his surviving grandchildren, if any.'

'But Nick lived in it all these years and Bel before him. I

can't be turned out. Where would I go?' Her voice rose as panic gripped her.

Mr Patterson took a deep breath. 'I understand how you feel. What are your instructions? I can do the search for the legal heirs but it will cost money, or we can leave things as they are. Since no other claimants have come forward in all these years, it's highly likely that you will be able to live out your life there.'

No, Jeannie silently cried. She needed to own it, know it was hers.

Her breath stuttered. She heard people walking outside, the beat of footsteps on the pavement, the dull rumble of a motor car, a child's laughter, a muted conversation in the room next door. 'What do you mean? Even as the surviving partner, I have no right to it?'

'Patterson shook his head and shuffled some papers on his desk. 'The property belonged to Daniel Reid and he left no will.' He repeated the words slowly as if Jeannie were hard of hearing. 'You do own Stonehill, however. You will not be without means.'

Means, she thought. Over the years Nick had kept her short. She had been forced to use the money she had found behind the picture in Stonehill whenever she wanted something extra. By the time she paid the lawyer for his time, there would be precious little left. If her father had left anything else, Nick had had it long ago.

'But Scartongarth was Bel's. She transferred it to Nick.'

'I'm sorry, It was never hers to transfer.' He stood up, 'If I can help you in any other way…' he began.

'Don't bother.' Jeannie grabbed her bag and stood up. No, this couldn't happen. With her security ripped away, she wouldn't be able to sleep easily in her bed, ever. Even if Annie Reid didn't come after it, there was her son. And her son would never inherit, she would make sure of that. Why should he, when her son was dead? Ignoring Patterson's outstretched hand, she stormed out of the office.

What would she do if she had to leave Scartongarth? Where would she go? Before she left her cottage of Stonefield, the thatch was rotten and the walls were streaked with mould. Furthermore, Nick had removed the door to give the animals a place to shelter. God only knew what state the place was in now.

Her stomach churned as she waited for the boat on Huna shore. Her hatred at that moment was strong enough that she could kill both Annie Reid and her son. All her life she had been put down, made fun of, made to feel useless. All her life she had dreamed of having her own place, being somebody at last. With everything she had gone through, she deserved that. By God, she deserved it! By the time the boat came, Jeannie was so distraught she could hardly breathe..

'Are ye all right?' asked Hughie as he helped her aboard. When she didn't answer, he shrugged his shoulders and rolled his eyes at Magnus who held the helm. She sat on the crossbeam, staring rigidly ahead and clutching her bag as the boat ploughed through the swell. Once on the island, Magnus helped her ashore.

'I'll give you a lift home,' he offered, but instead of answering, she stared at him for a full minute before nodding.

'Bad news then?' asked Magnus, as he helped her into the truck.

'No, no, why would ye think that?' she snapped. What had it to do with him? Without speaking, she stared out of the truck window. Perhaps it would be better if Annie remained free. If she left the island and took her son with her it was unlikely they would ever return, whereas if she was locked up, the boy would grow up here and might well come for his inheritance one day. He wouldn't have it. He wouldn't.

Back home, Jeannie paced the floor.

Very possible, very possible, you could live out your life there, the lawyer had said. the words spun in her head. That wasn't good enough. Scartongarth was hers.

Ye never deserved anything, ye fat pig, came the voice of her father, but now he was joined by another voice, that of Nick Sinclair. *She actually thought she could kill me and have everything,* he said, and they both laughed.

Chapter 54

Jeannie: Raumsey 1942

Jeannie let the letter fall from her hands. It was happening. She had reread the letter twice, but the words screamed at her even louder the second time.

MacDonald and Son, lawyers and Estate Agents. *We have to inform you that the legal owners of Scartongarth are making a claim*... it had said.

Her breath hitched and she stopped in her tracks, staring at the iron range that had been her pride and joy when she first moved here.

The thought twisted in her mind like a cruel joke. This house — *her* house — was the last thing she had left. She had worked so hard to make it hers; now, it would be taken away, reduced to nothing more than a line on a piece of paper.

'No,' she whispered to the empty room, her voice shaking with defiance. 'Annie Reid will not have it.'

She paced the floor, wringing her hands and with every step her anxiety grew. Before her was an all-consuming black hole waiting for her to step too close.

Ye'll be in the poor house where ye belong, she imagined the gruff voice of her father. *And ye're such an ugly slut with yer horse face they'll use ye, and it won't be good.*

Her father would not shut up and now it was Nick's voice joining him. *Annie Reid is yer enemy. She wants Scartongarth. There's only one way to stop her getting it.*

She put her hands over her ears. 'Ye're not real,' she shouted. 'Mam, where are ye? Make them go away.'

But they were laughing at her now. Harsh, cruel laughter. *Get her child,* said Nick. *She killed your bairn because she knew ye were not fit to be a mother.*

Yer mam has gone,' said her father. *Down to hell, with yer bairn. Where Annie Reid means to send ye. She killed yer bairn. Kill hers.*

'No. no, the boy is innocent,' Jeannie covered her ears.

Take the knife ye skin rabbits with, said Nick. *It's the only way to pay her back.*

They were here, in the house, the men who had made her life hell. Somewhere deep inside, she knew she could never harm the boy, and something else clicked too. The knowledge that Annie Reid had not harmed her baby.

But the ghosts of her tormentors would give her no peace until she did as they asked.

She had to destroy them or destroy herself.

Her eyes darted around the room, landing on the wooden box perched on the mantle. It contained matches. She approached it slowly, almost reverently, as though some invisible force was guiding her.

After striking a match, she watched as the spark became a flame sputtering to life, a tiny, flickering light in the darkness.

In that moment, a clarity she hadn't felt in weeks swept over her. If she destroyed the house, she would destroy the men who tormented her. It was that simple. It was the only solution that made sense. The fire would consume everything, erasing the memories, the pain, the loss. And Annie Reid would never have it.

The paraffin was kept in the back porch. She brought the can into the kitchen and poured some over the ends of the curtains, over the fireside rug, then with a mad sense of glee, splashed it over the bed in the wall recess.

She moved with purpose now, striking matches and holding them against the hem of the curtains. The fabric smouldered, curling up in fiery tongues, and soon the flames spread, hungrily licking up the walls. Jeannie didn't flinch, instead, she watched with a detached fascination as the room transformed before her eyes, the fire growing, feeding on the years of history contained within these walls.

She stepped back into the hallway, the heat almost unbearable now, the air thick with smoke. Yet, she felt no fear. Instead, she felt an odd sense of peace, as though she was finally doing what she should have done a long time ago.

Before moving upstairs, she paused long enough to take one last look around. The fire had taken over the entire bottom floor of the house. The home she had coveted her whole life was dissolving into nothingness, and would soon be reduced to ashes.

Chapter 55

Annie: Raumsey 1942

A sudden hammering on the door startled Annie. By the time she came downstairs, her mother was standing in the doorway. Ada's youngest, Billy, stood there gasping and trying to catch his breath. 'Scartongarth is on fire,' he stammered.

'What?' yelled Annie, and dashed outside. From over the hill, in the distance, she could see a flickering glow of flames.

'Stay with Dee,' shouted Donald to his wife, as he came running from the study and followed Annie to the top of the hill. They stopped, frozen in shock. The hungry tongues of flames had burst through the downstairs windows of Scartongarth and were licking upwards. Already crofters were running from their houses collecting pails of water.

'She's probably knocked over a lamp,' said Donald. 'She'll still be in there.' He grabbed Annie's hand and together, they raced down the hill.

Donald released her, surged ahead and reached the cottage door minutes before her. He put his shoulder to the locked door and burst it open. In the sudden rush of oxygen, the flames burst out towards them and he staggered backwards to fall on the damp ground.

Other islanders were already rushing to form a human chain from the well to the house, passing buckets of water along. In spite of their haste, the water that splashed against the flames was barely enough to be effective as they grew in ferocity.

'Jeannie, where is she?' cried Annie, spinning around in panic. 'Has anyone seen her? She must still be inside.'

The remaining windows burst outward with a shattering crump.

Suddenly, a dark outline appeared at an upstairs window. Thankfully the flames seemed to be concentrated downstairs. Jeannie stood still, her arms crossed over her chest, a manic grin on her face. 'Annie Reid, ye'll never have Scartongarth,' she shouted, her voice lost in the roar of flames.

'I wasn't going to put you out,' screamed Annie.

Jeannie threw back her head and laughed, a hysterical laugh.

This was her fault, Annie thought. Having seen mothers who had suffered a deep depression after childbirth, commonly known as baby blues, she should have realised how desperately ill the woman was. Jeannie, as well as losing the child, had the added trauma of Nick's death. And now, the thought of losing her home had tipped her over the edge.

'No,' Donald shouted. 'This can't happen. We have to get her.' Jeannie was a sad creature but he was sure she wasn't entirely lost. Taking her own life like this was condemning her soul to damnation. He had to save her. 'Stay here, Annie,' he ordered. 'The back way might still be clear. I'll get her.'

'Be careful. Don't put yourself in danger. Wait, I'm coming too.'

But Donald hadn't heard her. He took a detour to the back of the cottage, where he knew there was another entrance. Most of the fire seemed concentrated at the front — there was still a chance. Annie followed him, heart pounding, every beat urging her onward.

'Donald,' she called. 'Take care.'

‘Go back,’ he shouted.

‘No, if you go in there, I’m coming with you.’ She was right behind him.

The smoke was everywhere, choking him, blurring his vision but he pushed forward.

‘Donald, no,’ Annie kept shouting, even as she followed him. ‘It’s too late.’

He didn’t stop. He climbed up the back stairs and crept towards the front of the house. Here, the flames had not yet taken hold.

When he got to the main bedroom, he pushed the door open. Acrid smoke that seared his lungs with each breath filled the air. Coughing violently, he dropped to his knees and crawled through the room, his eyes locked on Jeannie’s still figure.

With a surge of adrenaline, he rose, ran and grabbed Jeannie around the middle. He pulled her backwards, just in time as creaking beams beneath them gave way, crashing into the interior. The heat was unbearable. Driven by the blast, the door slammed shut, trapping both Donald and Jeannie inside.

‘Help me,’ Annie screamed and tried to force the door open with her shoulder. The burning wood scorched her skin. The flames were gaining purchase, but she didn’t care. It was her fault, her obsession with Scartongarth, her disregard for Jeannie’s mental state. Now Donald was in danger.

Suddenly, Magnus was beside her, joining her in the desperate attempt to open the door. At last, it gave way to reveal a scene from hell. Flames licked along the ceiling and down the walls.

Donald was lying flat, edging backwards, dragging Jeannie with him, but it was obvious his strength was failing. Magnus bent low. crawled in and grabbed Donald’s leg.

‘Keep going,’ shouted Annie. ‘Over here.’

Together they managed to get to the back stairs and slid down on their bellies.

With a final, desperate lunge, they burst through the back door, tumbling into the cool night air, the flames roaring angrily behind them. Annie's body ached, her lungs burned, and both Donald's and Jeannie's clothes were already smouldering.

They lay there, coughing and spluttering and then there were people around them, throwing water on them, covering them with coats and blankets and dragging them out of the range of the ever-encroaching flames.

'Thank God. I heard you shout for help and I thought…' Magnus's voice gave way to emotion. 'What in the name of the Almighty were you thinking, Annie?' Magnus shouted.

Then he was gathering her in his arms. 'I thought ye were gone,' he said. 'When you disappeared after Donald, I came after ye.'

For what seemed an age, Annie lay, coughing, gasping for breath, her vision swimming. Then, slowly, she became aware of the other people around them. She sat up, pushing aside the coat that covered her shoulders. 'Donald,' she cried when she could get a breath. Her throat was hoarse and burning, her eyes streaming, her voice raspy but she was alive.

'I think he'll be all right,' someone said.

'Jeannie?' she asked.

Magnus, despite coughing and spluttering himself, bent over the other woman. 'She's badly burned, but she's breathing.'

Jeannie's eyes fluttered open, her gaze unfocused and dazed. 'Why did… ye save me?' she whispered weakly, her voice barely more than a breath. Her body went limp and her eyes closed.

'Is she alive?' Annie asked.

'She's alive.' Magnus said.

The fire crackled behind them, but it was distant now, no longer a threat.

'It was my fault,' said Annie. 'She must have got the letter.

I meant to see her first…' She took another fit of coughing. 'She must've been so unhappy. And we could have lost Donald. All because of me.'

'Hughie's gone over for the doctor,' said Magnus as he helped her to stand.

Her head spinning, she leaned against him. 'You…saved us.'

'Take them to the manse,' Magnus said.

'Jeannie too?' asked another voice.

Annie nodded. 'Jeannie too. She's got nowhere else to go.' She looked at Donald, who had struggled to his knees, for confirmation. He nodded, although he still could not speak.

Later, when Annie sat up in bed drinking milk laced with honey, enjoying the administration of her mother, she asked again about Donald and Jeannie.

'Donald has a few burns, but Jeannie is much worse. Rose is with her but she needs something stronger than a nurse can give her. The doctor should soon be here.'

'Has she spoken?'

'Only to ask, "why, why, why."'

Chapter 56

Jeannie: Raumsey 1942

Jeannie's eyelids fluttered, heavy and disoriented, as she slowly drifted out of the fog of unconsciousness. The world around her was a blur of muted light and soft colours, the sterile scent of antiseptic mingling with something faintly floral. Her limbs felt like lead, her mind sluggish as she tried to piece together where she was and how she got here.

As she struggled to focus, the fog began to lift, revealing the outline of a small, cosy room. She wasn't in a hospital; that much was clear. The bed she lay in was soft, the sheets smooth against her skin. A single window let in a sliver of sunlight, warming the pale walls decorated with delicate, hand-painted pictures of flowers.

Where am I?

Her throat was dry and raspy, and when she tried to swallow, it felt like sandpaper scraping against her insides. And then the pain hit. Her face, her arm, her back, searing burning pain. She attempted to sit up, but a wave of dizziness washed over her, forcing her back down. Panic bubbled up within her, memories of the fire flashing in her mind like jagged shards of glass. The smoke, the flames, the suffocating heat — she remembered the terror, the feeling of her body giving out, and then… nothing.

The door creaked open, and Jeannie turned her head weakly. A figure entered the room, moving with careful, deliberate steps. As the person came into view, Jeannie's heart skipped a beat, and her stomach twisted with a mix of shock and confusion.

Annie.

The woman Jeannie had despised for so long, the woman she had sworn to never forgive, stood before her, holding a tray with a steaming bowl of something that smelt of chicken soup. Annie's face was etched with weariness, her eyes shadowed with exhaustion, but there was a softness there that Jeannie knew she did not deserve.

'You're awake,' Annie said, as she set the tray down on the bedside table. There was a tremor in her hands. She brushed a stray lock of hair behind her ear. 'How are you feeling?'

Jeannie opened her mouth to speak, but no words came out. Her throat tightened, her mind reeling. Why was Annie here? Why wasn't she in a hospital? Why… why did Annie care?

'I know you must be confused,' Annie continued, her gaze avoiding Jeannie's, as if afraid of what she might see there. 'But Doctor Anderson kept you sedated. The pain of the burns is severe.' She crossed to the nightstand, lifted a bottle of something and poured a small amount into a glass. 'I'm going to give you some medicine now. Eat the soup and then you'll sleep for a wee while.'

Jeannie gratefully swallowed the liquid. Her burns were beginning to be unbearable.

Annie continued to talk. 'After the fire, you were too ill to transfer to the mainland. You would not have survived the journey. The doctor said you needed time to heal and, well, there was nowhere else for you to go. You're safe here.'

Safe. The word echoed in Jeannie's mind, stark and foreign. Safe wasn't a word she associated with Annie. Yet here she was, in what was clearly the manse, being cared for by the very person she had wished to never see again. 'Why?' Jeannie finally croaked, her voice rough and barely audible.

'Ye could have hanged because of me.'

'You must be a very unhappy person. I didn't realise how unhappy till now.' Annie's voice wavered just a little. 'I couldn't leave you to fend for yourself after everything that happened. I know I have every reason to hate you, Jeannie, but I couldn't let you suffer. Not when I could help.'

'I did it, didn't I? I killed Nick.'

'You didn't mean to. You did it to save me. He was attacking me, remember?'

'I think so. But it's hazy. It's so hazy. I was taking Phenobarbital, you remember, Rose gave it to me after I lost the bairn.'

'It can cause confusion, right enough.'

'And the minister? He saved me.'

'Donald has some burns as well, mostly on his hands, and his lungs are still recovering from smoke inhalation. He'll be in to see you in a wee while. I'll look after you in the meantime. I'm still a nurse.'

This was the last thing Jeannie expected. Annie had every reason to leave her to her fate, to wash her hands of the past and be done with the animosity between them, instead, she was willing to help her and care for her as if she were someone who mattered. The minister probably saw it as his Christian duty, but Annie had no reason to be kind.

Her thoughts were spinning, a whirlwind of conflicting emotions. 'It wasn't ye. They were there in the house, Nick and my paw. I had to get rid of them.' Then her voice faltered. She felt so weak, so drained by the weight of what she had done.

'What do you mean?' said Annie.

'They were saying horrible things. They wanted me to hurt Dee, but I wouldn't. I'd never hurt a bairn. I had to get rid of them, ye see.'

'Who? Who did you have to get rid of?'

'My paw and Nick. But they'll be gone now. I burned them. I deserve the agony. It's my punishment.' She screwed up her face in pain.

As Annie went downstairs, her belief that her diagnosis was correct had grown stronger. Jeannie was suffering from a lot more than baby blues. Although she had never witnessed it before, she had attended lectures on the new concept of postpartum psychosis as part of her training and found it extremely interesting.

'Many medical professionals do not agree that it can be caused by childbirth and is temporary,' the lecturer had said. 'They do not see it as a separate issue to other mental illnesses and many women have been unjustly imprisoned in mental institutions.'

'Do they recover?' Annie had asked.

'With family support, therapy, and the use of barbiturates, I'm confident many patients can make a partial if not a full recovery.'

She suspected this was what happened to Jeannie. Why hadn't she realised sooner?

A few days later, Annie sat across the table from Doctor Anderson. 'I've discussed Jeannie's problems with my colleagues,' he said. 'We all agree that a period in an asylum in order to assess her is the best way to go. It seems she could be a danger to herself as well as others.'

Annie had heard stories about the inhumane conditions in these places. 'What treatment will she receive?' she asked.

Doctor Anderson shrugged. 'Lobotomies are popular, or psychiatric drugs like Thorazine. Moral Therapy is the preferred way to go nowadays. I have to be honest, these places are overcrowded and conditions are not ideal. But I can see no other option. She set fire to Scartongarth.'

'She's desperately unhappy,' said Annie. 'I think she has been for a while.'

'She's definitely mentally ill,' said Doctor Anderson. 'But

that's not my area of expertise.'

'It's my guess that she's suffering from postpartum psychosis. But it's best she is assessed by the experts. My stepfather is investigating Church of Scotland-run institutions.'

'You've done all you can, Annie.' Doctor Anderson nodded at her. 'Do not feel any guilt about how things turned out.'

'I think the letter from the lawyer telling her that I was looking into the ownership of Scartongarth finally tipped her over the edge. I should have made sure she knew I would never put her out before I pursued it.'

'Then we'll make sure she gets the help she needs.' Doctor Anderson patted her hand.

Chapter 57

Jeannie: Raumsey 1942

The next time she woke, Reverend Donald Charleston was sitting on the end of her bed. His hands were bandaged and his cheeks and nose were an unhealthy shade of red, but thankfully not blistered. The front of his hair was frizzled and singed. She blinked and blinked again. 'I believe ye saved my life,' she croaked.

'I didn't think of it in the moment,' he replied. 'I should have helped you more. I should have come to visit, despite Nick's objections. I should have tried harder.'

'Ye should have left me to die. I'm a bad person. I don't deserve to live.'

'You deserve a second chance.'

'Tell me, Minister, am I damned to hell?'

'Not if you are truly repentant for your sins.'

'Even for murder?'

'You didn't mean to kill him.'

Jeannie shook her head. No, she hadn't meant to kill Nick, but instead of striking him, if she had screamed, would he have stopped? Possibly.

'I do repent,' she said, knowing that would never be enough, because she *had* meant to kill her father.

'What more can I do to be saved?' she asked, longing for that peace.

‘Confess to your sins and repent with all your heart. Ask our Saviour to forgive you.’

‘I’ll tell the constable it was me. That I tried to blame Annie. But…’ By now she was sobbing.

‘But?’ He raised his eyebrows.

She wanted to say, *I killed my father*. But those words wouldn’t come. Instead, she said; ‘If I hang, I don’t care. I can’t cope any more. I can’t cope now.’ *I’m going to hell,* she thought. *I’ll be damned to spend eternity with my father and Nick.* She began to shake.

‘Calm yourself, Jeannie. I’ll get Annie to give you something to help you.’

‘Get the constable. I’ll tell them everything. What does my life matter? When did it ever matter? I’ve nothing left, not even a roof to put over my head.’

‘I’ll do that, but every soul matters. Let us pray together,’ said Donald.

She closed her eyes as his words simultaneously soothed her and distressed her. Because she had so much more to repent for, but she didn’t know if she ever could.

‘Just rest now.’ He patted her hand, rose and, opening the door, he called for Annie.

Over a week had passed and Jeannie’s scars were healing well. She no longer heard her father or Nick, but her melancholy persisted. The medicine Annie made sure she took seemed to keep her permanently drugged.

‘Have you heard your father or Nick speaking to you lately?’ asked Doctor Anderson.

‘No. I burned them in Scartongarth,’ Jeannie replied.

Doctor Anderson indicated that Annie follow him downstairs.

‘I’m satisfied that she’s not hearing voices any more,’ he said. ‘But I can’t convince her that she never heard them in the first place. I’d be happier if she wasn’t under your roof. I’ve arranged a hospital bed for her now that she’s strong enough to be moved.'

'Thank you, Doctor,' said Annie, feeling relieved that the responsibility would soon be lifted from her shoulders.

'You're a good woman, Annie.' Doctor Anderson set a hand on her shoulder. 'I've been reading up on postpartum psychosis and I agree with you. It's possible that with support she may recover, but it's not a given.' He took a deep sigh and carried on. 'As soon as she's medically and mentally fit, she will face charges. She will likely be sent to an asylum rather than prison.'

When Annie told her she was going to be transported to the hospital, Jeannie nodded. 'I expected it,' she said.

The bitterness that had fuelled her for so long now felt hollow and she couldn't reconcile the image of the woman she hated with the one standing before her now. 'Why would you do so much for me?' she whispered.

Annie's expression softened. 'Because I know only too well what Nick Sinclair was like.'

Jeannie didn't know what to say, what to feel. All she knew was that everything had changed and maybe, just maybe, the minister was right. Her soul could be saved even if her life wasn't.'

'Say ye forgive me? I may hang, but I need ye to forgive me.'

Annie reached out, hesitated, then gently took Jeannie's hand in hers. The touch was warm, comforting in a way Jeannie hadn't expected. For the first time in what felt like forever, she felt something other than hurt. It was small and fragile, but it was there.

Hope.

Chapter 58

Annie: Raumsey 1942

The hall filled up. It looked as if every islander fit to walk the distance had come to hear what Annie had to say. Since the fire, speculation had been rife, accusations thrown, and gossip spread as fast as the fire itself.

'I've brought you here today to explain the situation,' said Annie standing up from where she sat on the platform. 'If you haven't already heard, Jeannie has admitted to killing Nick. I have been cleared, although I blame myself for not realising sooner how ill she was.'

There was a muttering spreading around the audience.

'I kent fine she wasn't right in the head,' said Nelly More, looking left to right and nodding at her friends, who nodded back knowingly.

'Aye,' agreed Helen, 'And losing that bairn would put her right off. We never blamed ye, Annie.'

Aye, right, thought Annie.

'But ye must admit it was affy risky, taking her into yer house after she's tried to burn down Scartongarth. We thought that was a wee bit of madness on yer part,' said Hughie. There were more murmurs of ascension, and nodding of heads.

Donald, who sat beside Annie cleared his throat. 'Where else could we take her? And she was so badly burned she would be hard pushed to rise from her bed. She was no risk at all.'

'Is she badly scarred?' asked Dolly who was always interested in looks.

'I'm afraid she will have scars that will be with her for life,' replied Annie.

'She was never a picture anyway,' said a voice from the back of the hall and somebody laughed.

'Don't be unkind,' said Annie. 'I don't know what will happen to her, but if she comes back to the island, we will all need to be understanding.'

'She'll surely no come back,' said a horrified Harriet, as she hefted her massive breasts from her stomach. 'I'll no sleep soundly in my bed if she does.'

'She is most probably suffering from something called postpartum psychosis and cannot be held accountable for her actions after having and losing the baby,' explained Annie. 'Whatever she has, she's not in her right mind.

'And will ye take her in if she does come back?' asked someone else.

'I don't think we'll need to do that,' said Donald. 'Remember, she still owns Stonehill.'

The murmuring had grown and filled the hall. 'She killed my brother,' shouted Dougal Sinclair. 'Surely, she'll hang for that. We don't believe yer new-fangled ideas about post whatever ye said.' He looked around and there were a few nodding heads.

Annie longed to say, *what interest did you ever take in your brother?'* Even after Bel died, he never went near him. She wondered briefly whether Nick would have been different if he had family around him.

'We all knew what Nick Sinclair was like. But did anyone do anything to help Jeannie?'

'We can't interfere with another man's life,' said Hughie.

'And what could we do?' said Connie. 'We made her welcome that time she came to the sewing circle, but she never came back.' There were more mutterings and agreements.

'We always spoke to her when she came to the shop. Even as a wee lassie. She always said she was fine.'

'You're right.' said Annie. 'There wasn't anything you could do. As for me, I wouldn't have got over the door. The main thing is, she has confessed. I hope her sentence isn't too severe.'

'Murder was a bitter thing to be accused of. We're all happy for ye, Annie.' Magnus stood up and looked around the hall. 'Aren't we?'

'Aye.'

'Yes.'

'Welcome back,' came the calls from across the audience. Magnus started to clap and the applause spread.

'I just wanted to clear the air.' Annie stood up once the noise had abated. 'And to let you know, I've been offered my old job back.' She turned to look at Nurse Pennington who also rose to her feet.

‘I’ve loved it here, darlings. But I’m ready to retire. If I can find a wee house, who knows, I’ll maybe stay.’

There was more applause, she had become popular.

‘You’re welcome to stay on at the nurse’s cottage,’ said Annie. ‘If the state allows it. Otherwise, it’ll just lie empty.’

‘What about Scartongarth?’ asked an old worthy, rubbing his whiskered chin. ‘I helped Owld Man Reid build it. It’s a sad day to see it now.’

‘I mean to rebuild it so that Dee can use it when he’s older, or any of the cousins if they want to come for a visit. But there’s not the money right now with the war and all.’

‘We’d all like to see it rebuilt. They’ll aye be willing hands,’ the old worthy spoke again, and there were more whispers and nods.

‘Thank you, everybody,’ said Annie. ‘Now some ladies have made sandwiches and baked cakes. If ye make your way to the kitchen area, there’ll be tea and all.’

Three years later

Chapter 59

Alexander: River Valley Road Camp 1945

Alexander once more walked through the streets of Singapore, or rather limped and stumbled, a very different spectacle from the handsome, healthy young reporter who had arrived with hope in his heart. Now he was one of an army of living skeletons, lice-ridden and clad only in loincloths. The destination was River Valley Road Camp.

The new camp was worse than the one he had left. The detritus of the previous tenants were scattered all around. Instead of latrines, there were shallow trenches, writhing with maggots. To one side of the camp, flowed a stinking, yellow river.

Overcrowding was at a peak. Plagued by bed bugs, mosquitoes and rats and suffering leg pain caused by beriberi, Alexander's nights were never peaceful. His old trick of going back in his mind to happier times didn't work anymore. Sometimes, unable to find comfort on the hard floor, he got up and walked around the camp. The guards mostly ignored him, at worst they would stare at him and mutter among themselves.

Sometimes he slept outside, finding the constant, rhythmic chirping of crickets and the high-pitched trill of tree frogs almost comforting after the moans of discomfort and despair within the overcrowded walls.

During the hours of darkness when it was freezing cold but free of bugs, he psyched himself up for another day of torture.

After Tenko, they had to walk three miles to the docks. Many of the guards were Korean and they were even more cruel than the Japanese. At the docks the prisoners were immediately set to work, unloading bags of rice and sugar. For any poor soul who dropped his load recrimination was fast and brutal. No one ever gave in and begged. To do so would bring an even harder beating on their heads. If the prisoners stood strong and tried to ignore the pain, the guards gave up.

Although they carried sacks of food all day long, stealing even the smallest amount was punishable by a fate worse than death.

Then one day, as the unforgiving sun beat on his head and as he hoisted the bag of rice onto his shoulders, the world went black and Alexander knew no more.

In the blackness, there was peace. He was walking barefooted through wet grass, laughing and a young black-haired girl was by his side. He looked, then looked again. Annie. The wind lifted her hair and she tossed her head back.

'You left me,' she accused.

'I didn't mean to,' he said. And then he disappeared into blackness again.

'I told you not to go.' It was his mother's voice.

'Mama,' he cried, fighting to see her through the thick grey web that was suffocating him.

The next time he opened his eyes, he was back in a pain-filled body and struggled to sink back into the dream world that was so much better than the hell he was waking up to.

'I'm Doctor Buchanan,' said a soft Scottish voice. 'You're in hospital.'

'Am I home?' he croaked as the face swam before him,

but as he breathed in the stale, hot air smelling of disease and human waste, he knew.

'Sorry. We're still in a prison camp. You're suffering from heatstroke accentuated by malnutrition among other things. Come on, I'll help you sit up. You have to eat something.'

'Let me die.' He no longer had the will to live.

'Not today.' Doctor Buchanan slipped an arm around his shoulders and levered him upwards.

'You can get through this,' said the doctor. 'We've seen American planes fly over. We can't give up now.'

Alexander tried to nod but his head felt too heavy for his neck to support. The doctor spoon-fed him on some rice. Alexander looked around. It was a long room with half a dozen beds. Most of the men were in a similar condition to himself. Some moaned softly and some looked already dead.

'You will have to go back to work as soon as I sign you as fit,' the doctor said. 'The guards aren't too bad here, but I can only get off with so much.'

Alexander gradually grew stronger, eating a little more rice every day and drinking as much water as he needed. Finally, although he could only stand on shaking legs, Doctor Buchanan came and sat on his bed. 'I've tried, but if you can walk, the Japs say you're fit to work. And with so many others coming in each day, we need the bed. I've declared you fit to leave the hospital but only to camp duties. I'll suggest you help out at the hospital. God knows we need it.'

Alexander felt like crying. He was still so tired and weak. 'Will they listen?'

'These jobs need to be filled, too,' he said. 'And living men work better than the dead.'

He returned later that day. 'What I said worked. They've agreed to let you do the job of an orderly.'

As the months passed, the prisoners began to sense something different in the camp. The demeanour of the guards, their constant jabbering together and worried glances at the sky made the prisoners believe that the war was not going well for them. Increasingly, they left the prisoners alone seeming to be glad to get out of the camp come evening.

Then, one day, the remnants of Red Cross parcels which had been looted by their captors, were finally made available.

'Something's going on,' said Doctor Buchanan. 'And it can only be good for us. We have to keep as many men alive as we can.'

Alexander had lost count of the days, the weeks, even the months. Time had blurred into one endless, torturous stretch of survival. His thoughts once more drifted to home, to the green fields of Scotland, the laughter of his family, and the life he had once known, to that cavernous place that knew no boundaries. But hope was a fragile thing in a place like this. It seemed clear that the war was going badly for the Japanese. American planes often flew over their heads, but help was taking forever to come. He wondered how much longer the seriously ill could hold on — how much longer *he* could hold on.

He was helping with a new batch of emaciated patients, carried more dead than alive into the hospital when he heard a weak voice call his name.

'Alex…?'

He bent down and looked at the face of the young man who had spoken, desperately searching his brain for recognition. The lad was hairless with few teeth, his eyes sunken, skin stretched over a skull.

'It's… Tommy,' the patient whispered. 'Hi… mucker.'

'Tommy? Is it really you?' Alexander clasped his hand feeling his eyes sting. This once plucky, healthy youth was reduced to this. 'How was the holiday camp?'

'It was… a blast.' The words sat on his breath as his eyes closed.

Day after day, Alexander sat by Tommy's side as he slowly regained strength until he was able to sit up and eat by himself. His eyebrows began to sprout a few hairs.

'You're coming back, lad,' Alexander said.

'Told you we'd meet again, didn't I?' At Tommy's first attempt at a smile, Alexander's heart filled with hope.

'I wouldn't have if it weren't for you,' Tommy said.

'What about the others? Have you any news of them?'

'We worked together for a while, but I don't know.'

A sudden explosion rent the air and Alexander rushed outside just as a large aircraft flew overhead.

Doctor Buchanan had joined him at the door. 'One of ours. They must be bombing nearby. We won't be here much longer.' He set his hand on Alexander's shoulder. 'I told you, didn't I?'

From then on, the bombing raids increased and with every explosion, the prisoners used what little energy they had to cheer and clap.

Early one morning they stopped work when they heard the drone of an aeroplane flying exceptionally low, so low that the American military markings could be clearly seen.

'The Japanese aren't shooting at it, why?' asked Tommy who by now was strong enough to spend some time outside.

'Can only be a good sign,' said Alexander.

As the plane disappeared in the distance, there were more explosions, each one adding hope to the half-dead men of the camp.

Later that night, when the men came back from the docks, they were in a high state of excitement.

'The Japanese are jumpy to say the least. We caught most of what they said and it seems there's been a massive raid on Nagasaki. They're bombing the shit out of the place,' said one. None of them dreamed at that time what had really happened at Nagasaki.

Alexander could not allow himself to be optimistic. 'If this is the end,' he said, 'What will the Japs do with us?' He had visions of them all being shot rather than allowing them to be rescued.

'I was wondering that, too,' said Doctor Buchanan grimly.

'Well, if they try to kill us, I'm going to fight till the death,' said a voice behind them. Tommy was standing there, small amounts of hair beginning to sprout, the skeletal face looking more recognisable. 'If I'm going to die after all that I've been through, I sure as hell am going to take a few of the buggers with me.'

Alexander squeezed his arm. 'Me too,' he said. 'Me too.'

'It's almost over,' Alexander told the patients as he cleaned their wounds and changed dressings with whatever he could find. There was barely enough water to drink and none to bathe fevered brows. Doctor Buchanan was constantly trying to find more ways to make the patients comfortable. The best Alexander could do was try to bolster their spirits. 'Hold on. Not long now,' became his mantra.

On the 21st of August, the prisoners were assembled before the Japanese commander who read out that a Declaration of Ending Hostilities had been called six days earlier. He then shouted orders to his men and they marched out of the gates, leaving them open.

The prisoners in the compound looked at each other not daring to speak for a few minutes. Was it really over? Had the Japs really left just like that or would they return at any minute and mow them all down?

Then Tommy spoke, much of his old character returning. 'Let's raid their kitchen.' There was some of the old measure of mischief in his words.

But to their disappointment, the kitchen shelves were bare. If there was little food before, there was none at all now and no indication when help would come.

'Can't we just go?' asked Tommy.

Alexander shook his head. 'We're too weak to go far and which direction would we go?' Outside the gates was the jungle and unknown dangers.

'There might be eggs or berries,' said Tommy.

'Maybe poisonous berries, and snakes and God knows what else. Help will come soon.' He put a hand on Tommy's shoulder, not knowing what was best to do.

Alexander went back to his duties in the hospital. 'The war is over,' he shouted to the apathetic patients.

Another day with no food at all and the men held a meeting on whether to leave or stay. Arguments were breaking out and the officers were losing control. The men looked to their superiors for guidance, but the officers in camp seemed to be as much at a loss as everyone else.

'We'd best stay,' was the eventual consensus. And Alexander agreed with that.

Despite warnings, Tommy ventured outside the camp. 'They didn't take the chickens,' he cried excitedly. 'I've found where at least ten of them are living.' He held out his cupped hands. When he opened them there were two lovely eggs. 'There are more. I couldn't carry them all.'

With no way of knowing how much longer help would take to come, the men argued whether to kill the chickens for food, or keep them for the eggs they provided. In the end, it was decided to collect as many eggs as they could and only kill the chickens as a last resort.

One morning, a droning filled the sky and as the plane passed over, it dropped hundreds of leaflets.

Stay where you are. We are coming to get you.

The question was, when?

Chapter 60

Alexander: River Valley Road Camp 1945

With rescue on the horizon, they killed some of the chickens and cooked them. The long-forgotten aroma of roasting chicken drew the salivating men around the chef as he divided the meat into barely more than bite-sized portions.

'Kill them all,' shouted one prisoner, 'Help'll be here soon.'

Around him there was agreement.

'It's too risky,' said Alexander. 'We don't know how long they'll take. We need the eggs.'

'We need a decent feed,' complained the prisoner, and turned to look at the others. 'What say you all?'

Captain MacLeod stepped forward. 'Alexander's right. We need to ration what we've got.'

Tommy strode up to Alexander's side. Doctor Buchanan positioned himself at the other side. 'Come on, mem, we're nearly there. I know how hungry you are, but we can't fall out now.'

The officers in the camp held a brief, murmured conversation.

Finally, Captain MacLeod returned. 'We will kill no more hens today,' he said in a commanding voice.

The men who had supported killing the chickens stood down, disgruntled. 'Bloody ridiculous. The Americans will be here tomorrow,' grumbled one, but he had been outvoted which was just as well. The following day there was no sign of the Americans. The instinct now was to run from this place and find food and shelter wherever they could, but still, the leaflets came from the sky urging them to stay where they were.

'And do what? asked Tommy, scrunching the latest leaflet in his hand and tossing it into the dirt. 'There's nothing to eat. I can't just sit here while we starve.'

'They could come at any minute,' said Alexander. 'They know better than us what's going on. Come on, man.'

The sun was at its height, beating down on the heads of prisoners slowly losing the will to live.

Tommy stood up. 'I'm going. I might die out there but at least I tried.' He turned to look accusingly at Alexander, who no longer had the strength to argue, when, in the distance came the low drone of an aeroplane.

'More fucking leaflets,' muttered Tommy. 'Do they expect us to eat them?'

Lethargic prisoners rose to their feet and looked up at the sky in hope.

'No, it's not leaflets,' shouted one.

They cheered as the Red Cross boxes fell from the sky and crashed into the dust narrowly missing some overeager prisoners. Despite their weakened state, the men, fuelled by a new surge of adrenaline, cheered and clustered about the prizes, tearing them open with weakened hands. There were bandages: penicillin, aspirin, soap, tinned milk, sugar, rice. But barely enough to go around.

Captain MacLeod, Captain Fulton and Doctor Buchanan took charge.

'Don't panic, men. We need to stay organised. I'm sure this is only the beginning,' said MacLeod.

'The sick must be a priority,' said the doctor. 'Otherwise, they won't make it.'

In spite of their desperate hunger, the men agreed.

Back in the hospital, Alexander helped Doctor Buchanan

to make sure all the sick had clean bandages and a nourishing meal, small though it was. One young lad, Oscar, who looked barely out of his teens, grasped Alexander's arm. His grip was no stronger than a baby's. 'I'm dying,' he said. 'I can't hold on any more.'

'You bloody well will,' said Alexander. 'Think of your parents and all the things you still want to do. Do you have a sweetheart?' He had to keep him talking.

'There was a girl,' Oscar said with a wavering grin, 'but she'll not be waiting for me.'

'She may be. What's her name?' He could feel the youth slipping away, but he couldn't let him give up now, he just couldn't.

'Caroline.'

'Tell me about Caroline.'

Oscar spoke slowly, his voice changing, gradually growing stronger as he spoke. 'Her family left as soon as there were warnings. My dad thought they were mad. He never thought this would happen.'

'Then she'll be safe on British soil.'

'I wish I was there too.'

'They've damaged our bodies but they cannot touch our minds,' Alexander said. 'Close your eyes and you can go anywhere you want.'

'And you,' Oscar said, 'where do you go?'

Alexander tilted his head. 'To where there's salt on the wind,' he said.

'Where's that?' asked Oscar.

'There's a place where cows and sheep graze on green, green grass under an endless sky and the sea rattles over the pebbles on the beach.' He closed his eyes and he was back there again. 'The seals bark and the gulls yelp and there is a girl. I see her now in the shadow of Scartongarth.'

Oscar, who had been born on a plantation in Singapore knew nothing of the United Kingdom except what his parents had told him was suddenly interested. 'Scartongarth?'

'It's a house. It's where she once lived. Where did your family come from?' he asked.

'My grandparents… came from a place... called Newcastle.'

'Can you try to eat some of this now? It's rice made with milk and sugar.' He slipped his arm under the boy's head and supported him as he lifted the spoon to his mouth. He managed to get the lad to finish the small amount.

'Don't leave me,' Oscar whispered. 'Tell me more about the place you call home.'

Alexander didn't leave until he was sure Oscar was sleeping naturally.

Chapter 61

Alexander: River Valley Road Camp 1945

In the days that followed, more life-saving canisters thundered to the ground. Sugar, milk, rice, aspirin, penicillin, bandages, cigarettes and matches. Doctor Buchanan always made sure the sick got the best food.

Alexander sat by Oscar's bed daily feeding him rice softened and cooked in milk. 'Won't be long now. We're going home,' he repeated, time and time again.

Oscar gave a weak smile. Doctor Buchanan had already given him a shot of penicillin. 'I'll try and hold on,' he said. 'But if I don't make it, you'll find my mum and dad?'

'You'll make it. You'll see them again yourself.'

Suddenly, a commotion swirled outside. Shouts, running footsteps, the unmistakable cheers of hope. Oscar tried to sit up. 'What … what's going on?'

'Just lie there. I'll find out.' Alexander pushed himself to his feet. He opened the door, just enough to peer outside.

American soldiers were marching into the camp.

'Oh my God, you don't know how pleased I am to see you,' said Alexander. His legs, suddenly weak, collapsed under him. Two soldiers rushed to his side, their strong hands supporting him. 'We've got you, buddy,' one of them said, 'You're safe now.'

Alex's vision blurred. 'Inside,' he whispered, his voice

cracking. 'The patients, they're in a worse state than me.'

The soldiers gently lowered him to the ground and offered him water. 'We're getting you all out of here,' the other soldier said, his tone resolute.

As Alexander gulped down the water, his hands shaking, he looked around at the other prisoners. They were cheering and clapping. The American soldiers moved among them, providing aid, offering words of comfort, and promising that their ordeal was finally over. Others were bringing in stretchers to transport those too weak to walk.

A commanding officer stepped forward, his voice carrying over the noise. 'Men, you're free. The war is over for you. We're going to get you home.'

Home. The word echoed in Alexander's mind, a distant dream. He closed his eyes, allowing the reality to sink in. He was going home. 'Do you hear that, Oscar,' he whispered, 'We're going home.'

Together, the prisoners began the slow, painful walk toward the gates, leaving the nightmare of the camp behind. laughing, crying and singing Rule Britannia.

At that moment, under the harsh sun and the watchful eyes of their liberators, Alexander felt the first stirrings of a freedom he had almost forgotten existed. Yet he could not relax. He expected Japs to jump out at any moment from every rock, nook or cranny. Then he let his mind turn to home. 'Is the war over? Is Britain free?' he asked the soldier walking by his side. Were his parents still alive? Was Annie? Would he really make it? Would Oscar?

'The war in Europe is over, buddy,' said the soldier. 'Germany has been defeated. Hitler is dead. More than that I can't say.'

He walked by Oscar's stretcher and held the boy's hand as they were loaded into lorries. 'We're going home,' he whispered when Oscar smiled weakly.

'They'll give us food, but remember, not too much at first,' said Doctor Buchanan. 'Your stomach will have shrunk and won't be able to cope.'

Once they reached the docks, they stopped and waited to be boarded on the largest aircraft carrier he had ever seen. On board, those on stretchers were carried to the sick bay, and the others were showered, fumigated and deloused then dressed in ill-fitting boiler suits. They were led to a dining room with long tables laden with all the food they could eat. Foods they had forgotten existed. Aromas that had been buried in the archives of memory assaulted their senses.

'Tuck in, boys,' said a large American Captain with a deep, booming voice. 'It's all free.'

Alexander was almost drooling at the smell of rich food.

'Don't eat too much,' came the voice of Dr Buchanan at his elbow. 'Slowly does it.'

Although all his instincts were to gorge on the food, he heeded the doctor's advice and chose a rasher of ham and a single slice of bread, and it tasted delicious.

Doctor Buchanan nodded his approval. 'That's enough for now.'

It was no use telling the other men though. Heedless of the warnings, they heaped their plates and within an hour, were desperately ill.

Row after row of camp beds were arranged on the decks. All Alexander wanted to do was sleep but he joined the others at the rail where, to the strains of a Glenn Miller tune, they sailed out of Singapore. looking back at the devastation the rulers of Japan had brought down on what once had been The Gibraltar of the east.

Chapter 62

Alexander's parents: Aberdeen 1945

The room was quiet, bathed in the soft glow of the setting sun. The air was heavy with the lingering grief that had been part of their lives since Alexander had disappeared. Sofia Garcia sat in an armchair, knitting aimlessly. Her husband, Robert, sat at the small dining table, flipping through a newspaper. A knock at the door broke the silence, startling them both.

'I'll get it,' said Robert, dragging himself to his feet.

He returned, staring at the envelope, his brow crinkling, his breath stalling.

'Sofia,' he whispered.

Sofia looked up and, seeing the expression on her husband's face, rose quickly. She hurried over to him, her heart thundering with a mixture of hope and fear. 'What is it? Robert, what's wrong?'

Without a word, Robert handed her the letter, his hand shaking.

She took it. Her eyes scanned the front. Something within her core trembled. It was unmistakable — the handwriting was their son's. 'Alexander.' Her breath hitched and she looked up at Robert, hot tears stinging her eyes.

‘Oh, Holy Mother of God, Alexander.’

Robert nodded, unable to speak. Sofia clutched the letter to her chest for a moment, then, with unsteady hands, tore the flap open. Carefully, she unfolded the paper inside and began to read aloud, her voice shaky.

‘Dear Mama and Dad,

I’m alive. I know you must have thought the worst, but by some miracle, I survived. I’ve been in a prison camp all this time, but now I’m free, and I’m coming home.

Your loving son

Alexander

Her voice broke on the last word and she looked up at Robert, her heart bursting with a mixture of disbelief and joy.

‘He’s coming home. Our boy is coming home.’

Robert, usually a man of few words, felt his outward mask crumble. He pulled Sofia into a tight embrace, his tears finally falling as he held her close. They stood there, holding each other, the letter crushed between them, a reminder of the miracle they never dared to hope for.

They stood there for a moment longer, lost in the flood of emotions, before slowly, they began to move as if waking from a long, dark dream. The house, which had felt empty and cold for so long, seemed to fill with warmth and light once more. The promise of Alexander’s return brought life back to this grieving couple, making them whole again.

Chapter 63

Tess: Glasgow 1945

The hospital hallway buzzed with the usual activity: doctors in white coats consulting their clipboards, nurses bustling between wards, and the soft murmur of patients. Tess Munro walked down the hallway, her sensible shoes whispering against the linoleum. Her thoughts consumed her, her mind overflowing with the endless to-do list that came with the afternoon shift.

'More men came in this morning, Nurse Munro. Poor souls. A lot from POW camps. They are in ward 10. We've had to send some of the walking wounded home to make way for the new arrivals.'

'Yes, Sister,' said Tess, suppressing a sigh. She had meant to write a letter to Annie later tonight, but with a new influx of patients, it didn't look like she'd get out of here before midnight.

She approached the first patient and picked up the chart clipped onto the bottom of his bed. 'Alexander Garcia,' she murmured, the name tugging at a distant memory. She paused, frowning slightly as she tried to place it. With a shrug, she stepped up to the sorry soul whose eyes remained closed.

He was thin, his skin slack over his bones, his eyes hollow, his sparse hair white, but even in his weakened state, there was something familiar about him. Garcia. It was the Spanish name that stirred her memory. And then it hit her. The schoolteacher from Raumsey. The man her friend Annie had been in love with. Was this *the* Alexander Garcia? The once vibrant man she remembered? *This* ghostly shadow?

'Alexander?' she asked, as she picked up his wrist to check his pulse.

His eyes flickered open, and for a moment, there was no recognition. Then, slowly, his gaze sharpened and he blinked in disbelief. 'Tess? Her name sat on his breath, hardly a word at all. He tried to smile, revealing the shape of his teeth beneath the thinness of his lips. The teeth that remained.

She checked her watch, her heart speeding up. 'Yes, it's Tess. Alexander, I can't believe it's you.'

'Me…neither,' he said, his voice dry and strained. 'It's been... so long. I never...'

Tess pulled a chair to the bedside and sat down, her eyes not leaving his face. 'Don't try to speak, Alexander. Time enough for explanations. It's a surprise to see you here, though. The last I heard, you were off to Spain. And then... nothing.'

He took a deep breath and closed his eyes. 'Japanese… POW.' His voice trailed away as he seemed to run out of the energy it had taken to form the words.

She had already heard rumours of the Japanese camps. Her hand reached out instinctively, covering his. 'I'm so sorry. I can't even imagine what you've been through.'

A shudder ran through his body. He took a deep breath

and spoke again. 'Tess...'

Tess squeezed his hand gently. 'You're home now and we can help you heal.'

He opened his eyes again, looking at her with a mixture of gratitude and pain.

Tess smiled softly. 'Let's take it one day at a time. That's what we're here for.'

As she rose to her feet, Tess couldn't help but think of the years that had passed, the lives that had changed.

'Do you…ever hear about Annie?' he asked.

She hesitated. She had hoped against hope that Annie and her brother would tie the knot, and she had the feeling that her next words might dash that hope to pieces. But she could do nothing less than be honest. 'Yes, we keep in regular contact.'

'How… is she?'

'She's doing well.' It was not the time to tell him of Annie's troubles.

'Is she…is she… married?'

For a brief second, Tess wanted to lie, tell him that Annie and Magnus were together.

'No. She never married. But rest now. We'll talk more later. You were almost unconscious when you were brought in, but you're going to make it. You're one of the tough ones.'

Alexander's eyes closed and a faint smile ghosted his lips. As soon as she was off duty, Tess would write to Annie, no matter how late, although she knew that if Annie still had feelings for the schoolteacher, it would break her brother's heart.

Chapter 64

Annie: Raumsey 1945

Still thinking of Magnus and wondering whether she had been hasty to turn down his proposal, Annie sat in the manse kitchen sipping tea while Dee slept curled up in the opposite chair. Her mother was hosting a sewing group in the new hall and her stepfather was holding a bible class in the kirk.

Outside the window, the sunset cast its fiery fingers over a sea that lay as smooth as pearly glass, and vessels both large and small sailed through the channel. She had hardly become used to the silence, the lack of gunfire from Scapa, the relief that it was finally over, not just here, but also in the Middle East.

The front door opened and Hughie the Post's voice echoed through the hall. 'There's mail for the minister the day. One for ye, too, Annie.'

'Leave them on the hall table,' she called back.

Still holding her cup, she rose, went into the hall, lifted the letters, closed the door, and returned to her chair. She flipped through the usual kirk correspondence, then stopped at a plain envelope with Tess's handwriting.

There had been no letter from Tess for quite a while. In the last one, she was working in a ward with traumatised and badly injured soldiers who had returned from the war. With her shifts sometimes fifteen hours a day, Annie guessed she didn't have much time to write. Sadly, many nurses had gone abroad to help in war-torn countries and never returned.

Annie opened the envelope and pulled out a neatly folded letter. As she read, she drew in a sharp breath, momentarily frozen. She read it again, to make sure she had understood the words.

'Alexander,' she said aloud, the letter trembling in her grasp.

He was alive. In a bad way, but alive. And he was asking for her.

She stood up, heat racing through every fibre of her being. He had been in a war camp and was suffering the effects of malnutrition and jungle fevers. Jungle fevers? But he'd been in Spain. What had happened in the intervening years that she knew nothing about? He was asking about her — so, like her, he had not forgotten. She had to see him.

Maybe, with everything that had gone on, she wouldn't feel the same when they met again, but she had to find out. She just had to. With memories of the past and the possibilities of the future in her head, an unbidden smile formed on her lips and she laughed out loud.

She headed towards her desk and pulled out a pen and paper. As she began to write a reply, her hand wouldn't stay steady enough to form the letters. Finally, she gave up. Needing to tell someone, she had to find Isa.

'I have to go to him,' she said. 'I hate asking you to look

after Dee…' She stopped, waiting, hopeful.

'You don't have to ask,' said Isa. 'It's always been Garcia, hasn't it?'

Annie nodded.

'You follow your heart, love, I know how that feels.'

'Thank you, Mam,' she said with blurred eyes.

Chapter 65

Annie: Glasgow 1945

Annie breathed in the antiseptic hospital smell. 'Alexander Garcia,' she asked.

The young nurse at the desk consulted a ledger in front of her. She looked up and smiled. 'Ward 6,' she said. 'He's nearest the door – in case you don't recognise him,' she explained.

Annie thanked her and fought down the urge to rush. As she strode through the hospital corridors, butterflies danced in her stomach until she thought she might be sick. Doubts had plagued her all the way here. What if, when she saw him, he no longer wanted her? What if his Spanish wife was sitting by his bed? If that were the case, she would go home and expect nothing more from him, but at least she'd know. But Japan! Stories had seeped through of the desperate suffering told by returning servicemen. Photographs appeared in the newspapers of living skeletons, barely alive. Why hadn't she known? Why hadn't she felt his pain in her heart?

She stopped at the door of the ward 6. Through the small window, she could see him, thankfully with no wife by his side, but this parody was nothing like the man of her memories. Was this really Alexander, or had some ghastly mistake been made?

Gathering her courage, she pushed the door open, stepped

inside and approached his bedside slowly, almost afraid he might disappear if she moved too quickly.

His lids flickered open and the minute the dark brown eyes found hers, she knew. Yes, even with his face skull-like, his once black hair white and thin, it was still those eyes that had haunted her dreams down through the years.

'Alexander,' she murmured.

For a heartbeat, he looked confused, as if trying to place her face. Then his lips trembled into a weak smile. Her eyes fixed on his as she tried to pour strength into him.

'Annie,' he whispered, his voice hoarse and barely audible. 'Am I dreaming?'

'I thought you were dead,' she said, her voice breaking. 'All these years, I thought you were either dead or were happy in Spain and didn't want to know me.'

He reached out, his hand trembling with effort, and she took it in hers, feeling the bones beneath the skin, the warmth and the reality of it.

'I nearly was…many times,' he said. 'God, Annie, you look so good.'

She thought he had fallen asleep again when he took a deep breath. His lids blinked apart. 'I dreamed of you…I had to see *you*.'

'But… your wife?' she asked.

'Wife? What…what wife?'

'You didn't marry?'

'But I told you there was no wife.'

He wasn't married! 'I wrote to you. When I heard nothing back, I assumed…' she said.

'I did write. When I got no reply, I thought…' His eyes shut again as if the words were exhausting him.

She realised this was not the time to discuss what had happened. 'Sleep now. I'm going nowhere.'

'I'm sorry, I can barely stay awake. Sleep is such a luxury, I can't get enough of it. It's like…I haven't slept in years.' His eyes closed, but his fingers tightened on hers.

They sat in silence, holding hands, the weight of lost time hanging between them. There was so much to say, so many questions to ask, but for now, just being together was enough.

'He's improving every day,' said Tess when Annie joined her, to glean more information. 'He already had treatment in an American hospital, before he was fit to travel further. Also, careful nursing in the hospital ship that brought him and many others home. It seems to be the case that they find the strength to survive the most terrible hardships, but as soon as they can relax, everything hits them at once.'

Annie shuddered. She didn't want to imagine how bad he was when rescued.

'He needs rest and good feeding now. I'm not going to lie to you, one more day and it might have been a different story.' Tess slipped her arm through her friend's. 'You're staying with me, I assume? I have a very comfortable settee.'

'Well, I had hoped,' said Annie. She glanced back at the ward door. 'Maybe I should stay beside him, though.'

'The best thing for Alexander now is sleep. I've a feeling he will recover a lot sooner after seeing you. Save your strength for when he comes home; he'll need support. I'll be off in half an hour. We've so much to catch up on.'

Chapter 66

Annie: One month later.

The rain had stopped an hour before, leaving the air with a fresh, new scent, as if everything had been cleansed. Out in the bay, a small boat sliced its way from the mainland. Annie paid little attention to it. There was no regular ferry service; boats came and went by request. Her parents had taken Dee to the mainland for the day, a visit to family already living there was long overdue. She would have been with them, except for Eliza, who was very ill and Annie had promised Ada to be there at the end. Yesterday, she held the heartbroken Margaret's hand and stroked the old woman's forehead with the other. Eliza had cheated death so often, it was unbelievable that she could finally let go of life.

The old woman opened her eyes and tried to speak but her voice was barely above a whisper.

Annie leaned close. 'Don't strain yourself.'

'Dear Annie, the black cloud has gone,' Eliza said, 'I had to wait and make sure…' Annie barely heard the words before the old woman finally drifted away.

The sky was a deep, endless blue the day Alexander Garcia stepped off the boat, his heart pounding with a mixture of anticipation and anxiety. The war had been over for months, but the scars it left behind were still fresh and raw. After spending time in the hospital and then with his parents, he was finally strong enough to travel north. Now, he was going to see her again.

The Island of Raumsey had changed little in his absence. The animals still grazed in the fields, the houses stood steadfastly where they always had, and the scent of fish and salt still filled the air. Seagulls still screamed, and the soft accent of the islanders brought memories back. Yet, everything felt different. He had changed and not just emotionally. His hair once as black as wet coal had grown back, but it was as white as cumulus clouds, his skin once smooth and firm was now sun-damaged and lined. Perhaps by his very appearance, he was no longer the man she once loved. And inside, he would be forever changed, in some ways for the better. He was no longer the unbending fundamentalist. Although she spent time with him in hospital, had she done it out of the kindness of her heart? After she left had she buried a ghost? They were both different people now.

'I have the truck there if ye want a lift,' said Magnus.

Alexander recognised him immediately, but it seemed that Magnus had no recollection of him. He shook his head. 'I need the exercise. But if you could take my luggage, I'd be grateful.'

'Where are ye going?'

'The retired schoolteacher, William Dick. I'm visiting him for a few days. I believe he lives in a cottage on the north side.'

'Aye, I ken fine where Willie lives.' He peered at Alexander with narrow eyes.

'Don't you recognise me, Magnus?'

Magnus's eyes opened wide. 'Garcia. Aye, it's the white hair and, man, ye look as though ye've been through the mill.'

'As you did after the Great War.' The two men faced each other for a moment before Magnus offered his hand and Alexander grasped it.

'Ye've come for her,' said Magnus. 'Ye're a lucky man.'

Alexander didn't miss the regret in the other's eyes and immediately understood.

'Thanks, Magnus.' He took a breath and started walking, his feet instinctively guiding him towards a place he had thought about every day since his release. It was the island kirk and manse where she lived, the girl who had occupied his thoughts and dreams. Annie Reid.

He hesitated at the door, his hand hovering over the doorbell.

Steeling himself, he listened to the familiar clang from deep inside. When there was no answer, he pushed the door open and called. 'Hello, anyone at home?' The scent of old books and polished wood filled his senses and, for a moment, he was transported back to a simpler time.

The kitchen door opened and Annie was standing there. Her dark hair fell in soft waves around her shoulders. Her lips parted but she didn't speak.

'Annie,' he said, his voice barely above a whisper.

Her eyes widened as they met his. For a heartbeat, there was silence. Then, she dropped the dishcloth she was holding and rushed towards him.

'Alexander,' she cried, 'why didn't you let me know you were coming?'

He put his arms around her, feeling the warmth of her embrace, the solidity of her presence. It was real. She was real. He was home.

'I wasn't sure when I'd arrive,' he said.

They stood like that for what felt like an eternity, neither wanting to let go. Finally, she pulled back slightly, her hands cupping his face as she looked into his eyes.

'You finally came,' she said. 'After I left the hospital, I wasn't sure, you know, how you would feel once you were well.'

'How could you doubt me?' he replied, brushing a tear from her cheek. 'I never stopped thinking about you, Annie.

You kept me going, even in the darkest times.'

She smiled through her tears. 'Like I told you, I never gave up hope. I would have stayed longer with you, but my son needed me.' She dropped her arms and took a step back.

'Yes,' he said. 'I understand that. About the missing letters, my mother told me what she did. I'm angry as hell, but after everything that's happened, life's too short to hold it against her.'

All the time, he drank in the sight of her, the flush on her cheeks, the eyes locking into his, and the scent of her, soft soap and rose water. A lump rose in his throat. For a long moment, he fought the desire to sob like a girl.

'I'm glad,' said Annie.

Silence reigned for a beat, then he found the power to speak again. 'I love my mother, but she tries to rule my life. I never was married. I couldn't go through with it.'

Annie moved backwards. 'Where are my manners? My parents have gone to the mainland for the day to visit my Aunt Chrissie, and they took Dee with them. I can make you tea, I've got some scones and mutton stew.'

He refused to let go of her hand. 'A cup of tea will be grand,' he said. 'And I can't wait to meet your lad.'

'You don't hold it against me? That I had a bairn with another man?'

He shook his head. 'How could I? If the boy's part of you, then I'll love him too.'

He followed her to the stove. 'Annie,' he said, liking the sound of her name on his tongue, 'I want you to know that I'm a different person than I was back then. I could never hold it against you, but I'm also broken. I have nightmares and I'm back there, and I wake up screaming. I can only eat small amounts at a time…what I'm saying— '

She reached up and set her fingers against his lips. 'Hush. None of that matters. We have all the time in the world. I'm a nurse, remember, and the island is peaceful, just the birds and the seals and the sea washing on the shore. The ideal place to heal.'

They spent the rest of the day together, talking and catching up on the lost years. Alexander told her some things about the camp, about the friends he had lost and the hardships he had endured, but there were things he could never talk about.

Annie listened, her heart aching for the pain he had gone through, but also filled with gratitude that he had survived. She didn't tell him about Scartongarth, about Nick, about Jeannie, there would be time enough for that.

As the sun set and the island basked in a golden glow, they sat on a bench outside the kirk, hand in hand. The future was uncertain, but they had each other, and that was enough.

Alexander turned to her. 'I know we've both changed, and the world isn't the same as it was. I wish I could build a future with you, but I don't want to burden you with my pain, my moods. I'll understand if you're wary. What I'm saying is, it's going to take me time. I can't expect—'

Annie silenced him with a wave of her hand. She slipped to the ground so that she was on her knees before him.

'I know it's not my place, and you might think me a brazen hussy, but I don't care. Alexander Garcia, will you marry me?'

He straightened his shoulders as if taken aback, and for a moment she thought she had gone too far. Then his eyes grew moist, 'You…are you sure? I'm crippled, inside.'

She nodded. 'I've been sure since the first time you walked into Connie's shop, and I was as silly seventeen-year-old lassie. Why else would I ask you to tutor me?'

'Because you wanted to better yourself.'

She turned her head to one side. 'Well, there was that, too.'

He laughed. 'Then yes, I will. Yes, a thousand times yes. I'll even let your stepfather do the honours.'

'What? Not a priest? I won't convert but I'm willing to make concessions.'

He shook his head. ‘I won’t give up my faith, but it’s the same God, and it’s the same vows. I’m sure we’ll work it out.’

In that moment, with the past behind them and a new beginning ahead, they knew that love had triumphed over everything. They had found their way back to each other and, together, they would face whatever the future held.

Epilogue

Donald

The heavy oak door creaked open as Reverend Donald Charleston entered the asylum. He paused and wiped his brow with a worn handkerchief. The stale smell of disinfectant and urine hit his nostrils and the distant cries of anguished patients hit his ears. Yet this institution, run by the Church of Scotland, was so much better than many of the state-run mental facilities he had visited.

He had been here before on a few visits to Jeannie Sinclair over the years, but it never got easier.

A nurse in a crisp, white uniform led him down the dim corridor. Their footsteps echoed in the hall, and his eyes passed over the small, barred windows of each room. Most patients stared blankly into space or muttered to themselves. Some curled up on their beds, looking like shadows of people rather than human beings.

'She's doing well, Reverend,' the nurse said, glancing over her shoulder. 'Really well, all things considered.'

At last, they reached a door at the end of the corridor that led outside to the asylum garden. It was one of the few places that allowed a glimpse of nature. The nurse pushed it open. The sun had begun its downward arc, casting a golden light over the overgrown hedges and stretch of garden attended by the fitter patients. Among the flowers and vegetables. a figure moved slowly and deliberately, humming quietly to herself.

'Jeannie,' the nurse called. 'You have a visitor.'

Jeannie turned from where she was kneeling by a flower bed. Her face barely changed when she saw the minister. She rose to her feet and walked toward him, her steps slow, almost dreamlike. Her hair, wild and unkempt during her trial, was neatly tied back now, and her face, though pale, had a calmness that made her seem like a different woman. The vicious scars left by the flames on one side of her face had lost their initial intensity and had settled into a white, shiny puckering.

'Minister,' she greeted him with a soft smile. Her hands, rough from manual work, extended toward him, but not before she carefully brushed them on her apron.

'Jeannie,' he said, grasping her hand. He was surprised. There was nothing left of the tortured woman he once knew. 'How are you?'

Her face remained calm. 'I'm well, I am.' Her voice was soft and still carried the island lilt. 'I've found peace here, Reverend. The Lord... He's been with me. I've confessed my sins to him and prayed, like you said.'

They sat on a nearby bench under the shade of a drooping willow tree, its branches swaying gently in the breeze. Birds twittered in the branches and the sun dappled through. Jeannie folded her hands in her lap, her fingers still dusted with earth. Her gaze was far off, as though she was lost in memories.

‘I help in the wards, too,’ she said at last, breaking the silence. ‘It’s... it’s good work. I change linens, read to some of the patients. I pray with them, too, if they ask.’

Reverend Charleston had heard about her change, the way she had embraced her role within these walls, how she had found solace in her faith. It was a far cry from the woman who had stood trial for culpable homicide just three years prior — eyes hollow with grief, haunted by fear of what was to come.

‘Jeannie,’ he began gently, ‘Is there anything you want to speak about today?’

She looked down at her hands, but she didn’t flinch. ‘I think about them every day, Minister.’ Her voice didn’t waver. ‘My father and Nick… but they don’t speak to me anymore. They were unhappy men and I hope they’ve found peace wherever they are. I forgive them, as I hope they have forgiven me.’

‘God forgives, Jeannie. He sees the sincerity in your heart.’

Jeannie’s eyes glistened. ‘I’ve come to terms with it here. I should be in this place. The others… they think I’m one of them.’ She gave a little laugh. ‘I’m not though. I’m perfectly sane.’

Donald placed a hand over hers. ‘Many people are broken in one way or another, Jeannie, but we can be made whole again through God’s grace.’

‘My paw went to the kirk. Every Sunday. And he made us say grace. But he wasn’t a good man.’

‘It’s what is in our hearts that counts,’ said Donald.

A long silence stretched between them, with only the wind rustling the leaves above and the persistent birdsong. Jeannie tilted her head back, letting the dying sunlight touch her face. For a moment, she looked serene.

'I don't think about getting out,' she said softly. 'I used to dream of walking free, living outside these walls again, but where would I go? Going back to Raumsey is not an option for me. I think I was meant to be here. Maybe this is my atonement.'

'Stonehill is still yours, you know.'

She shook her head. 'Too many bad memories. He'll still be there ye know, my paw.'

Donald studied her face and saw contentment. Whatever path she was on now was the one she needed to walk.

'Perhaps you are right,' he said. 'God's love is infinite. He sees the good you are doing.'

'I'm happy to stay here. I feel... I feel safe, at peace.'

He rose slowly, giving her hand a final squeeze. 'You are in God's hands, Jeannie. Never forget that.'

'Tell Annie and Isa I'm asking after them.' Then, she rose and returned to the flower bed without looking at him again.

'Goodbye, Jeannie,' he said to her bowed shoulders

She did not reply.

If you've enjoyed the final story in the Raumsey saga, please leave a review on Amazon and Goodreads and tell your friends. It only takes a few minutes, and written reviews greatly help a struggling author. Thanks in advance.

https://www.amazon.co.uk/Shadows-Scartongarth-Raumsey-Catherine-Byrne/dp/199958306X?ref

Printed in Great Britain
by Amazon

59665770R00179